Bennett Hillary Springer Meghan Parrish Broo~~~~ ~~~~ Emma
in Budish Chris Whalley Elaine Hobson Peter A~~~~ ~~~~offy
~~~~aroline Knaggs Heather Anderson Cathy Slate~~~~ ~~~~lin
~~~~ Bailey Bill Carden-Horton Stuart Baron Malcolm English Pau
~~~~ue-Williams Eugene Bay Ian Farnfield Richard Beaumont Sarah
~~~~Bennett Sherry Wales Debora Berardi Jonathon Sleeman Helen
~~~~en Heron Kate Stevenson Carol Bossman Tim Cole Pierre Boyre
~~~~ Gilmore Jeremy Britton Ian Newman Myriam Loda Tim Britton
~~~~Ian Norman Paul Browton Neil Murphy Giovanna Brunello Danie
~~~~Rowntree Alison Cane Roberto D'Andria John Scott Caroline
~~~~Colin Frewin David Ives Elena Reznikovitch Peter Chodel Tom
~~~~d Collins Elina Berzina Derek Fieldman Joffy Connolly Edward
~~~~ St Lawrence Ron Cregan Andrew McCall Simon Critchley Ian
~~~~oger Kenchington Claudene Davies Caroline Jewitt Lisa Davies
~~~~ackell Shelly Davies Chris Lightfoot Tanja Schlager Hamish
~~~~sca Queirazza Max Dubois John Bolt Roger Hardy Denise Maas
~~~~on Edge John Hughes Colin Elston Martin Campbell Dominic
~~~~n Stefano Fabrucci Ken Corsie Julie Farber Chris Barber Kevin
~~~~hessian Elena Chuvakhina Paul Bagshawe Jonathon Ford Alex
~~~~n Neil Fruen Melissa Smith Claudene Fuller Damien Schogger
~~~~rd Crisp Catherine Geraghty Mark Doodnath Valerie Gibbons
~~~~ert Downing Sue Witherden Carrie Cummins Tim Leahy Mat
~~~~nez Stephen Hodgson Jim Tochas Tony Meeuwissen Roy Gray
~~~~anni Caselli Morton Langenbaek Sophie Gunther Krystina Lyon
~~~~ll Adam Halliway Kimberley Priestley Garrick Hamm Mike Gilling
~~~~n Bruce Duckworth Glenn Harrison Paul Langsford Hazel West
~~~~Simon Williams Adam Helliway Lisa Fredericks Julie Hewitt

Tony Blurton Caroline Hiam Kat Gomez Frixos Aixentiou
Geoff Hockey Sarah Duncan Martin Ayer Robertson
Geoff Holliday James Duncan Leigh Fry Mark Holt Jimmy
Yang Stuart Naysmith Matt Horseman Maria Glynn Carolyn
Sweet Neil Howe Andrew Crighton Ruth Goddard Ter
Howes Laura Bastick Felicity Hunt Abigail Ireland Andrew
Porter Kate Hutchinson Beverley Gibbons Lucy Isherwood
Brendan Martin Rosa Jawad Rob Davie Andrew Jephson
Peter Brookes Denise Fairweather Alfie Peters Carmalinna
anelli Manu Joshi James Hagger Smilynne Joukovski Michael
Bettis Vanja Karas Brian Couzens Paul Groves Caroline
Nembhard Adrian Kilby Pamela Conway Jim Fitzpatrick Kate
Kileen Aubrey Hastings-Smith Nadia Kokni Martin Maidstone
David Haggie Stuart Lang Ian Firth Laurence Lassalle John
Gorham Carole Laugier Geoff Halpin Anton Petrucelli Chris
Lee Gareth Rutter Ro Brockbank Giles Lenton Alison Murray
Marina Leopardi Shamoon Keevah Dumont Barbara Lewis
Dorothy MacKenzie Simon Lince Liz Edler Lara Clifton
Catherine Lloyd Maudie Parkinson Frances Lovell Mark
Pearce Clive Gross Liz Lydiate Peter Berners-Price Stuart
MacKay Nick Corney Robert Silver Fiona MacLeod Lynette
Grass Lindsey Maidment John Bound Alan Manham Hilary
Boys Jane Mann Keith Bowen Miguel Mazarrasa Alvear Chris
Keeble Stephan Wichman Clare Fitzgerald Vanessa Elliot
Kevin McGurk Ana Gonzalez Maree McNicoll Linda Grischott
Wendy Mellors Ash Smith Paul Brand Sheona Michie
Di Picard Ian Miller Stephen Woodward Alan Newnham

Yes Logo

**40 Years
of Michael Peters
Branding, Design
and Communication**
Sarah Owens

YES

LOGO

black dog
publishing
london uk

Contents

7 **Dedication**

9 Foreword **Sir John Hegarty**

11 Introduction **Jeremy Myerson**

15 **ONE—FORMATIONS 1941–1969**

17 **David Hillman**

18 **Timeline 1959–1969**

21 Early Years

25 A Born Salesman

28 The Designer's Apprentice

29 Student Days

38 The Bauhaus Legacy

46 A Mecca of Design

57 Return to London

57 Setting Up Shop

61 **TWO—VIBRATIONS 1970–1982**

63 **Bev Whitehead**

64 **Timeline 1970–1982**

67 Michael Peters and Partners

69 Breakthroughs

72 A Second String to the Bow

75 Team Players

79 The Outsider

80 Interpretations

83 Innovations

86 Designing a Company

143 **THREE—FLOTATIONS 1983–1990**

145 **Glenn Tutssel**

146 **Timeline 1983–1990**

149 Joining the Club

160 A University of Design

164 Rubik's-Cube

168 The Midas Touch

174 A Designer Decade

177 Initiatives and Innovation

179 New Territories

185 Fall from Grace

235 **FOUR—CONSOLIDATIONS 1991–2008**

237 **Carole Laugier, Jimmy Yang, Dana Robertson**

239 **Timeline 1991–2008**

243 Phoenix from the Ashes

246 Re-fighting the Fight

249 Driven by Creativity

251 Links and Mergers

253 On Familiar Terms

255 Foreign Relations

258 A New Millennium

259 The Shape of Things to Come

308 **Designer Index**

312 **Index**

318 **Credits**

319 **Thanks**

319 **Acknowledgements**

319 **Colophon**

Dedication

This book is a huge thank you to my darling family.
To Jo, my wife, to my son Gary, my daughter Sarah,
and my daughter-in-law Anna, and Jonathan, my
son-in-law. And to their children: Jacob, Sam,
Alfie and George.

A special person in my life has been my late
mother-in-law, Rachel, who was totally supportive
of everything I have ever done.

I must, however, reserve my lasting love and
thanks to Jo who has supported me through both
good and difficult times. She has been a complete
source of inspiration and this book is dedicated to
her. With my love and affection.
Michael Peters, London 2009

Foreword **Sir John Hegarty**

t was 1967, the summer of love. The Beatles had just released *Sgt. Pepper*, *Bonnie and Clyde* was smashing box office records and loon pants with 24 inch trouser bottoms were all the rage.

I was a young art director at Cramer Saatchi the forerunner to Saatchi & Saatchi. We had just moved into new offices on the corner of Goodge Street and Tottenham Court Road.

Over the next three years 16 Goodge Street was to become one of the most influential addresses in the rise of British creativity. On the first floor David Puttnam had just set up his groundbreaking photographic agency, representing David Bailey, Terence Donovan and Lord Snowdon.

Alan Parker was developing film scripts in conjunction with Cramer Saatchi that would later be produced by Puttnam—and help propel Alan into one of Britain's greatest film directors.

On the floor above that a new young agency was opening its doors, Boase Massimi Pollitt, where a young art director, by the name of John Webster, was about to convince UK housewives of the superiority of an instant mashed potato called Cadbury's Smash.

And on the very top floor, the floor we all envied, sat Klein Peters. The uber hot design duo. It was a time when art, commerce and music were crashing into each other. The scent of possibility was everywhere.

I first met Michael when we were working on a new product idea for instant porridge. I wandered up to the top floor to talk to Michael about our ideas. We wanted him to work on the packaging. They had a spiral staircase. Now, that might not seem much now, but back then a spiral staircase was the business. I thought this is definitely it. I had arrived, I was in awe. But once I got over the staircase it was Michael I was most in awe of.

I had studied graphic design at the London School of Printing. But under the manic, mesmerising, influence of the legendary John Gillard I pursued advertising as a career of choice. I realised it was ideas that turned me on. Much as I loved design, I relished the challenge of a 'blank page'. And now at last I was talking to a designer who understood that process.

Michael talked ideas. He started thinking conceptually before he thought typographically. He wanted to know the story. What were we trying to achieve, how could design be part of that narrative.

Form over content will always be transient. Of course we create for the moment, work is always a reflection of the era it's created in. But great work stands the test of time—and sorts the thinkers out from the colourists. If you're trying to make a lasting impression then your thinking has to last.

Michael was never afraid of the big picture. He understood the design business but also wanted to expand the business of design, elevating its role in a demanding commercial world. Doing this, of course, does take courage and does mean you'll make mistakes. And he certainly has made some. But as someone said "nobody stumbled while standing still".

And Michael has never stood still. Constantly innovating and changing. Despite all that change, the thing that has remained constant is the quality of the work he's produced and inspired.

This book, then, is a testament to that commitment. It charts a remarkable period in British history as we moved from a manufacturing based economy to a thinking one.

Looking through the pages of work and the progress of Michael's career you get to see Britain in a unique and original light. And what a wonderful glow it casts.

That original meeting with Michael never materialised into a piece of work. But what it did materialise into was a lifelong admiration of the man and his creativity. And eventually a partnership in one of his design companies.

Michael is a true renaissance thinker. Bringing the art of design into the heart of business. He wasn't afraid to engage with the brutal realities of commerce and turn that challenge into a creatively led business admired the world over.

But what really makes this book great is Michael. He's mad, brilliant, crazy, thoughtful, impossible and inspirational. That's why I love him. And why I love his work.

Introduction **Jeremy Myerson**

As an art director and design entrepreneur, Michael Peters has revelled in being cast in the classic role of outsider for almost his entire career. When we look back at the dominant personalities in British design of the past 40 years, it is hard to think of another individual who has exerted such a central influence on the shape of the design profession while busily and self-evidently doing his own thing.

Michael Peters joined the design industry in Britain in its infancy, when it was small and unformed and unremarked upon, and he lacked even the most basic resources and contacts most would consider necessary to get ahead. He was destined never to be part of the 'club'—he was never really interested in learning its rules. Instead, armed with a formidable self-belief, he propelled himself forward and found strength and inspiration in being free to forge his own design path.

Over the next four decades, Peters would break the taboos that separated design from business, graphics from other disciplines, and designers from brands. An entire generation of his former disciples marched through the doors that Michael Peters opened, setting up their own entrepreneurial design businesses and going on to brand companies in ways that had only been entrusted to large advertising agencies before.

In the process, Michael Peters made people jealous of his success, but also hugely admiring of his talent for merging the creative with the commercial. He raised the design fees charged in the industry by pushing clients to the brink to accept his terms. He challenged every visual convention in how packaged goods should be presented. He tested the limits of the big, publicly quoted design firm to the point of destruction. Then, after being broken on the wheel of the City, got back on his feet, dusted himself down and devised a new and different model for the design business.

He was and remains irrepressible, leading one of his many collaborators quoted in this book to comment: "Michael is like Marmite, you have a real opinion about him. You either love him or hate him." I prefer to see Michael Peters not simply as a love-hate figure, a creative controversialist, but

as someone far more complex—a character akin to Woody Allen's Zelig. In Allen's 1983 film, the part of Leonard Zelig played by the New York director is a human chameleon who crops up at all the critical moments in American history in the early twentieth century. Allen skillfully inserted his character into old black-and-white movie newsreels, so that Zelig is both observer and participant in the key moments shaping the times.

So it is with Michael Peters. It is extraordinary how he crops up, Zelig-like, at key moments in British design history, brushing shoulders from the very start with many of the central characters in the evolution of the profession, darting in from the wings to play a leading role in the drama, the unknown searched out by the spotlight. Who else could land an apprenticeship as a teenager via the Jewish Board of Guardians with a German graphic artist, Hans Arnold Rothholz, who had designed posters for the 1951 Festival of Britain? Who else would be taught as a rookie student at the London School of Printing by Harry Beck, designer for the iconic 1931 London Underground map?

From Luton where he grew up on the outside looking in, Peters quickly found himself in the influential company of two future Pentagram partners: Alan Fletcher, whose time spent studying at Yale persuaded Peters to go to America, and David Hillman, whose very first job after studying alongside Peters at the London School of Printing was on *The Sunday Times Magazine*, where a typical day's work was asking Man Ray to photograph Catherine Deneuve for a magazine cover.

It took the bizarre intervention of a *Daily Mirror* campaign to get the penniless Michael Peters to Yale—even Woody Allen would have struggled to make that one up. Once there in the early 1960s, this Zelig of design found himself in the company of teachers Paul Rand, Herbert Matter and Alexei Brodovitch, and under the influence of Josef Albers, one of the greats of the German Bauhaus who had fled Europe to resettle in America. Thus Peters was later able to claim with some justification that his giant multi-disciplinary design firm of the 1980s was a "new commercial Bauhaus", mixing as it did all his early influences from Yale.

At Yale, Peters found a way to reconcile the overtly commercial basis of American design that he so admired with a moral European sensibility imparted by so many of its émigré teachers. It was more than a marriage of convenience—it would drive him on, beyond Yale, where he nearly got to work for Charles Eames but did secure a job with Lou Dorfsman's revered CBS network in New York, and back to London in 1965. There he was headhunted by David Puttnam to set up a design department within the famous Collett Dickinson Pearce (CDP) ad agency, sharing creative space with Charles Saatchi and future film director Alan Parker and displaying once again that uncanny, Zelig-like knack of being in the right place with the right people at the right time.

Much has been written about the London design scene of the 1960s, often by unreliable witnesses. Michael Peters caught the tail end of it. Suffice to say that by the time he set up his own firm with Lou Klein in 1967, he was well-placed to benefit from the gains made by such pioneering groups as Wolff Olins, Minale Tattersfield and Fletcher/Forbes/Gill, whose founders he knew and whose methods he studied. Within 20 years he would outstrip them all in scale and ambition, for a brief glittering period at least.

The 1960s can now be seen, with all the benefit of technicolor hindsight, as a golden age for British graphic design and print, a rich kaleidoscope of new and often radical visual ideas in which young designers could find their milieu. The 1970s, by contrast, lacked the creative coherence and sustained energy of the previous decade and was far more messily individualistic and fragmented. The break-up of The Beatles in 1970, replacing one universally recognisable group with four diverse characters each going their own unfathomable way, acted as a symbol for the bigger changes afoot.

That same year, Peters launched his own firm, Michael Peters and Partners, and slowly established himself in the sleepy cottage industry of design while many of his former colleagues grew rich quickly in the burgeoning world of advertising. CDP, his former employers, were the undisputed kings of adland in the 1970s, but Peters was canny enough to bide his time, learn on the job and build for a future in which British designers would begin to command the big fees and juicy retainers that the ad agencies regarded as their birthright.

In the 1970s, an era of state monopolies, public sector strikes and ailing smokestack industries, Peters kept his rampant free market philosophies stuffed under an artist's beret and sought out clients like Winsor & Newton that would let him simply strut his stuff as an award-winning art director. His gifts for graphic pastiche and mastery of different styles would allow the companies he worked for to cash in on trends such as that inspired by the 1977 publication of *The Country Diary of an Edwardian Lady*.

The story might have ended there with a successful if essentially small-time creative entrepreneur finding his own comfortably affluent niche. But the rise of Mrs Thatcher—who came to power in 1979 and for whom Michael Peters later re-designed the Tory torch logo—changed the landscape so dramatically with her savage economic reforms that the entire design community was transformed. Amid deregulation and state sell-offs to the private sector, British graphic designers were borne on a wave of business opportunity in the 1980s and decisively lost their commercial virginity.

This was Michael Peters' moment to become the boardroom wheeler and dealer he had always wanted to be since Yale. The shackles were off. The design soloist could also be the business supremo. Michael Peters and Partners was transformed in the 80s into an international supergroup encompassing a complex Rubik's-Cube matrix of design disciplines, companies, countries and clients. Through acquisition and growth, through the hype surrounding a steady flow of great projects, his power and influence grew. It was no longer just about packs and print but also about products and environments too. Significantly, Peters returned to America and purchased design companies there. Such acts would be his undoing.

In many ways, we can now see Michael Peters himself as a symbol of a complex and contradictory era. The 1980s was a time of private affluence but public squalor in Britain: conspicuous consumption, red braces and yuppies in the City balanced out by ferry, tube station and soccer stadium disasters and the slow drip-feed of misery caused by the constant rate-capping of local councils.

Amid the turmoil, Peters cut an almost schizophrenic figure in his efforts as a designer to remain a social idealist while making a mountain of money. This was the man who adored the

Conservatives and loved the thrill of the commercial chase—who could forget his story of booking onto Concorde just to strike up a conversation with big shot client Ralph Halpern of Burton in the next seat? But he'd also find time to dash up to the north-east to aid a Design for Recovery programme for small firms in Middlesborough, or lovingly support a foundation for the applied arts. Such a combination of idealism and opportunism was unusual in design, which was traditionally reticent about getting ahead in business. For those who flinched at Peters' provocative commercial tactics, he would suggest that they, unlike him, had never been poor.

It was in the early 1980s that I first ran into Michael Peters when I was working as a journalist on *Design* magazine. Early in our relationship, I attended the City flotation of his firm and saw a designer in a crisp pinstriped suit and starched white shirt, but no tie, captivate his audience with an origami prospectus. Peters was always determined to do things his way, even at the most critical financial junctions.

When I launched *DesignWeek* in 1986 as its founding editor, Michael Peters was supportive where other established designers were sniffy. *DesignWeek* was Britain's first weekly business magazine for designers and their clients and Peters wasn't scared of the competition. He wanted an open market and wanted his peers to know how well his share price was doing. The first issue of *DesignWeek* analysed the setting up of the Design Business Association, Britain's first trade body for design firms. Naturally, Peters was among its prime movers.

When *DesignWeek* ran a survey of client opinion in 1988, we discovered that Michael Peters was the best-known designer in Britain. Zelig was no longer on the edge of the picture—he was right at the centre. Of course, Peters thought he could walk on water and was even photographed in a bowler hat attempting the feat for the front cover of an American advertising magazine. He couldn't.

When the 80s party was over, the Michael Peters Group imploded horribly and traumatically in 1990. But within two years, its founder had established a new vehicle for new times. Its name was Identica and it anticipated many of the key themes of the 1990s, an era which saw the rise of the big global brand and of digital technology.

The rules changed completely in the 1990s as branding blurred the boundaries between design and advertising and digital platforms enabled communication to be rolled out successfully around the world.

Michael Peters, sobered by his crash and that of the entire British design industry, anticipated it all with that keen radar of his. Identica would sell not on design but on brand strategy, not on a charismatic named leader but on a cool, client-oriented collective. Don't mention the D-word was the motto throughout the entire sector. Once again Peters managed the transition more effectively than most, working globally for big brands like Nike and Universal Studios, expanding into new markets such as Israel and Russia, for whom he re-designed Aeroflot. Within a few years he had built a global network more robust than his global group of the 1980s.

Today, after four decades of innovation, provocation and success in design and branding, Michael Peters has entered his post-Identica phase as determined as ever to reinvent himself. His significance lies in helping to create a more professional and entrepreneurial design industry in Britain while retaining a truly creative commitment to craft and ideas inherent in the very best of his art direction. He has been a radical in both organisation and output, full of chutzpah and unafraid to confront the accepted wisdom of each age, as the title of this book, with its dig at the Naomi Kleins of this world, suggests.

His is a tale that needed telling and many of us spent years advising Michael Peters that he needed to consolidate his life and works in one publication. He never listened. He was always too busy chasing the next project. Now at last *Yes Logo*, with its elegant and spare commentary by design writer Sarah Owens, a graduate of the RCA's History of Design programme, has assembled the entire story with clarity and style. Its message is that Michael Peters remains the classic outsider and all the more persuasive for adopting that stance.

Formations
1941–1969

David Hillman

I met Michael Peters at the London School of Printing in 1959 when we were enrolled on the same graphic design course. His ambition as a designer was evident even back then, and as a friend I have followed the many turns his career has taken over the years with great interest. Our graduation in the early 60s was at the beginning of an exciting period in history as well as in the development of design.

The decade has so many key figures and iconic events that they are too numerous to mention, but from Kennedy and Martin Luther King to Twiggy and The Beatles, there was never a dull moment. Ban the Bomb, race riots, Elvis Presley, Men in Space, Women's Liberation and miniskirts were enough to inspire our generation and its designers too.

It was a time of renewal. Not only did we say farewell to rationing and the austerity of the post-war years, we also saw the beginning of a huge shift in the design profession. We had to complete our apprenticeships under the watchful eyes of the grand old men of the day but there were many new and exciting developments around the corner. Initially we had to learn our professional craft, which alongside design and draughtsmanship included hand lettering, typesetting, block-making, and other now long-forgotten skills, but we learned from the best.

The major influence on graphic design at the start of the decade was the typography of the new Swiss School and the graphic communication style of the USA—but we were inspired by many different design greats like—Eckersley, Smith, Cowan, Birdsall and Beck. The influences of jazz, modern cinema, magazines and mass communication meant there was a rich diversity of design influences on young British designers and we all became aware of the work of Saul Bass, Paul Rand, Herb Lubalin and Vignelli which was out there alongside that of Brockman, Henrion, Milner Gray and Mischa Black. Too many names to mention but incredibly inspiring times. I worked for the newly created *Sunday Times* colour supplement and *Nova* magazine finding my own design voice and like Michael saw enormous changes in this period. Much of the work from this period still has great power, but imagine the shock of the first Pirelli calendar, or the introduction of Helvetica, the epitome of Swiss design, and how about the unveiling of the Lotus car or the public adoption of the Ban the Bomb symbol? Heady times indeed.

	1959	**1960**	**1961**	**1962**	**1963**	**1964**
Politics	• Castro to power • First known human with HIV dies in the Congo • Start of the Vietnam War	• Martin Luther King receives Nobel Prize • Nelson Mandela sentenced for life • Jawaharlal Nehru dies	• Bay of Pigs • Berlin Wall is built	• USA and Russia avoid nuclear war • First black student in US (University of Mississippi)	• Kennedy assassinated • Martin Luther King "I Have A Dream" speech • Profumo scandal	• Robert Kennedy runs for president • France tests first atomic bomb
Music	• Buddy Holly dies • Billie Holiday dies • Cliff Richard is the best-selling British artist	• *Top of the Pops* premieres on BBC television • The Beatles and the Rolling Stones break into the USA	• *West Side Story* is released on film • New York debut of Bob Dylan	• The Beatles release their debut single, "Love Me Do"	• Edith Piaf dies • Beatlemania	• The Beatles make their debut in Hamburg, Germany • Highest chart position: Elvis Presley "It's now or never"
Art	• Homage to Surrealism exhibition celebrating the fortieth anniversary of Surrealism • Mark Rothko—*Black on Maroon*	• Edition of Duchamp's *Bicycle Wheel* • Harpo Marx dies	• Young Contemporary Show • Hemingway commits suicide • Louis-Ferdinand Céline dies	• Marilyn Monroe dies • Sidney Janis Gallery mounts The New Realists—the first Pop Art group exhibition in an uptown gallery in New York City • *That Was The Week That Was* first aired	• First episode of *Dr Who* is aired • Bond film *From Russia with Love* • Georges Braque dies	• Hitchcock *Psycho* • Fellini *La Dolce Vita* • Andy Warhol Campbell's Soup • *Beyond The Fringe* conceived by Robert Ponsonby
Design / Architecture	• Frank Lloyd Wright dies—his Guggenheim museum in NY opens to the public • Launch of the Mini motorcar	• BT tower, London, topped out • Flaminio Bertoni dies	• Panton's plastic furniture	• Introduction of Castiglioni's Taccia table lamp and the Arco and Toio floor lamps	• Bankside Power Station in London, designed by Giles Gilbert Scott, is completed • Launch of the Aston Martin DB5	• Kenwood Mixer • Giles Gilbert Scott dies • Birdsall designs Penguin book covers
Innovation	• Russian probe Luna 2 sends back first photos of the far side of Earth's Moon	• Two planetary probes leave for Mars	• Yuri Gagarin, a Russian, is the first man in space	• *The Sunday Times* gets colour supplement • The first transatlantic television transmission occurs	• Russia sends first woman, Valentina Vladimirovna Tereshkova, into space	• Lambretta Scooter • Nikon F camera
Fashion	• Pantyhose introduced • Dior red cabbage dress • Yves St Laurent invents the hobble skirt	• 'Discothequery'—shorter, skinnier fashions • Rudi Gernreich makes headlines designing the first topless bathing suit for women	• Fashion mirrors the styles of Jackie O with short crisp hairdos and underfitted suits as well as that of Audrey Hepburn following the 1961 release of *Breakfast at Tiffany's*	• 'The Teddy Boys' influences the Mod look	• In Spain Armancio Ortega Gaona founds Inditex—the world's fastest expanding makers of fashion clothing	• Beatniks • Dr. Martens • Marc Bohan takes over fashion house Dior
Sport	• Ingmar Johansson becomes first non-American world Heavyweight Champion since Italy's Primo Carnera, 25 years previous, by beating Floyd Patterson	• Cassius Clay dismisses Sonny Liston to win the World Heavyweight Championship • Tokyo Olympics first to be broadcast worldwide on television	• Tottenham wins double cup and League Cup	• Rod Laver wins Grand Slam	• Jim Clark wins world championship—Grand Prix • Sonny Liston wins Heavyweight Championship of the World by knocking out Floyd Patterson in the first round	• Real Madrid wins European Cup • Rome Olympics sees the arrival of Cassius Clay—Mohammad Ali
Projects		London School of Printing (LSP)		THE DI-VINE REL-ATIVITY	YALE LAW REPORT	The Last Angry Man / GEORGE ROSE ENTERTAINS

18

1965

- Churchill dies
- Malcolm X is assassinated
- US troops are sent into Vietnam

- The Beatles awarded MBEs
- Dylan releases influential album *Highway 61 Revisited*

- Roy Lichtenstein *Girl with Hair Ribbon*
- TS Eliot dies
- Stan Laurel dies

- Le Corbusier dies
- Crosby/Fletcher/ Forbes is formed

- Non-crease fabric introduced
- First US astronaut walks in space

- Jean Shrimpton sun hairstyle
- Mary Quant's Miniskirt

- Footballer Stanley Matthews retires

1966

- Mao proclaims Cultural Revolution
- Race riots flare up in the US

- The Jimi Hendrix Experience form
- *Pet Sounds* by the Beach Boys

- André Breton dies
- Hans Arp dies
- Giacometti dies

- *Complexity and Contradiction in Architecture* by Robert Venturi
- Superstudio founded in Florence

- Luna 10 enters orbit around the Moon
- VTOL aircraft, Dassault Mirage III

- Twiggy launches career
- Mary Quant is awarded an OBE

- England wins the FIFA World Cup beating West Germany 4–2

1967

- Six-day War won by Israel
- Large demonstrations against Vietnam War in US
- Che Guevara is killed

- Elvis Presley and Priscilla Beaulieu are married in Las Vegas
- BBC Radio 1, BBC Radio 2, BBC Radio 3 and BBC Radio 4 are all launched

- René Magritte dies
- Michael Fried publishes *Art and Objecthood*—a critique of minimal art

- Queen Elizabeth Hall is opened in London
- Moscow's 537 metre tall Ostankino tower is finished

- First Boeing 737 (100-series) takes its maiden flight
- The first UK colour television broadcasts begin on BBC2

- Mini Mals—a type of surfboard—and pork pies launched
- 'Maxi' length launched

- Billy Jean-King wins Wimbledon for second time

←**SPACE'FITTA"**→

1968

- Nixon elected president
- Martin Luther King is assassinated
- Paris May 68

- *Hair* opens
- Johnny Cash performs live at Folsom Prison

- Radical feminist Valérie Solanas shoots Andy Warhol, wounding him
- Marcel Duchamp dies

- Lake Point Tower in Chicago is completed
- Saul Bass wins an Oscar for the short film *Why Man Creates*

- Apollo 8 enters the moon's orbit
- First beanbag chair is produced

- The first of Biba mail order catalogues launched
- Fashion 'permissiveness'

- Manchester United wins European Cup
- Mexico Olympics

1969

- Richard Nixon becomes the 37th President of the US
- Northern Ireland riots
- The Stonewall riots in NYC—start of the modern gay rights movement in the US

- John Lennon and Yoko Ono: Bed In and Give Peace a Chance
- The Beatles give their last public performance
- Woodstock Festival

- Samuel Beckett is awarded the Nobel Prize
- *Easy Rider*
- *Midnight Cowboy*

- Bank One Plaza in Chicago is completed

- Man lands on the moon
- Dr Denton Cooley implants the first temporary artificial heart
- First Concorde test flight

- Levi-Strauss starts to sell bell-bottomed jeans
- First Gap store is launched

- Robin Knox Johston becomes the first person to sail around the world solo without stopping
- Pele scores his 1,000th goal

Early Years

Michael Peters was born in Luton, Bedfordshire, as the only son of Hyman and Claire Peters, and grandson of Mr and Mrs Gabriel Patashnik and Mr and Mrs Herschel Pievsky. The Patashniks were émigrés from Poland who, prior to the Second World War, had fled to London via Paris to escape persecution, survived the London Blitz and finally settled in Luton. The Pievskys had emigrated from Kiev, managing to get on a ship which they were told was heading for America—instead, they were taken to Liverpool. Peters' immediate family had moved from London to a rented accommodation in 31 Lincoln Road, Luton, when Hyman Peters, once a successful furrier with his own manufacturing workshop in Great Portland Street, lost his business due to a change in fashion.

Thus, private misfortune met the already bleak situation many Britons found themselves facing during and after the war. Not only did the nation have to come to terms with tremendous losses and devastations—as a young child, Peters witnessed firsthand the bombing of his home town—it also had to cope with a high unemployment rate and economic recession. The years after the war were marked by pragmatism and austerity, as the state responded to the shortage of materials by regulating the production and consumption of food, clothing and furniture, and rationed these under the 'Utility Scheme' up until the mid-1950s.

Throughout the hardship, Peters and his younger sisters, Elaine and Rosalind, grew up in close camaraderie. Although his parents failed to encourage any kind of artistic pursuit, music entered the household in the shape of Hyman's brother Abe Pievsky, a violinist in the Royal Philharmonic Orchestra. The young Peters quickly became enamoured with his uncle's tales of music; he was furthermore provided with a musical introduction to Mozart, Beethoven, Schubert and finally, Shostakovich. He was equally captivated by the concerts he was taken to, where he experienced "more than just black notes on bars, but the blending of instruments and ideas". This was a very first encounter with the notion of achieving a higher goal through collaboration—one that would accompany him throughout his later career.

As a young boy, Peters read avidly, and his natural inquisitiveness led him to favour books with a touch of mystery. His favourite fictional character was, in fact, a detective in the Hardy Boys series

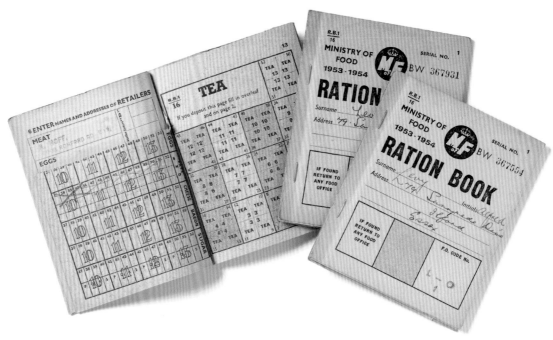

Top: At the beginning of the Second World War—The Ministry of Food issued Ration Books in October 1939 to all members of each family. Each person was allowed (in lieu of a coupon from the Ration Book) a specific amount of food, from meat to tea and from cheese to sugar. The scheme finally ended in 1954.

Bottom: This painting of St George and the Dragon, now in the National Gallery of Art in Washington DC, was painted by Rafael in 1504. It was part of a BBC series devoted to explaining famous paintings. Peters avidly listened to these broadcasts heightening his interest in the world of fine art. Courtesy Bridgeman Art Library/National Gallery Washington.

Opposite: Michael Peters' parents Claire and Hyman in happier days, strolling along the promenade in Cliftonville, near Margate in Kent, in June 1948.

by Franklin W Dixon. He also regularly listened to daily radio serials, including the BBC's *Journey Into Space* and *Dick Barton: Special Agent* (which was first broadcast in October 1946). During the 50s and 60s, the radio played a significant role in the life of most Britons, forming the centrepiece of the living room around which families would gather in the evenings.

The radio, or more specifically, the BBC, then provided one of the turning points in Peters' life when it launched an art programme for children. After subscribing, young art lovers received via mail roughly a dozen reproductions of famous paintings, ranging from the works of El Greco to those of Picasso. Each painting was then presented on the radio. Peters recalls being most intrigued by Rafael's *St George and the Dragon*, and the precise geometric analysis and vivid description given by the programme. It immediately sparked his interest in the visual arts, and he started doodling,

drawing, and tracing postcards of paintings. As he grew older, his tracing obsession expanded to include interesting photographs from newspapers, and, as he admits, "ladies scantily clad" from the popular girlie magazine *Tit-Bits*, which he had to hide from his displeased parents.

At age 11, Peters took the 11 Plus, a test introduced in 1944 which measured the scholastic ability of students in their last year of primary school. The test determined whether the student was suited to enter a secondary modern school or grammar school, and thus, would be provided with the education to take up a respected profession. By passing the 11 Plus, Peters had an entry ticket to Luton grammar school, where he was immediately put into the D-stream. These were the "dunderheads, the dunces, the renegade bunch who were good at sports, but had the rubbish teachers", he recalls. They were the polar opposites to those in the A-stream, who were "bright and clever and loved science". Peters, however, found his academic subjects rather boring, and instead continued drifting towards the visual arts.

His artistic interests, however, soon conflicted with his religious education, as the Patashniks were strongly observant orthodox Jews and wished for him to study at a Yeshiva, a religious school teaching the Torah and Talmud. Peters had never mentioned his newfound interests out of respect to his grandparents, however, roughly a year after his Barmitzvah, he could no longer keep his secret. He announced at the family Passover dinner that he had decided not to attend the Yeshiva, and in the ensuing shocked silence added that he had been considering visiting the local Polytechnic to study art. After a long and very serious conversation, Peters' grandfather came to realise the passion his grandson felt, and assured him of his blessing to attend an art college upon finishing grammar school: "If art school is your Yeshiva, then that's where you must study."

Couple's Adventurous 50 Yea...

TRAVELLED EUROPE, SETTLED AT LUTON

Son From Australia At Golden Wedding

Mr. and Mrs. G. Patashnik, of 54, Leagrave-road: Sunday was their golden wedding day. —M9300M.

MARRIED in Poland, "exiled" from France, blitzed in London, and now happily settled in Luton— that is part of the story of the 50 years married life of Mr. and Mrs. Gabriel Patashnik.

On Sunday this 71-years-old Jewish couple, of 64, Leagrave-road, celebrated their golden wedding. One son travelled from Australia for the event. Now they are at Cliftonville on their "second honeymoon."

Born in Poland, Mr. Patashnik has led a varied life. He was a Russian soldier in 1906, has travelled in Switzerland, Germany, Austria and France, and has been a Paris tailor.

On holiday, came to England in 1914 ... of Europe changed, and he found that it would be impossible for him to return to Paris.

With his wife he settled in London and by 1941 they owned a manufacturing business at Highbury. A German bomb ended that venture, and they started life once again—in Luton.

Before that, said Mrs. Patashnik, "we went through a hell of a life."

Here they took over the store in Leagrave-road, which they have turned into a homely drapery shop.

On Saturdays the shop is closed, because Mr. Patashnik is a devout worshipper at Luton Synagogue.

ENGLAND THE BEST

They had a tribute to pay to England.

"Although we have loved every country we have lived in, we wouldn't change any country for England—it's the best country in the world. It is also the most honest country." They have always kept their business among working people.

On Sunday their family — one daughter and four sons— travelled to Cliftonville to give them a celebration in their hotel. At the end of a fortnight they can look forward to another celebration in London.

Said their daughter, Mrs. C. Peters, who is a vice-President of Luton and Dunstable Zionist Group: "They are the most wonderful parents children could ever wish to have."

A Born Salesman

In his mid-teens, and while still at grammar school, Peters began working Saturdays at Jefferson's, a menswear shop in Luton's George Street. For a wage of £1.50 per day, he was hired to do the cleaning and sweeping, but soon also assisted with the sales. The job unearthed new talents, as Peters learned that he was quite a good salesperson: "I could literally sell a suit of clothes and a tie and shirts to anybody. I had a natural feel for selling." In an interview with *Creative Review* in 1981, he was certain that "If I hadn't gone into design I would have gone into retailing. They're both the same—I have to convince people to buy my goods."

Peters then had the chance of employing both his artistic talent and business sense when he was asked to dress the shop windows and design posters for special occasions. He realised that window dressing was less straightforward than it seemed—that he had only one chance to sell a shirt while people passed by the window, and therefore, that he had to instantly capture their imagination. This was a first nudge towards his later design approach: to apply his artistic skills and business insight to commercial problems, and to find the best and most beautiful solution possible.

After the war, the business of solving commercial problems had increasingly regained importance, as consumerism once again blossomed. The Festival of Britain on London's South Bank,

which marked the 100th anniversary of the Great Exhibition, celebrated in 1951 the British advances in technology and design, allowing a newfound optimism and belief in scientific progress to enter the hearts and minds of people. The majority of Britons had also become more affluent, as Harold Macmillan confirmed in 1957.

Meanwhile, Peters was failing in grammar school, and there was little hope that he or his fellow pupils in the D-Stream would pass any O-levels. The headmaster of the school thus decided to take drastic measures by transferring two A-stream teachers—one for mathematics, one for English literature—to the rambunctious D-stream. These teachers "brought their subjects to life", Peters recalls, "for the first time I was really interested in reading books by HG Wells and Shakespeare". It was his maths teacher especially, who through

Opposite: This cutting from the Luton News *in June 1956 celebrates the 50th Wedding Anniversary of Adele and Gabriel Patashnik. Peters was very close to his grandparents and spent a great deal of time in their company.*

Top: Created by Peters, this hand-lettered advertisement was published in the Luton News *in July 1960, for Jefferson's Menswear Shop.*

Bottom: Peters with his mother Claire and his two sisters, Elaine (right), and Rosalind (left), in their garden in Lincoln Road, Luton.

Part of the audience that attended Speech Day, 1953, with file of recipients of awards at far side.
(LN-LMC)

The Literary and Scientific Society listened to a fascinating Presidential Addres
by Mr Donald Sutcliffe called 'Travellers' Tales' which ranged from Mandevill
to Shipton's Abominable Snowmen. The joint debate with the H
that 'In this new Elizabethan Age the costume
be revived'. It was proposed by D
d Les Young; the n

his ability to express mathematics in visual terms
ignited in Peters a lifelong appreciation for
geometric and abstract art. He passed his
O-levels in maths and English literature effortlessly—
interestingly however, he failed those in art. "I
was a bit of a rebel", Peters explains, "I had just
discovered the Bauhaus and painters like Wassily
Kandinsky and Paul Klee, and wasn't interested
in the realistic representation demanded by my art
teacher. If they asked me to draw a nude woman,
I would do it the way Braque would have done it."

In 1957, the year that the Soviet launching
of the Sputnik satellite triggered the race to
the moon, 16 year old Peters graduated from
grammar school. He was undecided on which
field to further pursue. On one hand, he had
already developed an interest in packaging by
indulging in fromology, the art of collecting cheese
labels. On the other hand, he had started to
become keenly interested in architecture after
reading Ayn Rand's novel *The Fountainhead*
and seeing the Hollywood adaptation starring
Gary Cooper.

His interest in architecture had also been
fuelled by a competition to design a showroom
for G-Plan, a range of modern and affordable
furniture launched in 1953 by EH Gomme and Sons.
Peters nicked hundreds of colour swatches and

paint chips from his local outlet, from which he cut
out and assembled little pieces of furniture to form
three-dimensional room sets. Much to his own
amazement, his submission won the competition
and was awarded the "princely sum" of One
Guinea (£1.10).

Encouraged by this achievement and
armed with his O-levels, Peters then set upon
applying to several architectural schools. However,
as he told *Communication Arts* in 1986, "the
examining bodies felt that I was lacking in some
of the prime requisites for the study of architecture"—
the prime requisites being five O-levels. His
mother, who at this time had separated from her
husband after an acrimonious marriage, then
decided to take matters into her own hands by
sending her son to the Jewish Board of Guardians,
an employment agency that assisted Jewish
immigrants and refugees. Upon arriving and
being interviewed in an old-fashioned building
in London's East End, where the Board was
located, Peters remembers haughtily being asked:
"Architecture? What kind of job is that for a Jewish
boy?" Nevertheless, the job agency managed to
secure him a place in what they thought was an
architectural firm. In fact, and unbeknownst to
Peters, it was the studio of the German graphic
artist Hans Arnold Rothholz.

Above: Arnold Rothholz, the German graphic designer gave Michael Peters his first job after leaving Luton Grammar School in 1957.

Right: This poster for RoSPA was one of a number designed by Rothholz for Second World War safety information.

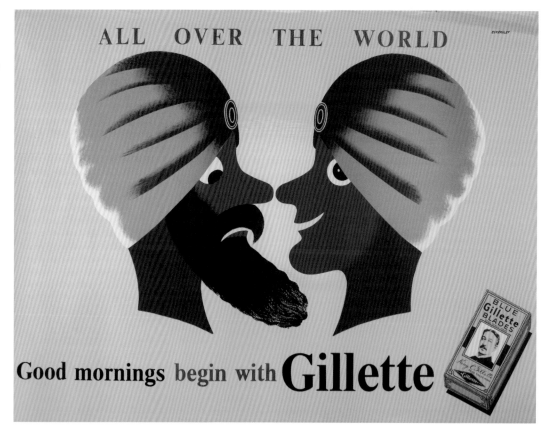

ALL OVER THE WORLD

Good mornings begin with Gillette

BLUE
Gillette
BLADES

The Designer's Apprentice

When Peters went for an interview with Rothholz—"a gruff, frightening, harsh man with a shock of white hair"—in his studio in Cricklewood, North London, he first encountered his future mentor at the window with a pencil in hand, conducting along with a piece of classical music playing at an ear-shattering level. The interview went well, and Rothholz agreed to take him on as an apprentice for £4.50 a week. Being apprenticed, however, also meant that Peters had to leave the house every morning at an "ungodly hour" (at 6:30 am), so that he could arrive early at Rothholz's second studio, where the employees worked.

There, Peters' responsibilities included stoking the boiler and lighting the fire, mixing the German Plakat paints, sharpening the pencils and sweeping the studio. He was also asked to clean Rothholz's car and teach mathematics

to his daughter. Looking back, Peters characterises this time as being "not so much a formal apprenticeship with a set programme, but rather learning by stealth. I was a lackey. I think he hired me purely because his daughter liked me and because I was good at maths."

Several months into his apprenticeship, he started wondering about the lack of architectural drawings or models in the studio, since he only ever saw the employees draw, letter and design exhibitions. Thus, while the master was out for lunch one day, Peters decided to sneak into Rothholz's private studio, where he imagined the architectural models and blueprints to be kept, only to find more exhibition graphics. Rothholz, upon discovering his utterly perplexed apprentice, explained that he was not an architect, but a graphic artist who had studied in Britain during the early 1930s. Due to his German citizenship, he had been deported to Canada at the outbreak of the Second World War, and had later returned to continue his work, which included posters for the Royal Society for the Prevention of Accidents (RoSPA), a programme for the 1948 Olympic Games, and the Dome of Discovery at the Festival of Britain.

Having grown aware of Peters' interest in the lettering work done at the studio, Rothholz began to educate him in the principles of typography. Peters learned to sketch even the smallest characters, since Rothholz would only have type set by an external source if it was smaller than a certain size. He also became more and more involved in general design work by assisting the painting of a mural for a Lyons Corner House restaurant in London, and

helping with exhibitions for the studio's main client, Shell. For Oxo, Rothholz had invented silly, but wildly popular paper glasses featuring green and red cellophane lenses. It was Peters' additional task to handle the everyday orders for the glasses, and to wrap and send them off.

It was during this time that he also got a first taste of freelancing when David Freedland, the manager of a camping equipment and outdoor clothing shop in Luton called Millets, approached him with a commission. Freedland, an acquaintance of Peters' grandfather, had seen the G-Plan showroom and, impressed by this achievement, asked him to design a poster for Lee Cooper Jeans. Putting his newly acquired graphic and lettering skills to the test, Peters painted his design on a two by three metre pegboard with Plakat paints, and was paid One Guinea for his work. Most significant however, was the linkage this freelance job established with the Freedland family, one of the countless linkages that later became important in Peters' life.

Working for Rothholz was tough, and Peters earned barely enough to go out for lunch once a week to a nearby kosher restaurant, where he would order chips and latkas (potato pancakes), since he could afford neither meat nor vegetables. But the master also introduced him to the world of graphic design, and enabled him to meet design luminaries George Him and Abram Games, who had worked with Rothholz for the RoSPA and who would, every now and then, drop by for a visit.

Through Rothholz, Peters discovered the work of corporate identity pioneer FHK Henrion and poster artist Hans Schleger (Zéró)—work which was to influence him greatly in his later career.

And Rothholz himself, despite his strictness, turned out to be a wonderful teacher, both by providing an example of how to run a successful design studio, and by being able to recognise and act upon the further needs of his apprentice. "It was he who after two years said I should be moving into a bigger world, and I too, wanted to quit in order to go to art school", Peters recalls. Making use of his contacts to other German émigré designers, Rothholz arranged for Peters to be interviewed by George Adams at the London School of Printing and Graphic Arts (LSP). He took the exams and due to the quality of his portfolio, managed to secure a place at the internationally renowned school.

Student Days

In 1959, the year that witnessed Fidel Castro take power in Cuba, and the deaths of creative pioneers George Grosz and Frank Lloyd Wright, Peters, now age 18, was enabled to fulfil his dream of going to art college. He enrolled on a three year course to pursue a National Diploma in Design at the London School of Printing and Graphic Arts. Every weekday, he travelled to and from Back Hill, Clerkenwell, which he recalls was a "bit of a Mafioso area—full of oil and leather shops".

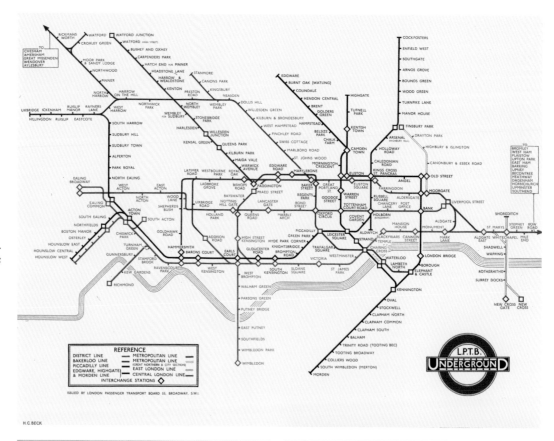

Studying with and learning from teachers and the other young students at the London School of Printing was the beginning of a whole new world for Peters. Here, he first met his lifelong friend David Hillman, and Hillman's first wife, Eileen. "I can't really remember why we got together", Hillman says, "it was just two spotting each other. He was probably the most ambitious person I'd ever met." Although all students had enrolled to study what was then called commercial art, Tom Eckersley, the head of the design department, soon split the course into two—and students from then on focused either on graphic design or typographic design. While Hillman was assigned to the graphics class, Peters due to his lettering skills went into typography.

It was only a superficial split, David Hillman recalls, since the students actually shared most of their tutors. However, it reflected the gradual professionalisation of the discipline: the vocational nature of commercial art, which was categorised into visualisation, typography, illustration or lettering, had since the Second World War increasingly turned professional, marked by the new, overarching term "graphic design". Peters' first and subsequent impressions of Tom Eckersley were rather negative, as he felt that Eckersley "looked down on us typographers, but loved the graphics class because

In order to supplement his income at the LSP—Peters created monograms and then found companies that had those initials as part of their company name. One such company was Arnold Cook in Islington. They clearly liked the design and paid Peters 21 Guineas (approximately £23.00) for the logo and stationery.

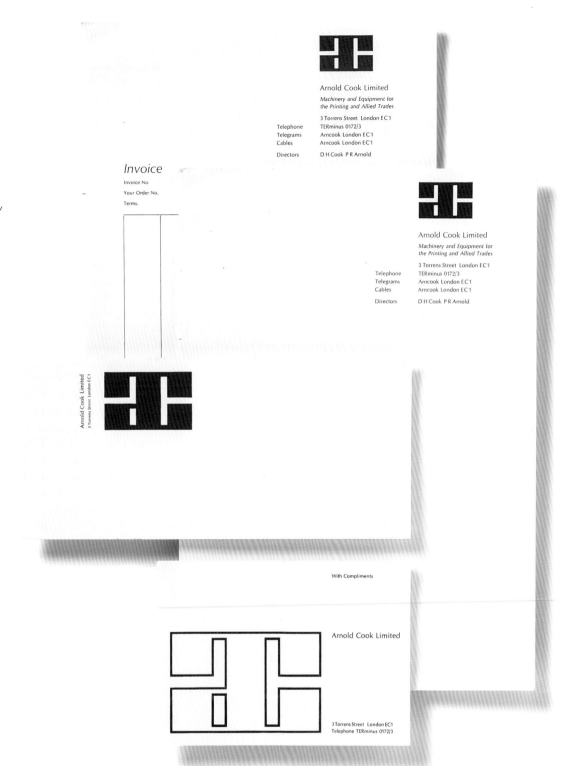

that was very much part of him. I could draw, but not quite to the standards he would have liked. I didn't realise at the time what a fabulous poster artist he was. He was able to think of a big, creative idea, and was able to implement this in the most beautiful, exciting way."

In the typographic design class, Peters was surprised to find himself taught by Harry C Beck, who was famous for creating the iconic diagrammatic plan of the London Underground system in 1931, a solution that later influenced the New York subway plan by Massimo Vignelli

and Bob Noorda and Erik Spiekermann's transportation plan for Berlin. "Beck was completely out of kilter with the rest of the teachers", Peters remembers, "he was a much older man who wore a three-piece suit with a fob watch in his waistcoat and shiny, polished shoes with cracks in the leather. One day, he excited us by showing his original sketches for the Underground map." Beck's ability to simplify complex issues such as transportation excited Peters immensely, and inspired him to work towards achieving this skill for himself.

Michael Peters setting type at the London School of Printing in 1961.

The students at the London School of Printing benefited from being taught by prolific designers and dedicated tutors. Peters met the typographer and font designer Fred Lambert, whom he described as a "beer-swigging, cigarette-smoking womaniser and a brilliant enthusiast", and met well-known typographers and designers such as Ivan Dodd, Derek Birdsall, Harold Bartram and John Gillard. Gillard was a maverick, beloved by his students, and the subsequent founder of the School of Communication Arts in London. Amongst his peers however, Peters was initially somewhat of an outsider. "I was the Jewish boy from Luton, 30 miles out in the sticks. And although I had two years' experience as an apprentice under my belt, I felt that they were much more advanced than me."

But he gradually came to feel like "one of the boys", and turned to his classmates for inspiration, since many were from the London area and thus knew the latest trends in music and film. Peters became a great jazz music enthusiast, favouring artists such as Duke Ellington, Lionel Hampton, Mel Tormé, Ella Fitzgerald, Lena Horne, Peggy Lee, Sarah Vaughan and Billie Holiday. Together with his fellow students, he frequented the Academy Cinema in Oxford Street to see the latest subtitled Italian films such as Federico Fellini's *La Dolce Vita*,1960, Luchino Visconti's *Rocco e i suoi fratelli* with Alain Delon,1960, and Michelangelo Antonioni's *La Notte* starring Marcello Mastroianni and Jeanne Moreau,1961.

Since the London School of Printing was, in essence, a printing school with an adjunct design department, its students focused mainly on design production. After assembling layouts

and taking photographs, they composed, set type and printed their works themselves. It was here that Peters learned his craft and discovered his passion for typography. "I came to understand what letterspacing meant, because I experienced having to put metal letters into the composing stick, binding the chase (the frame) and then printing the text. Getting the ink under the fingernails was a crucial part of understanding what typography was." David Hillman adds that it forced one to decide more carefully, "because the minute you committed yourself to type, there was no going back. If you made a mistake, you had to pay for it to be reset".

Peters, like many in his class, was also involved in doing freelance work. Using the school telephone box as an office, he would draw initials and then search the phonebook for a company with a corresponding name. An early success was selling a logotype to a hot and cold metal typesetter called Arnold Cook in Torrington Place, London. "It was a horrible logo, but I was paid 21 Guineas, an absolute fortune for me", he recalls.

While in his second year at the London School of Printing, one of the teachers, Keith Cunningham, played a deciding role in Peters' life. Having noticed that his work had a very 'American' style to it, Cunningham—"a wonderful mentor and exhibition designer with a great sense of humour"—suggested that Peters should consider continuing his studies in the United States.

Indeed Peters had developed a passionate interest in American graphic design. He was greatly influenced by the work of John Massey, who in 1961 had become advertising and design

manager for Container Corporation of America. He was impressed by film titles and posters designed by Saul Bass. "I loved his work for *Man with the Golden Arm* and *Bonjour Tristesse*. I loved the absolute simplicity with which he conveyed a very complicated message; the dramatic colours he used and their intensity. In one poster, you could read almost the entire film." He was equally inspired by the innovative magazine art direction

originating from the States, including Sam Antupit's *Esquire*, Henry Wolf's *Harper's Bazaar* and above all, *McCall's* designed by Otto Storch. "His magazines were full of intrigue, wonderful illustrations and photographs. Storch brought a kind of freshness to the magazine, and the whole page, not just the text, talked to you. It became our Bible."

The very thought of going to America thrilled Peters. Surviving the war nearly unscathed,

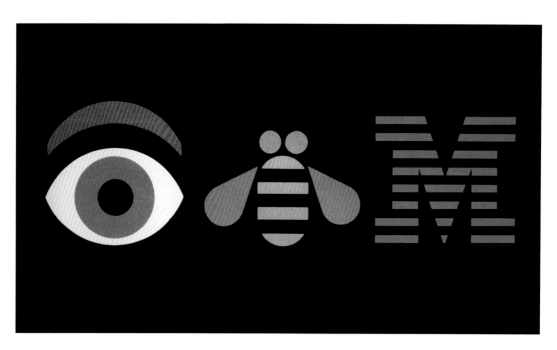

the United States had by the end of the 1950s become ever more commercialised and affluent, and the American Way of Life was aspired to by many Europeans, which indirectly supported the cultural hegemony of the USA. American Rock 'n' Roll had, through Bill Haley and Elvis Presley, already, since the mid-50s, dominated the British music charts, and Hollywood films and advertising allowed American trends in lifestyle and fashion to cross the Atlantic.

Pursuing graduate studies in graphic design in the United States was, however, even in the early 60s rather unusual for a young Englishman. Since Peters lacked the financial resources to travel to and support himself abroad, the notion of studying there seemed nearly impossible. Keith Cunningham, however, continuously encouraged Peters to apply to American art schools, and finally helped him meet two designers who were to play key roles in Peters' life: Alan Fletcher and Lou Klein. Fletcher had just returned from the United States after studying at the School of Art and Architecture at Yale and working for *Fortune* magazine in New York. By the time Peters met him, Fletcher was in the process of founding Fletcher/Forbes/Gill with his former classmate Colin Forbes and the American graphic designer Bob Gill.

Lou Klein at this time worked for the Charles Hobson advertising agency in London and was one of a number of American designers including Bob Gill, Robert Brownjohn and Bob Brooks who were making things hum in the London design scene. Klein had also studied at Yale, and persuaded Peters that his portfolio was good enough to make it into the graduate programme. With Lou Klein's and Alan Fletcher's encouragement, Peters began the Yale interviewing process during his second year at the London School of Printing, however receiving only little help from Tom Eckersley: "He thought I was pushy, and not really worth going to Yale. He would just about give me a reference."

This was the beginning of what Peters later describes as probably one of the roughest journeys of his life: getting to Yale without having the money to pay for it.

The Yale School of Art and Architecture in New Haven in the early 60s boasted an illustrious faculty with art and design greats such as Alvin Eisenmann, head of the graduate programme in design, Paul Rand, Norman Ives, Josef Albers, Herbert Matter and Alexei Brodovitch. The United States throughout the 50s had established itself as one of the leading forces in design by combining the modernist sensibility that had been brought along by émigré artists and designers with the home-grown idea of using design as a means to further the economy.

Yale, along with the New Bauhaus in Chicago, also furthered the modernist legacy by employing former Bauhaus luminaries such as Josef Albers. Peters was determined to make it to Yale, and started writing to charities in the hope of raising money, but to no avail. After passing the university's rigorous examination and interview programme, he learnt that there was one European Fellowship available to all disciplines. Fortunately, he was also promised a grant towards his airfare and expenses by the County Education Authority in Luton—but only if he managed to secure the fellowship.

In May 1962, Peters in a rare coup indeed won the prestigious, two year European fellowship. Only a few weeks later however, the Education Authority decided to withdraw its offer. He already saw the once-in-a-lifetime opportunity of studying abroad slipping through his fingers, and time was running out. His dilemma then came to the attention of Michael Freedland, a journalist for the *Luton Pictorial* and the son of David Freedland, Peters' first freelance client. The story gained momentum and was taken up by a popular daily newspaper, the *Daily Mirror*, which questioned the authority's decision.

A. L. CHATTELL LTD.

Member: National Chamber of Trade
Radio & Television Retailers Association

Directors : A. L. Chattell, K. E. Chattell (Mrs.)

Retailing Radio, Television
and Electrical Appliances

**40 High Street North
Dunstable, Beds.**

Telephone : Dunstable 62141

ALC/MH.

8th August, 1962.

Mr. M. Peters,
31 Lincoln Road,
Luton,
Beds.

Dear Michael,

     I thank you for your letter of the 4th of August in which you confirmed the verbal arrangements we made together for assistance in connection with your Yale University Scholarship.

     I enclose a cheque for £600 which represents the interest free loan of £500 which I promised you together with £50 each from Mr. M. Lewin of 33 Kingscroft Avenue, Dunstable and from Mr. B.G.England whose business address is, B.G.England(Dunstable) Limited, Half Moon Hill, Dunstable. This loan is interest free on the understanding that the repayment will be made within 2 years of the completion of your studies in America.

     I trust that this assistance will enable you to obtain the benefit of the Scholarship that has been awarded to you and that you will have an instructive and interesting time during the course of your stay at Yale.

Yours faithfully,

(A. L. CHATTELL)

Enclosure: cheque value £600.

Pictorial

No. 4661   Postage on this issue is 3d.   TUESDAY, JUNE 26, 1962   © Home Counties Newspapers, Ltd., 1962.   3d.

"Mac" Subdues C.N.D. Hecklers At Luton Hoo Fete

PRIME MINISTER, Mr. Harold Macmillan met with cheers and jeers when he delivered a policy speech to a mass meeting at the Luton United Liberal and Conservative Fete at Luton Hoo on Saturday.

CHEERS came from thousands of Conservative supporters —they had come from a wide area to converge on the lovely Luton Hoo site—who were stirred by his fervent 30-minute "two-point" speech.

...Young C.N.D. Marchers On Way To Fete

Pictures ABOVE LEFT (SR365) and LEFT (SR3864) show the enthusiastic Campaign For Nuclear Disarmament supporters, who congregated on the Moor and marched through the town to the Midsummer Fete at Luton Hoo on Saturday. Some of the marchers attended the mass meeting and persistently heckled the Prime Minister during his half-hour address. They also raised their banners and chanted "Ban-the-Bomb"... but they met their match with "Mac."

JEERS came from a small, but persistent, group of hecklers — mostly young C.N.D. campaigners, and a few Labour supporters — who only once managed to distract the Prime Minister from his oratory objective.

And even then he gave as good as he got, by wise-cracking: "You haven't paid your subscriptions!" He also encouraged the ban-the-bomb hecklers to chant louder, paused for a minute, and then silenced them in determined, dominating style.

While making a conducted tour of the fete, accompanied by Lady Dorothy, Dr. Charles Hill and Mr. L. K. Toms, Mr. Macmillan was surrounded by a protective squad of Police and "Specials." But there was no trouble from the obviously-unorganised C.N.D. people.

The extremely-well organised afternoon's entertainment began at 1 p.m., with the opening of the stalls, boat and cage bird shows.

And throughout the afternoon, there was a wide variety of attractions—ranging from helicopter flights, to bingo, water ski-ing, Hovercraft demonstrations, fashion shows to sales of produce and lucky draw competitions.

Before the afternoon reached its climax, with the Prime Minister's address, the thousands who had assembled on a specially-prepared mass meeting site were entertained by the Luton Girls' Choir.

Then came the climax, Mr. Macmillan spoke for just over 30-minutes on a range of subjects, stating the cause and the case for the Conservatives.

In a speech delivered with determination, he came right out in favour of the Common Market, hinting at the effect on Europe and the Commonwealth. Another subject was wages and the Pay Pause.

Later in the evening, hundreds of young people went to the Midsummer Fete Dance, at which the music was provided by Terry Lightfoot and his New Orleans Jazzmen.

● Pictures from the afternoon's events—Page 12.

The Rt. Hon. Harold Macmillan, Prime Minister, tours Saturday's fete at Luton Hoo.

YOUNG PEOPLE ALSO ON THE MARCH

HUNDREDS of young people from schools all over the town were on the march last week. But this wasn't a protest parade.

Scene was the Wardown sports ground. Occasion—the march past of some 1,800 competitors in the Luton Schools' Sports Association athletic championships.

And there to picture the scene was "PICTORIAL" photographer RUSSELL BAKER, who provides this week's "Camera Close-Up" feature presented on Page Three.

On the Centre Pages are published the results of an investigation we have conducted on the subject of air rifles — lethal weapons on sale to youngsters at prices ranging from 35s. 6d. to £2½.

This report assumes even more importance at a time when strenuous efforts are being made to introduce legislation restricting their sale.

Facts are presented here informatively — comment is invited from readers.

LUCIE TIMPSON this week jots her indictment on funerals. And her comments are to be found on Page Two, which she shares with DEBATER's opinions concerning the future of Stockwood Park.

Film Guide by TERRY ALLEN appears on Page Four; the week-end news is on Page Five; and the sports scene is reviewed by CHILTERN on Page Eight.

Pick of the pictures from the Hoo Conservative Fete are featured on the back page.

Lifetime-Chance Of American Degree May Be Turned Down Unless Michael (21) Obtains Study Grant

YALE SCHOLARSHIP IS IN JEOPARDY

A TWO-YEAR scholarship to study for a degree at Yale University in the U.S.A. may have to be turned down by a young Luton student at the London School of Printing and Graphic Arts.

Due at Yale in September, 21-years-old Michael Peters has so far been unsuccessful in efforts to finance this chance of a lifetime.

The University would meet a proportion of Michael's tuition fees. But the big problem that remains is the difficulty of getting a grant towards the estimated day-to-day expenses of about 5,000 dollars for his two-year stay in the States.

A former Luton Grammar School pupil, Michael worked for a commercial artist in London for two years and attended a Typography course at the Luton College of Technology.

He showed great potential and was advised by the head of the Art Department to take up full-time studies in London, later to gain even more distinctions.

Only son of Mrs. Claire Peters, of 31, Lincoln-road, he was offered a fellowship at Yale when the Principal came to this country last year.

Michael, now awaiting the results of his Diploma after three years' study, eagerly accepted. He was anxious to further his ambition to work on magazine layout and to get experience on one of the major American publications.

Now he understands that the County Education Authority, who have given him a grant and travelling fee for the past three years, are unlikely to extend the grant to cover his two years' work for a degree at Yale, where his aim was to work his way through College.

"This really is a chance-of-a-lifetime," mused Michael, at the week-end," but if I don't get a grant of some kind, it looks like I will have to turn the offer down.

He said the Education Authority CAN and DOES make grants to students going abroad. But, despite pleas on Michael's behalf by Mr. Skinner (head of College of Technology), Dr. Charles Hill, the Royal Society of Arts, and the head of the London School of Printing and Graphic Arts, the County has declined to offer any help.

"I am working hard, and hope to raise something like £200 by September, but that's nowhere near enough," commented Michael.

****
ANXIOUS WAITING

★ MICHAEL PETERS—for this 21-years-old Luton student, it's a time of anxious waiting. . . . He expects the result of a recent Diploma examination any day, and is also living in hopes of gaining a grant towards his upkeep at Yale University, America.

****

GALLOPING GRANDPA PLANS TO BEAT HIS RECORD

THAT galloping grandpa, marathon walker Bill White, came into the "PICTORIAL" offices last week and declared: "I reckon I could do the walk from Land's End to John O'Groats in 19 days —three days less than it took me to walk from John O'Groats to Land's End.

"All I want is some sportsman to donate half of my expected £25 expenses. I've got someone else who will give me the other half."

Bill, a Wellington-street second-hand furniture dealer, who will be 60 next month added:

"I could do the walk anyway. I'm always in training. I smoke 40 cigarettes a day. I would be doing it to prove I'm faster from Land's End to John O'Groats than from John O'Groats to Land's End, which is the usual route."

He explained: "In long distance walks it takes a few hundred miles for your feet to harden. Starting at John O'Groats you have to cover really rough roads while your feet are still tender. If you start from Land's End your feet are really hard and tough by the time you reach the rough roads in Scotland.

If anyone knows, Bill should. In 1960 he competed in the country-long Butlin walk, and completed the 900 miles, plus distance in 23 days, 14 hours, and 40 minutes. He was the second oldest man to complete the distance.

"Reckon I could cut three days or more off that time," so saying Bill left the "PICTORIAL" offices to return to his shop—walking, of course!

ABOVE (SR3840), A finalist in the 1960 "Miss Luton" contest, Miss Linda May Bunker, the first daughter of Mr. and Mrs. L. E. Bunker, of 7, Bancroft-road, Luton, was married at Luton Parish Church on Saturday. Her bridegroom was Mr. Nicholas Gerard O'Connor, the first son of Mr. and Mrs. W. G. O'Connor, of The Chequers Inn, Whipsnade.

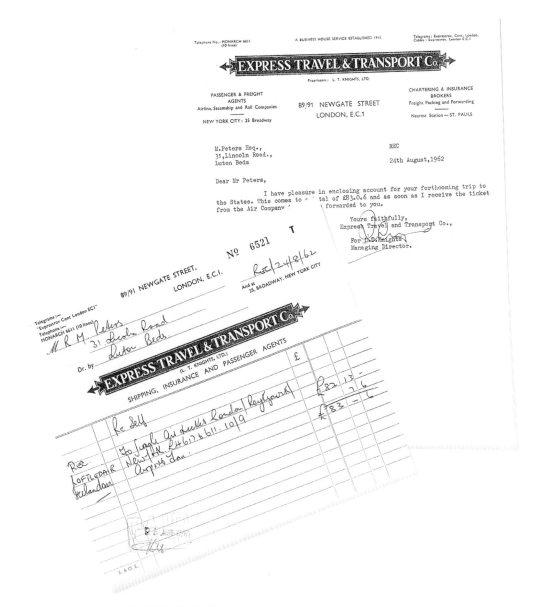

Interestingly, the authority replied that they did not recognise Yale University's School of Art and Architecture as an 'Institute of Higher Learning'.

It was therefore back to writing letters to charities with little response, until one day, Peters received a phone call from the principal of the College of Further Education in Dunstable, Bernard Armstrong. Armstrong had taken a personal interest in the case and asked whether Peters wanted to explain his predicament to the local Rotary Club. This he did, and soon received another phone call from one of the Rotarians, AL Chattell, who dealt in electrical appliances.

Then followed a rather mysterious episode in which Peters, invited to visit Chattell in Dunstable on a hot summer's day, encountered the Rotarian sitting in a wingback chair in front of a roaring fire. On a small wooden coffee table, he discovered a file labelled "Michael Peters, Yale University", full of newspaper clippings documenting his quest. After conversing for a couple of minutes, Chattell offered him a loan of £600, to be paid back within two years of the completion of his studies. Stunned,

incredulous, and rather unclear about Chattell's motives, Peters initially felt he should decline the offer. Chattell, however, explained that he and five other benefactors had been following Peters' progress for some time, and, impressed by the tenacity with which he had tried to raise money, had decided to support him.

Peters promised to pay back the generous loan, and with his stateside studies thus guaranteed, was able to make arrangements to travel to New Haven, Connecticut. He was joined by 20 year old Jo Levy from Ilford, Essex, whom he had met a few months earlier at a charity event and who, by chance, was also planning to go to America. A year later, she became his wife. Peters graduated from the London School of Printing in 1962, while David Hillman, who had also initially inquired into Yale, upon his graduation felt that he had had enough of being a student. "I wanted to go off and sample the real world", he says. He started as a design assistant at the newly introduced and very soon, highly influential *Sunday Times Magazine*.

The Bauhaus Legacy

In September 1962, Peters arrived in the USA as a "starry-eyed European", thrilled at having been accepted to one of the most renowned design schools in the world, but not quite knowing what to expect. He had flown to Idlewild Airport via Reykjavik with Loftleidir—the Icelandic airline was the cheapest way to cross the Atlantic—and was met at the airport by Fred Palmer, the head of a host family provided to him by the United States Information Service.

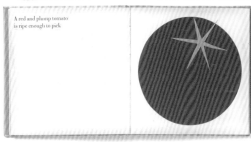

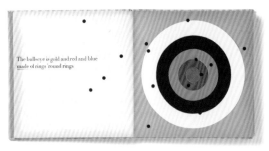

Driving from Idlewild up to New Haven, Peters recalls, "was like driving through an American movie. Big cars, huge highways and hamburger signs everywhere. It was big and colourful, brash and exciting. What amazed me most was that everybody was so welcoming, there was genuine hospitality." The Palmers introduced Peters to the world of American politics by taking him to fundraising events. "At one of these fundraising dinners", Peters recalls, "I was announced as the guest from England, and encouraged by the Republican Senator Lucy Hammer to ask a question about politics. So I wanted to know from her what exactly the difference was between the Republicans and the Democrats? The Palmers were so embarrassed that they threw me out of the house." Peters thus ended up staying with two Jewish host families during his studies.

To cover his day-to-day expenses, Peters had been given two bursary jobs. One was to design book jackets for Yale University Press, and the second was to work as a waiter in the Law School. He was, however, not too keen on waiting tables, and thus negotiated that he would instead design the *Yale Law Report*. For the *Report*, he was able to sit in on moot court hearings, and still remembers drawing the first high court black judge, Thurgood Marshall. Marshall in 1954 had won the landmark case of Brown vs Board of Education of Topeka, which declared segregation in schools as unconstitutional. Peters also worked for the B'nai B'rith, one of the oldest Jewish humanitarian organisations, and designed and mimeographed striking black and white posters for the weekly Shabbat services.

Like Alan Fletcher before him, Peters studied under the famous Paul Rand, Alexei Brodovitch and Herbert Matter, benefiting from their expertise and knowledge of design practice. "Paul Rand was the greatest teacher, he taught graphic design like nobody I'd ever encountered. I took photography with Brodovitch and basic

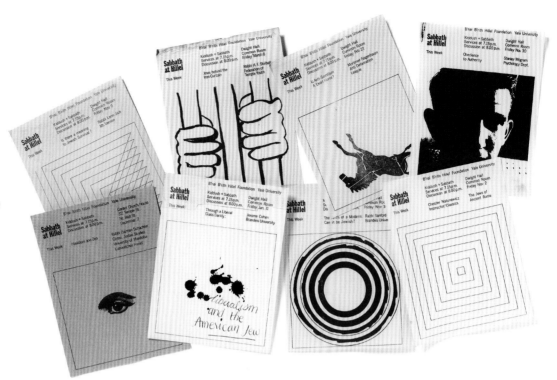

design and collage with Matter. Their teaching was based on their own experience, but everything came together when we were given tasks such as designing a piece of packaging, a poster or a book jacket." Peters was made to work hard. He was expected to formulate questions, to conduct independent research and to be able to justify his work. He still remembers being severely criticised by his taskmasters—Rand especially was known for his harsh criticism—but continuously learning from his mistakes.

Paul Rand, seen by many as the "father of modern American graphic design", because of his ability to fuse European modernist influences with American business pragmatism, had been teaching at Yale since 1956. "What I learned from Rand was the importance of sticking up for my ideas, believing in myself as a person and translating this self-confidence into business values", Peters says. Rand had through his work for the likes of IBM and ABC Television, his teaching, and also through his writings, incessantly sought to establish graphic design as a respectable profession, capable of both artistic integrity and commercial sensibility.

Herbert Matter was a Swiss designer best known for his posters for the national tourist office in Switzerland; Alexei Brodovitch had art directed and shaped *Harper's Bazaar* for nearly 25 years. Both were highly influential for Peters. "Matter taught me to experiment, whereas from Brodovitch I learnt to be my own person." Yale also rekindled Peters' passion for architecture, because even though he was placed in the graphic design department, he could "see what the architects were doing". During his second year, his department moved into a building designed by Paul M Rudolph, the head of the Department of Architecture at Yale.

During Peters' studies at the London School of Printing and throughout the early 60s, Swiss typography was all the rage. "Our heroes were Müller-Brockmann, Gerstner and Kutter, Herbert Bayer", David Hillman remembers. Sans-serif typefaces such as Helvetica by Max Miedinger and Edouard Hoffmann, and Univers by Adrian Frutiger had found widespread usage. This typographic style, however, left Peters "a bit cold, because it was very clinical and formulaic. It all looked the same."

He felt that American typography had a sense of warmth and character which was directly opposed to the cold aestheticism of Swiss typography. He was also intrigued by the way American typographers crafted their letterforms and logotypes, often blending characteristics of various typefaces together. Peters' typographic work during this time, he explains, was very much an attempt to combine both the beauty of Swiss typography with the imagination and verve of American designers and typographers. At Yale, he was also immensely fortunate to meet Bradbury Thompson, the prolific designer of *Mademoiselle* magazine, and to discover Will Burtin's *Scope*, a medical journal revolutionising the design of scientific knowledge.

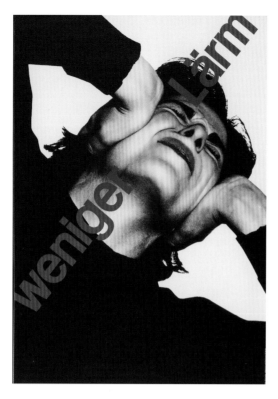

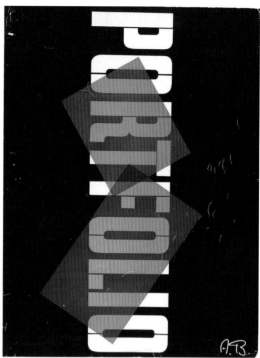

Apart from Paul Rand, the person who made the greatest impression on Peters during his studies was Josef Albers. Albers had taught the *Vorkurs*, the preliminary course, at the Bauhaus; at Yale he taught the colour course. He was one of the first masters to emigrate to America after the German design school had been closed by the National Socialist regime in 1933, and while the Bauhaus pioneer László Moholy-Nagy established the New Bauhaus in Chicago, Albers lectured at the Black Mountain College, at Harvard University and finally, at Yale.

Josef Albers gave Peters the opportunity to earn some money on the side by working with him in his studio, and assisting him with publicity. "He was a much milder and kinder person than Rand, who was extremely tough, even aggressive", he states, "but Albers was also the most shy and insecure individual I have ever met. He used to come in with piles and piles of the same magazine with articles about himself, and make me cut them out to send to his friends or put into folders." Albers' colour course was tremendously inspiring. "He made us do collages, measure colour and showed us that colour was an optical illusion." Peters also very much enjoyed working for the master. "I helped him mix paints in the studio, and people say that he only used standard Winsor & Newton paints, and never mixed these, but he did. I know because I did the mixing."

Albers spent hours talking and debating about the Bauhaus with his protégé, who was particularly interested in the Bauhaus ideal of the intersection of various art and craft disciplines, as well as its aim to overcome the gap between art and technology through collaboration. This ideal, coupled with Paul Rand's notion that design could indeed be beneficial to commerce, led Peters to conceive a "commercial Bauhaus", a group of like-minded creators who would combine their strengths and skills to solve commercial problems. Through this idea, he also grew increasingly interested in the relationship and possible co-operation between art and commerce. For Peters, the Bauhaus was the

ultimate prototype of a modern, multi-disciplinary design company.

Between his first and second year, Peters married his sweetheart Jo, courtesy of a Yale University bursary, which allowed them to return to London for the wedding. He also received his Bachelor of Fine Arts after his first year, with the agreement that he could pursue his Master of Fine Arts (MFA) the following year. In fact, he had persuaded Alvin Eisenmann to let him drop the foundation year recommended by Yale, and to encapsulate three years of study into two by promising to simply work "twice as hard".

While in his second year at Yale, Peters witnessed the tremendous social and political turmoil which held the United States in its grasp, from the invasion of Cuba at the Bay of Pigs and the Cuban Missile Crisis to the Freedom Marches under Martin Luther King, culminating in his "I Have A Dream" speech in 1963. Betty Friedan's *The Feminine Mystique* resuscitated the American feminist movement, while Bob Dylan's "Blowin' in the Wind" became the anthem of peaceful anti-Vietnam protesters. On 22 November 1963, the assassination of John F Kennedy and subsequent shooting of his assumed assassin Lee Harvey Oswald by Jack Ruby left the nation in shock. Peters remembers working on his MFA thesis and listening to the radio at that fateful moment. "Afterwards, I took my bicycle back to Yale to be there with everybody else. People put on their

black gowns and their mortarboards as a sign of respect. And there were students sitting on the curb, crying", he recalls.

His MFA thesis was an alphabet box that encouraged children to playfully learn about letterforms. Peters had become interested in this project through the Gesell Institute of Child Development at Yale, which had explained to him that young children could often not comprehend why there existed both lowercase and uppercase alphabets. He thus created a box full of lowercase letters, which were divided into hand-painted, plywood pieces and could be refigured into uppercase letters and numerals. "When the Gesell Institute tested it", he says, "the most important thing was that children loved that they could take apart the letters, feel comfortable with them and discover the shapes for themselves. Josef Albers simply and shrewdly commented: 'This makes sense out of nonsense, and nonsense out of sense.'"

After several months of hard work for his thesis, Peters received his MFA in June 1964 —an achievement of which he was immensely proud. His benefactor AL Chattell was equally pleased, and wrote his sincere congratulations. Peters had proved himself by graduating, and knew Yale had been yet another turning point for him. "The London School of Printing was remarkable, but my real learning was at Yale. Going to America changed both my life and career."

Michael Peters created Alphabetica™ as his graduating thesis at Yale. This project was inspired by his discussion with the Gesell Institute (of Child Development at Yale University). The idea was to create a playful modular alphabet that would demystify the difference in shape between lower case and upper case letters, and allow children to creatively discover the alphabet. The box contains all 26 lower case letters in different colours, (and with the aid of a diagram) enables the child to create all uppercase letters and numerals, as well as produce abstract patterns as part of their play.

An Art School assignment set by Paul Rand. The brief was to design for Borden's (a large US dairy company) a package of assorted cheeses. Peters' solution was to use the Dutch edam shape, with each segment wrapped as a different cheese.

If your Harvey Probber chair wobbles, straighten your floor.

Every piece of furniture that Harvey Probber makes at Fall River, Mass. is placed on a test platform to make sure it's on the level. If you get it, it is. Mr. Probber loses a lot of furniture this way.
Mr. Probber's furniture has an almost luminous satin finish. It is produced by a unique machine that has 5 fingers and is called the human hand.

This luminous finish takes a long time to achieve, but it lasts a long time. The lovely chair above could be made with 14 less dowels, 2 yards less webbing, thinner woods and so forth. You wouldn't know the difference, but Harvey Probber would. Of course, in a few years you would know too.

BOSTON/CHICAGO/DALLAS/DENVER/MILWAUKEE/NASHVILLE/NEW YORK/ST. LOUIS/
HARVEY PROBBER DESIGN BOOK, ONE DOLLAR; DEPT. T517, HARVEY PROBBER, INC., FALL RIVER, MASS.

A Mecca of Design

After graduating from Yale, and with Paul Rand's support, Peters secured a job with Charles Eames, whom he admired for his multi-disciplinary approach to design. "Eames was incredible, because he was a designer, a furniture maker, a filmmaker, an exhibition designer, a toymaker—he was everything." Peters was particularly excited about Charles and Ray Eames' 1961 Mathematica exhibition, which revived his appreciation of the visual depiction of mathematics. However, two weeks before he was due to join the Eames' workshop in California, he received a call from Eames' secretary. "She said that Charles had fallen seriously ill, and had to take time off. I was terribly disappointed."

He then decided that he wanted to work at Columbia Broadcasting Systems (CBS) in New York, which at the time was a 'mecca' for design. Its in-house design department worked with highly talented writers, filmmakers and art directors to create a total corporate identity for the company, overseen by its director of design, the famed Lou Dorfsman.

New York itself had turned into a hothouse for creativity in general and advertising in particular through the innovative work of agencies such as Doyle Dane Bernbach (DDB) and Papert, Koenig, Lois (PKL). Both radically transformed the look and feel of American advertising by enabling a close collaboration between copywriting and art direction. The results relied on the clever and often unexpected interplay between image and copy,

Top left and right: Celebrating all holidays— Christmas, Jewish New Year Greetings cards (featuring Jo Peters— blessing the candles) produced while in New York.

Bottom: Although Peters worked full time at CBS—he had a number of freelance clients including Time magazine. This promotional piece was designed for the Russian market to entice US advertisers to promote their products and services in the Russian edition of Time.

Gary, Josephine and Michael Peters wish you a joyful holiday

YEAR

a style that became known as the "New Advertising". Peters especially admired an ad for the furniture manufacturer Harvey Probber by George Lois, head of PKL, which read: "If your Harvey Probber chair wobbles, straighten your floor." This was a perfect example of a vital component of the "New Advertising", the execution of a big, brilliant idea both through image and text.

Paul Rand introduced Peters to Dorfsman, and one Thursday morning, Peters took the train down from New Haven to the CBS building at 485 Madison Avenue in New York, to be interviewed and to show his portfolio. It was a difficult

conversation. Dorfsman, despite liking the portfolio, denied Peters the $100 per week he needed to support himself and his wife Jo, who by this time was pregnant. "He said, 'You're kidding. I'll give you $75, take it or leave it'. And when I answered that I couldn't afford it, he ended the conversation with 'Listen, kid: CBS didn't make your wife pregnant!'" Dorfsman's secretary, who had overheard the conversation, then arranged for Peters to meet Ted Andresakes, an art director of one of the design divisions at CBS.

Both struck up an instant rapport which led Peters to sign with Andresakes and to stay at CBS

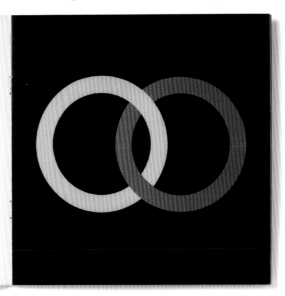

БОРЬБА ЗА ДОБРОЖЕЛАТЕЛЬНОСТЬ

Начать дела на иностранных рынках проще, если правительство вас понимает. Легче развивать дела, если печать и представители общественного и частного мнения относятся к вам доброжелательно. Чем больше предприятие рассказывает им о себе, тем благоприятнее будут решения этих влиятельных групп относительно этого предприятия—решения, основанные на фактах, а не на слухах, на знании, а не на предположениях. Информация посредством объявлений может создать признание вашего предприятия. То, что вы говорите в ваших объявлениях может создать доброжелательность и понимание.

HARRIS & SLOAN BROKERAGE CO. INC.
H&S
INSURANCE
WH 3-6870
75 MAIDEN LANE, NEW YORK, N.Y. 10038

No.

Date

Unexpired Premium and Remarks

Premium

Location

Term   Expires

Company

Policy No.

Amount

Stateme

Opposite: Through painter and designer Elaine Lustig-Cohen and her publisher husband Arthur Cohen, Peters met Harris and Sloan—a very large New York Brokerage Company. This identity and all of its applications was designed in 1965.

Top and bottom: This 40 foot (12 metre) long and eight and half foot (2.6 metre) high mural, conceived by Lou Dorfsman in 1965, was, for Peters, an example of the brilliance of Dorfsman and his fellow consultant designer Herb Lubalin. The design and construction of this great work of art was for the canteen/restaurant in the new CBS building (Black Rock), on 6th Avenue in New York. The mural locks up a series of 3-D letters, with simulated food ingredients, packaging, kitchen implements and sculptures 'designed and set' among the beautifully crafted 'food' letterforms similar to a printers job case. Courtesy Lou Dorfsman.

for nearly two years, designing diverse material such as advertising, promotion, sales kits, signage, and corporate identity work. "One day we would design an ad for a programme the next night, another day would be a poster, the day after that would be a promotional leaflet for a big American football game. They used to threaten to fire me if I didn't spend lots of money on the graphics. Money was no object at CBS."

Ted Andresakes' division, which included the designers Herb Levitt, Joan Lombardi, Peter Rauch and Peters, was directly responsible to Dorfsman. Dorfsman was particularly inspiring because of his skill in bringing various talents together. "He was a ringmaster in the circus, a catalyst and visionary, one of the best art directors in the world", Peters

says. Through Dorfsman, he met and befriended the leading lights of the American advertising and design world, including Bill Bernbach, John Bernbach (Bill's son), who became a lifelong friend and mentor, advertising maverick George Lois and designer Herb Lubalin.

New York was immensely exciting for Peters and his wife Jo, who had started to work for The Beatles' attorney at a time when they had reached the height of their popularity in the States. "In the office, they were so worried that the fans would get in, that they had policemen on patrol", Jo Peters laughs, "but of course nothing happened." She worked there until their son Gary was born in 1964, and the young family moved to the fashionable neighbourhood of Brooklyn Heights.

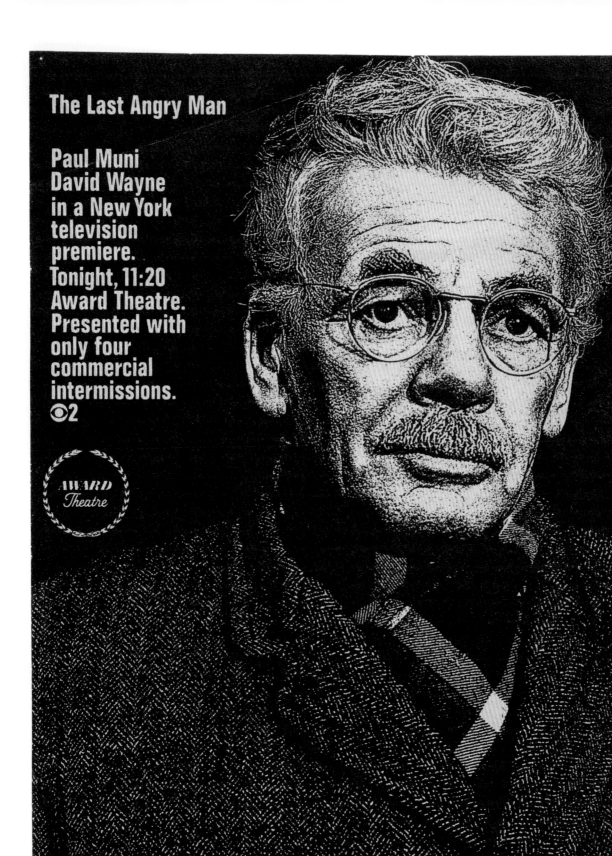

The Last Angry Man

Paul Muni
David Wayne
in a New York
television
premiere.
Tonight, 11:20
Award Theatre.
Presented with
only four
commercial
intermissions.
◉2

AWARD
Theatre

The Last Angry Man *and* George Rose Entertains *were both aired on CBS's Channel 2 in 1965. Peters designed the publicity for these showcase events through print advertisements, posters and special promotions. Very often the designers and writers were given no more than 48 hours to design and produce all communications.*

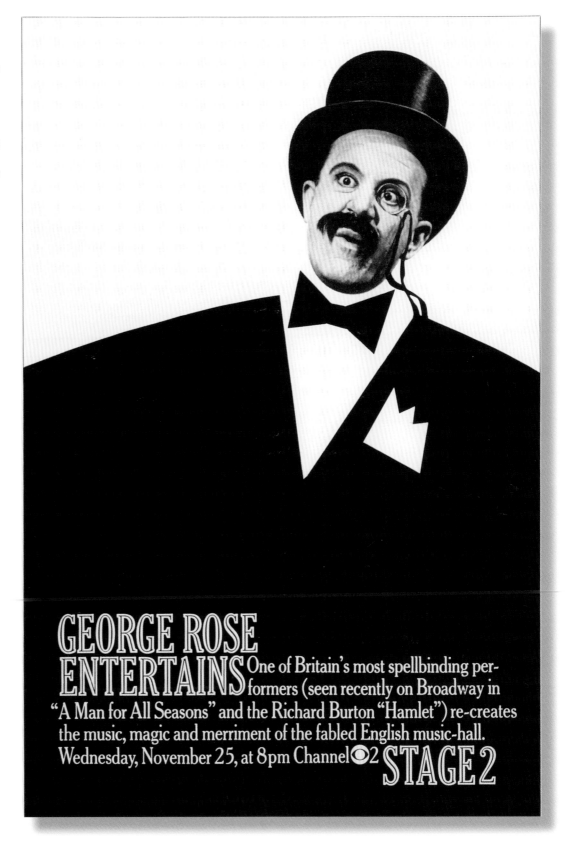

GEORGE ROSE ENTERTAINS One of Britain's most spellbinding performers (seen recently on Broadway in "A Man for All Seasons" and the Richard Burton "Hamlet") re-creates the music, magic and merriment of the fabled English music-hall. Wednesday, November 25, at 8pm Channel ●2 **STAGE 2**

"Rx for the Losers" Tonight at 7:30 ◉2

"My child is an addict"—the most terrible words that a parent can speak. Yet it can—*and does*—happen. How does teenage drug addiction start? Why? What are the symptoms? And most important, what can we do about it? WCBS-TV talks to the experts, to parents, and to teenagers themselves for some straight answers to agonizing questions. The narrator is Jim Jensen.

Although the pressure to produce these advertisements at speed was huge, Peters had the benefit of working with great copywriters to jointly create big ideas for CBS's special programmes. "RX for the Losers" and "On a note of understanding" are examples of communication turned around from briefing to delivery within 24 hours.

FAR MORE ELOQUENTLY THAN WORDS, MUSIC CREATES A BRIDGE BETWEEN PEOPLE OF DIVERGENT TONGUES AND CULTURES. ITS LANGUAGE, UNIVERSALLY UNDERSTOOD, SPEAKS DIRECTLY TO THE HEART. THIS WEEK, WITH "INTERNATIONAL HOUR: FESTIVAL OF MUSIC," THE FIVE CBS OWNED TELEVISION STATIONS—CHANNEL 2 IN NEW YORK, LOS ANGELES, CHICAGO; CHANNEL 4 IN ST. LOUIS AND CHANNEL 10 IN PHILADELPHIA—INAUGURATE THE FIFTH ANNUAL INTERNATIONAL PROGRAM EXCHANGE. THE OPENING PROGRAM (CONSULT YOUR LOCAL LISTINGS FOR TIME AND DATE) WAS PRODUCED ESPECIALLY FOR THE EXCHANGE BY KMOX-TV ST. LOUIS, AND FEATURES MUSIC FROM THE AMERICAS—AARON COPLAND, GEORGE GERSHWIN, CARLOS CHAVEZ, PETER MENNIN,

ERNEST GOLD, JEROME KERN AND LEONARD BERNSTEIN—PERFORMED BY AMERICAN BORN BARITONE ROBERT MERRILL, THE FAMOUS PIANO TEAM OF FERRANTE AND TEICHER AND THE ST. LOUIS SYMPHONY ORCHESTRA, THE SECOND-OLDEST SYMPHONIC ORGANIZATION IN THE UNITED STATES, UNDER THE BATON OF BRAZILIAN CONDUCTOR ELEAZAR DE CARVALHO. IN FOLLOWING WEEKS, THE FIVE STATIONS WILL BRING THEIR VAST AUDIENCES MUSIC AND DANCE PROGRAMS PRODUCED IN SUCH FAR-OFF PLACES AS AUSTRALIA, JAPAN, MALAYSIA AND VENEZUELA. IN TURN, AS IN YEARS PAST, ALL INTERNATIONAL HOUR PROGRAMS WILL BE FREELY EXCHANGED AMONG ALL PARTICIPATING NATIONS—A POTENTIAL OVERSEAS AUDIENCE NUMBERING IN THE

MILLIONS. (BY SPECIAL ARRANGEMENT WITH THE FIVE CBS OWNED STATIONS, THE SERIES WILL ALSO BE SEEN ON 14 STATIONS OF THE EASTERN EDUCATIONAL NETWORK IN SUCH MAJOR CITIES AS WASHINGTON, D.C., BOSTON, PITTSBURGH AND BUFFALO.) ON THIS WEEK'S SEASONAL PREMIERE, THE DOWNBEAT WILL ORIGINATE IN ST. LOUIS. BUT THANKS TO THIS UNIQUE ADVENTURE IN GLOBAL TELEVISION, THE MUSIC WILL ECHO THE WORLD OVER...EACH NOTE SERVING TO STRENGTHEN FURTHER THE VITAL BOND OF UNDERSTANDING BETWEEN COUNTRIES AND THEIR PEOPLE. **CBS TELEVISION STATIONS** ⑤ A DIVISION OF COLUMBIA BROADCASTING SYSTEM, INC., OPERATING WCBS-TV NEW YORK, KNXT LOS ANGELES, WBBM-TV CHICAGO, WCAU-TV PHILADELPHIA, KMOX-TV ST. LOUIS.

As part of working in the promotional department at CBS, designers were given sizable budgets to create special advertising promotions. This is an example of the Autumn/Winter Football Schedule for the CBS owned stations in 1965 in which Peters commissioned special photography, and lettering. The design was printed in eight colours—no expense was spared for these very important communications, which were intended to entice advertisers to commit to spending large budgets on TV advertising.

KICKOFF '65! It's the year's most exciting sports-action ticket: NFL football on the five CBS Owned television stations (Channel 2 in New York, Chicago, Los Angeles; Channel 10 in Philadelphia; Channel 4 in St. Louis). This convenient tear-out guide has a complete schedule of NFL games to be broadcast in your area during the coming season. And, if business takes you on the road, the other four major-market grid schedules may come in handy, too. Big games draw big audiences...and if advertising is your game, you're probably already wise to the sales-building potential of announcements adjacent to thrill-packed televised NFL football. Why not huddle with your CTS National Sales representative? He'll be glad to help you get the latest facts and figures? He'll be glad to help you get back your sales campaign to a winning season.

WHAT HAPPENED TO GOLDWATER?

The Inside Story of the 1964 Republican Campaign

By STEPHEN SHADEGG

WASHINGTON, Nov. 4— Senator Barry Goldwater lost his bid for the presidency of the United States long before the polls opened yesterday morning. The voters performed the ritual of marking ballots and pulling levers almost precisely as predicted.

The outcome was no surprise, but not even the most partisan of the Johnson supporters was prepared for the lopsided landslide Democrat victory.

The Goldwater rocket, fueled with such high re-

SEN. GOI

solve in San
zled on its l
Long before tl
all counted
questions wer
What happene
Continued

To supplement his income, Peters continued working freelance in the evening for the publishing company Holt Rinehart & Winston. He had acquired this job through Elaine Lustig-Cohen, first wife of design pioneer Alvin Lustig, who together with her second husband Arthur Cohen had taken Peters under their wings. One of his projects involved designing a jacket for a book about Barry Goldwater, the US senator who had spectacularly lost out to Lyndon B Johnson in the 1964 presidential election. It mirrored Peters' ambition to reconcile his sense for good design with the Big Idea thinking he had acquired while working at CBS. As David Hillman confirms, "Michael came out of the advertising industry as a much more rounded graphic designer than if he had stayed in England. He was extremely lucky and bright enough to work for the people who actually mattered." Indeed, American advertising and graphics were setting the tone during the late 50s and early 60s, and several years had to pass before Britain caught up with the giant.

Return to London

1965 saw the Vietnam War escalate, and in the spring of 1965, Kennedy's successor Johnson ordered the first napalm air strike against the Vietcong. Because Peters possessed a green card to work at Yale and at CBS, granting him the rights of a US citizen (which included fighting for Uncle Sam), he soon started receiving call-ups from the army. By chance, he simultaneously received an offer of setting up a London branch of the Cincinnati-based design group Studio Art Associates, who had heard of him through a former Yale graduate.

Peters was relieved to avoid being drafted into the American army by returning to Britain, and since Jo had also begun to feel homesick, the young family decided to leave New York. Back in London, Peters formed a company called Cato Peters O'Brien with two colleagues, Mac Cato and Dick O'Brien from Studio Art Associates. He learnt how to commercially cost jobs out in order to get clients to pay an appropriate price for design work. However he soon found that Cato Peters O'Brien did not care enough about the actual quality of the work (the quality being very important to Peters), and was instead mainly concerned with making money.

It was generally a difficult time for Peters, having just left the United States, which he adored, and having returned to a Britain that had changed, both politically and culturally. Prime Minister Harold Macmillan had in 1963 almost been brought down by the Profumo scandal, and after his resignation due to ill health, successor Harold Wilson heralded a new era for Britain, setting much hope in technological change. Sir Winston Churchill's death in 1965 was a political and cultural watershed. As more and more young people decided to break with staid traditions, the 60s, depending on one's point of view, came to signal both liberation and moral deterioration. In any case, it was the beginning of a cultural revolution, and in terms of design, golden years had begun.

The Sunday Times Magazine had been launched in 1962, the year Peters had left for Yale, and was soon followed by other newspapers, all of which triggered a need for photographers, illustrators and typographers. Disciplines mingled and established a symbiotic relationship, from the art of David Hockney and Peter Blake to the fashion of Barbara Hulanicki and Mary Quant and the designs of Terence Conran. Penguin Books had been restyled (by Romek Marber), as had the signage for the British road system (by Jock Kinneir and Margaret Calvert). The British film industry meanwhile was shaken up by the arrival of the flamboyant, fashionable James Bond movies. London had become a melting pot for talent, and exported this talent: more than 73 million Americans watched The Beatles appear on The Ed Sullivan Show.

After six unhappy months at Cato Peters O'Brien, Peters was headhunted by David Puttnam, who later became a well-known film producer (*Chariots of Fire, The Killing Fields*), and again received an offer he could not refuse. He was to join the newly created design department at Collett, Dickenson, Pearce, at the time one of the best and most innovative advertising agencies in Britain. Peters went to speak to John Pearce, one of the co-founders of CDP, and Colin Millward, its creative director. He was promised a significant level of responsibility and money, and thus, quickly agreed to work for the agency. After all, he had to support a family which again grew when his daughter Sarah was born in 1967.

Peters remembers being greeted by a letter on his desk on his first day of work. "It said, 'Dear Michael, welcome to Collett, Dickenson, Pearce, I decided last Friday to leave the agency to start my own business. You are now the head of the design department. Good luck, David Puttnam.' So I started on a Monday, expecting to be his assistant, and then had to run the department!" The very same day, he was taken out to lunch by Colin Millward, together with the new recruits Charles Saatchi, Alan Parker and John Salmon, all of whom later made names for themselves in the media and culture industry.

Setting up a design department in an advertising agency was an innovative step in Britain, although it had already been tested in the United States. Peters' task was to devise a way in which advertising and design could synthesise to make an even stronger impact on the business world. Advertising and design were at this time largely separate industries—whereas advertisers worked on identities and brochures, designers were simply, as Peters notes, "the backroom boys". Working at CDP strengthened his conviction that he could apply his design skills to solve commercial problems, and that design was indeed a means to increase profitability and a better return on business investment.

One of his first jobs for CDP was a sales kit for the fibre manufacturer Monsanto-Chemstrand. Peters had become quite interested in sales kits, as he liked the idea of giving sales people quality material to work with, and because it provided him with the chance to put his idea of linking design and commerce to the test. Together with the illustrator Alan Cracknell, he created a three-dimensional, vividly coloured "House of Monsanto", which earned a Design and Art Directors Association (D&AD) silver award in 1967. It was his first design award, with many more to come.

Setting Up Shop

The world changed with the student revolutions and iconoclasm of the late 60s, and graphic design changed along with it, triggered by protests against the gradual commercialisation of society, and in

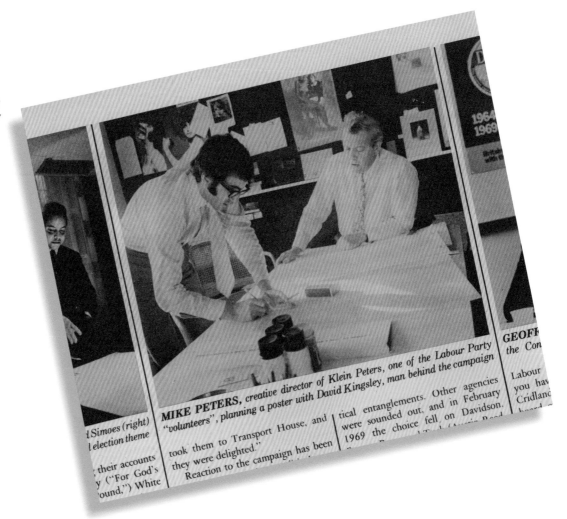

MIKE PETERS, creative director of Klein Peters, one of the Labour Party "volunteers", planning a poster with David Kingsley, man behind the campaign

Simoes (right) election theme

their accounts ("For God's ound,") White

took them to Transport House, and they were delighted." Reaction to the campaign has been

tical entanglements. Other agencies were sounded out, and in February 1969 the choice fell on Davidson,

GEOFF the Con

Labour you hav Cridland

particular, against the role of the designer as a henchman of capitalism. Ken Garland in his First Things First manifesto called for graphic designers to attend to worthier activities than consumer selling—running counter to the ideas Peters was developing—while in the United States, designers and typographers such as Milton Glaser and Herb Lubalin through their work created a completely new, playful and eclectic visual style.

In 1967 Lou Klein, whom Peters had throughout the years kept in close contact with, suggested a business partnership. Collett, Dickenson, Pearce promised them a generous financial advance as a backing, in exchange for a one-third share. The newly formed Klein Peters also took on several projects for the advertising agency. They settled in a building in Goodge Street near London's Tottenham Court Road above a fast food place called The Golden Egg, sharing the building with Puttnam and Peters' former colleague Charles Saatchi. Saatchi had teamed up with Ross Cramer, who later distinguished himself as a commercials director; both were joined by ad-man Sir John Hegarty, who went on to co-found TBWA and Bartle Bogle Hegarty (BBH). On the first day of their business, Klein Peters received a huge black stove-enamelled sign with a horseshoe with congratulations from Fletcher/Forbes/Gill.

Klein Peters was in good company. From the mid-60s up until the early 70s, and only within a few years of each other, a wave of designers had begun setting up consultancies, many of which grew to be highly influential. These included Minale Tattersfield & Partners, set up by Marcello Minale and Brian Tattersfield in 1964, Wolff Olins, formed by Michael Wolff and Wally Olins in 1965, Bill Moggridge's first company of 1969 which later turned into IDEO, and Pentagram in 1972, which had grown out of Crosby/Fletcher/Forbes. Design in Britain had slowly matured from being a cottage industry into a market force to be reckoned with. This development was supported by the founding of the Design and Art Directors Association in 1962, which aimed to raise both the profile and fees of designers by establishing professional standards and the D&AD pencil award (which had been designed in 1966 by Lou Klein).

Klein Peters enjoyed almost immediate success due to Lou Klein's ability to secure excellent clients and designers including Rod Springett, Klaus Wuttke, Jim Northover, Michael Waters—some of which later joined Peters at his subsequent companies. "I learned a lot from Lou about handling people, clients and staff", he states. As a newcomer, he was eager to prove himself as a junior partner and to gradually make a name for himself. In the same year that Klein

campaign

The newspaper of the communications business   May 22 1970   3s

Doug Maxwell joins up with top U.S. designer

DOUG MAXWELL, former joint creative director of Doyle Dane Bernbach, is getting together with Herb Lubalin, one of America's foremost independent designers, to set up a new company, Lubalin Maxwell, which will operate on both sides of the Atlantic.

The company, of which the two men will be joint managing directors, hopes to work on a wide range of design and product development problems for international clients.

But Lubalin Maxwell's ambitions go beyond servicing clients. The two partners have plans for going into small-scale manufacturing themselves to exploit some of their bright new ideas in the consumer goods field.

Actual production would be done under Lubalin Maxwell's brand name by an established manufacturer. The new company would control advertising, packaging and marketing both in Britain and the U.S.

Without disclosing what spe-

Klein Peters design group to break up

THE design consultancy of Klein/Peters is on the point of splitting. Lou Klein confirmed this week that he and his partner, Michael Peters, had agreed in principle to separate. Details remain to be worked out.

The consultancy was set up three years ago, with three-part ownership. Besides the two partners, a third of the shares is held by Collett Dickenson Pearce.

Peters was an art director at the agency before he decided to team up with Klein, then a freelance. The consultancy was very successful, gaining clients such as Birds Eye, Jaeger and ICI and winning awards from the Designers and Art Directors Association for its packaging work.

But recently differences of opinion have developed between the two partners, and they have decided it would be better to go their own ways. Peters, who is at present on holiday in Minorca, is understood to be planning to go into business on his own. Klein may join another design group.

Klein, a 38-year-old American, began his career as an art director and promotions man with *Time* magazine. Later he became creative director with Charles Hobson and Grey in London but left to work on his own.

Peters is also known for his voluntary work for the Labour Party. He designed a recent Labour poster which used a "Noddyland"-type technique to illustrate the Government's achievements.

The consultancy has specialised in packaging and point-of-sale material.

Colletts wins £½m bonus gifts account

Sam Rothenstein . . . passed over

COLLETT DICKENSON PEARCE has won the new bonus coupons account run by the Glen- total concept of the bonus gift operation. He does not envisage any conflict of clients. "The

Special 5-page report on the AA conference
Pages 43-49

Magazines wait for World Cup victory
Page 21

Who will Annan listen to ?
Page 25

Peters was launched, Peters was elected into the D&AD committee, along with Ross Cramer, David Puttnam and Michael Wolff.

Klein Peters specialised in packaging and point-of-sale material, two areas which to the partners seemed especially lucrative. A remarkable example of their approach was a carrier bag developed for the Sexton Shoe Company, which featured prominent, tightly-spaced typography combined with simple, black-and-white photography by the celebrated photographer Terence Donovan. It was rewarded with a D&AD award in 1968. For the Van Den Bergh company, Klein Peters was commissioned to create in close collaboration with art director Ron Collins, photographer Tony Elliot and copywriter John Salmon at CDP. This commission once more firmed Peters' ideas about the advantages of a collaborative creative effort.

However, as Lou Klein began devoting a significant amount of his time to teaching at the Royal College of Art, Peters found himself running the business almost on his own. "It became very apparent that I wasn't able to cope with that level of responsibility. Lou felt let down by me, his junior partner, and I felt he was letting me down because he was spending too much time teaching. We just had different philosophies." He was no longer willing to sustain the partnership with Klein, and in the Spring of 1970, roughly two months after The Beatles officially stated that they would never work together again, the Klein Peters situation culminated in an acrimonious split.

"We let the clients and staff choose who they wanted to come with, but decided to divide everything in the office 50/50, so we tossed a coin to see who would get first choice", Peters recalls. "I took this chair, he took that chair, and the same thing with the books, the pencils and the paintbrushes. It came down to that the only thing left was a rubber plant. I wanted him to take the plant, but he insisted, took a Stanley knife and whop! With the accuracy of a surgeon, had cut it into two. Ten years later, my half was thriving while Lou's plant had died within two weeks."

After the split, Peters felt chastised by a number of people in the design industry: "because I was the young upstart and seen as very aggressive. And I very much regretted that we had fallen out." In May 1970, he revealed to *Campaign* magazine his plans to expand Klein Peters into a larger company. While Lou Klein went on to act as both an art director and designer at his own company, Klein Design, Peters decided to stay on in Goodge Street and put his plan into practice by founding Michael Peters and Partners.

Vibrations
1970–1982

Bev Whitehead

I n a period of great turbulence, that saw Watergate, the IRA and mass unemployment dominate headlines, there was also great diversity in other areas of contemporary culture. From platform shoes to Disco and Punk, from Warhol, Hockney and Bowie to test tube babies and the Rubik's-Cube, this period defies definition. It was, however, a period of great change and that is never a bad time to be a designer.

Around the time Michael Peters set up shop on his own there were two distinct areas of competition. First, the old guard who had been producing packaging for years like PJ Amos & Partners, and the ad agencies like McCann Erickson and Garland Compton who developed packaging for their clients as an add on service. Then there were the new, young design studios and several independent designers that also made up a group of potential competitors. Agencies such as Crosby/Fletcher/Forbes, Wolff Olins, Minale Tattersfield, Nicholas Thirkell Associates, and Springett Wuttke were variously involved in publishing, corporate identity and packaging. There were also independent designers who had achieved recognition for their innovative work in areas similar to those then attained by Michael, notably John Blackburn, John Brimacombe, John Gorham and John McConnell along with Robert Brownjohn and Bob Gill.

Given this array of new talent and existing businesses it is interesting to pinpoint how, within a few short years Michael Peters and Partners became *the* packaging design consultancy.

There are differing reasons why the various competitors became more niche or added other corporate services, and Michael Peters and Partners also had other design skills at its core, reinforcing the quality of its offer, but I don't think these diversifications were a major reason for its rise to the top.

What I believe is that the combination of the focus on packaging design and the sheer determination of Michael's vision is what carried the business forward. He saw design not as an exclusive practice, but as a broad spectrum inclusive activity. He firmly put innovation at the core of the consultancy, and never underestimated the intelligence of the consumer. He was an especially good editor, able to select significance from diversity, and was as committed to 'The Business of the Future' as to future business. Michael's success was in no small part due to his ability to recognise the big picture and also appreciate the minutia. He combined the brio of a showman with the detail obsession of a typographer, which was a combination that worked equally well for clients and designers. Macro Micro Michael.

Perhaps it is this split personality that made the business so successful and attractive to clients, knowing they were getting scrupulous attention to detail and craft by a team that also understood the bigger picture?

The business was run in Michael's collaborative style, with emphasis given to his fundamental belief in the collective method. Delegation abounded—faith was shown in the ability of others, errors were forgiven, and there was a generously inclusive recognition of success. The work reflected this, relevant, nuanced and engaging, it had the diversity and humanity missing from so many contemporary design consultancies. It was spirited and independent, democratic, never formulaic and very much at odds with the soulless chic of 'high graphic design'.

This really was the era when the radical graphics of consumer communication found packaging as its true medium.

	1970	1971	1972	1973	1974	1975
Politics	• Salvador Allende is elected Chilean president • Paris peace talks to end the Vietnam War continue for a second year without progress	• Doctors in the first Dutch abortion clinic start to perform *abortus provocatus* • East Pakistan (now Bangladesh) Independence is declared	• Watergate first break-in and scandal • Jane Fonda tours North Vietnam • Bloody Sunday	• UK, Ireland and Denmark enter EEC • Yom Kippur War ends • Last US soldier leaves Vietnam	• In response to the energy crisis, daylight saving time commences nearly four months early in the United States • Nixon resigns	• IRA bomb Westminster Hall • Thatcher made Tory prime minister • General Franco dies
Music	• Janis Joplin dies • Jimi Hendrix dies • The Beatles disbanded • *The Who: Live at Leeds* recorded	• Jim Morrison dies in Paris, age 27 • Electric Light Orchestra release debut album	• Don McLean *American Pie* • The Rolling Stones "Brown Sugar" • Roxy Music	• David Bowie biggest seller since The Beatles • *Dark Side of the Moon* by Pink Floyd	• KISS debut released • ABBA wins Eurovision song contest	• Breakthrough year for Bob Marley and the Wailers • Bruce Springsteen releases his third album, *Born To Run*
Art	• Robert Smithson *Spiral Jetty*—Land Art and Earth Art • Mark Rothko commits suicide	• *Amityville* by Willem De Kooning • Pablo Neruda is awarded the Nobel Prize	• MC Escher dies • *Mao* by Andy Warhol	• Picasso dies • JRR Tolkien dies • Pablo Neruda dies • First solo show by Nan Goldin	• *Coyote I like America and America likes me* by Joseph Beuys • *The Destruction of the Father* by Louise Bourgeois	• Barbara Hepworth dies • Charlie Chaplin knighted • Stage sets for a production of the 1951 Stravinsky opera *The Rake's Progress* at Glyndebourne by David Hockney
Design / Architecture	• Construction begins on the Sears Tower in Chicago, designed by Bruce Graham and Fazlur Khan (of Skidmore, Owings, and Merrill) • Ford Pinto introduced	• Walt Disney World opens in Florida • Rothko Chapel in Houston, Texas, designed by Mark Rothko and Philip Johnson is completed • Arne Jacobsen dies	• The Transamerica Pyramid in San Francisco, California, designed by William Pereira, is completed • Massimo Vignelli's NYC subway map	• Queen Elizabeth II opens the modern London Bridge • Construction of the CN Tower begins • The World Trade Center towers, designed by Minoru Yamasaki, are opened in New York	• Warsaw radio mast completed (tallest structure ever built) • National Assembly Building in Dakka, Bangladesh, is completed • Hello Kitty launched	• Architect and city planner Clarence S Stein dies in New York • Completion of the Seoul Tower in Seoul, South Korea
Innovation	• Fibre optics begin to replace copper wires for high-speed data transmission • Liquid Crystal Display by George Gray	• First Microprocessor, the Intel 4004 • E-mail	• Digital watches are introduced • Polaroid SX-70	• A patent for the ATM is granted • Genetic Engineering USA by S Cohen and H Boyer	• MRI scanner • Bar codes (UPC—Universal product code) • Pocket calculators start to appear in shops	• VCR introduced in the US by JVC • Sony introduces Betamax videotapes • BIC launches first disposable razor
Fashion	• Known as Halston, Roy Halston Frowick dominates 1970s with pantsuits, sweater sets, form-fitting dresses, knit wear	• Coco Chanel dies • Platform shoes • Afro haircut • Belgian-born US dress designer Diane von Furstenberg, 24, opens a one-woman business	• Crushed velvet • Knee-high boots • Tinted contact lenses	• Big clothes and bigger hair • Glam rock • Tattoos	• The naked year—streakers and nudism	• Lounge suits • Introduction of the "overdressed" look and the "Big Dress"
Sport	• First New York marathon • Brazil defeats Italy 4–1 in FIFA World Cup	• Joe Frazier defeats Muhammad Ali at Madison Square Garden • Chelsea win FA Cup	• Munich Olympics • Bobby Fischer defeats Boris Spassky in chess becoming first American Chess Champion	• England FA Cup: Sunderland wins 1–0 over Leeds United	• Rumble in the Jungle: Ali beats Foreman • FIFA grants Colombia the right to host the Football World Cup 1986	• West Indies win first Cricket World Cup • European Cup: Bayern Munich defeat Leeds United 2–0 in a controversial final at the Parc des Princes, Paris
Projects	SEXTON	PARK VILLAGE PRODUCTIONS	Home Bake Rhubarb Pie			

1976

- Mao dies
- Jimmy Carter elected president

- Generation X
- Stevie Wonder signs $13 million-plus contract with Motown Records
- The Sex Pistols sign contract with EMI Records

- Carl Andre's bricks at the Tate Gallery
- Josef Albers dies
- *Untitled Film Stills* (black-and-white photographs) by New Jersey-born artist Cindy Sherman, 23

- National Theatre on South Bank officially opened
- The CN Tower in Toronto opens as the tallest freestanding structure
- Alvar Aalto dies

- First laser printer introduced by IBM, the IBM 3800
- The Olympics, broadcast from Montreal, Canada, draw an estimated one billion viewers worldwide

- Start of Punk—safety pins, studs, piercings and the Mohawk—with Vivienne Westwood and Malcolm McLaren as its championing designers

- Bjorn Borg wins Wimbledon
- 1976 European Championship— Czechoslovakia beat West Germany 5–3 on penalties to win

1977

- Steve Biko dies
- Jimmy Carter becomes US president

- Maria Callas dies
- Elvis dies
- Sex Pistol's #2 "God save the Queen"

- *Annie Hall* by Woody Allen
- Vladimir Nabokov dies

- Centre Pompidou
- The Space Shuttle makes its maiden flight

- NAVSTAR Global Positioning System GPS inaugurated by US Department of Defence
- The Commodore computer is introduced

- Disco-shiny white polyester pants and shiny shirts are at the height of fashion following the release of *Saturday Night Fever*

- Pelé plays the final game of his career
- After 13 years and 82 contests, including 14 title defences, World Middleweight Champion Carlos Monzon retires undefeated

1978

- Red Brigade kidnap Italian ex-premier
- Sadat and Begin share Nobel Peace prize
- Golda Meir dies

- The 12 inch single— Boomtown Rats

- De Chirico dies
- Soviet authorities permit a Moscow show of avant-garde paintings to open, but only after a score of works have been removed for ideological reasons

- Charles Eames dies
- *Delirious New York: A Retroactive Manifesto for Manhattan* by Dutch architect Rem Koolhaas

- First baby born from test tube

- New Wave: sharp suits, Brothel Creeper shoes, mohair jumpers and Slim Jim ties
- Velcro first used in fashion

- Argentina wins World Cup at home
- Leon Spinks defeats Muhammad Ali by decision in 15 rounds to win the World Heavyweight title

1979

- Vietnamese reveal Pol Pot's mass graves
- Thatcher wins election
- UK Winter of Discontent

- Ska & 2Tone
- The Clash *London Calling*

- Woody Allen's *Manhattan*
- Collector Peggy Guggenheim dies
- *Children Playing with Game* by Duane Hanson

- Reebok running shoes are introduced in the United States
- Charles Moore designs the Piazza d'Italia in New Orleans

- Remington shaver
- Sony introduces the Sony Walkman costing $200

- Designer jeans: Calvin Klein, Levi's

- Boxing Day disaster at Hillsborough Stadium as Sheffield Wednesday beat rivals Sheffield United 4–0 in the Steel City Derby
- Nottingham Forest win European Cup

1980

- Mugabe selected Zimbabe president
- UK recession

- John Lennon shot dead

- *Mulholland Drive: The Road to the Studio* by David Hockney

- Royal Gold Medal awarded to James Stirling
- Memphis founded

- International debut Rubik's-Cube
- Ergonomi Design Gruppen Eat/Drink Cutlery

- *Fame* musical —leggings/loose tops/ leg warmers

- Bjorn Borg wins Wimbledon for fifth time
- Britain decides against a boycott of the Moscow Olympics

1981

- Pope John Paul II shot
- Attempt to assassinate Reagan
- Charles and Diana wed
- Sadat assassinated
- Brixton riots

- Bob Marley dies
- New Romantics: Duran Duran, Human League

- Basquiat's first solo show in Europe

- Albert Speer and Marcel Breuer die
- Carlton sideboard by Memphis

- Delorean car (prototype)
- TGV makes first journey
- Space Shuttle Columbia flight
- IBM PC XT introduced

- Olivia Newton-John— aerobics wear

- John McEnroe beats Bjorn Borg

1982

- Unemployment in Britain tops three million
- Prince William born
- Argentineans invade Falkland Islands
- Israel drive PLO out of Beirut

- Glen Gould dies
- Culture Club form

- *Sophie's Choice*
- David Puttnam wins Oscar for *Chariots of Fire*
- Henry Fonda and Ingrid Bergman die
- *E.T.*
- Richard Serra— *Tilted Arc*

- Barbican Arts Centre, London, opened
- Lamy pens designed by Walter Fabien

- Fibre optics replace wires/chips more powerful and cheaper
- Barney Clark receives artificial heart
- Sinclair Executive first pocket calculator

- Hair: Mullet/ra-ra skirts/following celebrity keep-fit wave, hairbands, leotards and ripped sweatshirts are fashionable

- Italy wins FIFA World Cup with 3–1 victory over West Germany

Michael Peters and Partners

Following the split with Lou Klein in 1970, Peters formed his own design consultancy, Michael Peters and Partners. It was a small, informal and homespun practice sited in the attic space formerly occupied by Klein Peters, which shared the 'cottage-industry' characteristics of most design studios at the time. Michael Peters and Partners could also count on the support of the creative companies it shared the building with, such as Cramer Saatchi, Boase Massimi Pollitt and the office of David Puttnam.

His timing was perfect: the creative energy unleashed in the 1960s had been carried over into the early 70s, and the optimism felt by many did not cease until 1973, when the first oil crisis sent the world into shock. Peters was thus able to benefit from the advantageous shifts in the perception of design by the industry, which had taken place during preceding decades, and was ready to take on the challenge of consolidating these new attitudes and resulting ideas into new structures.

Peters had decided that his new company would specialise in consumer packaging, as this was an area to which he could apply the skills he had acquired at Collett, Dickenson, Pearce and Klein Peters. Furthermore, packaging for Peters represented a link between his interests in architecture and graphics. "Regardless of whether I was designing a bottle, or a piece of packaging or retail design, I would think of this piece as an architectural structure", he explains.

The beginning of a ten year relationship with frozen food manufacturer Birds Eye. The design of this pie range was influential in the company reassessing and identifying all its packaging needs. Michael Peters and Partners then went on to re-design nearly all of Birds Eye's packaging.

Most importantly, he thought that the British industry despite gradual improvements still paid too little attention to design—and felt that as a result, the British industry did not apply the highest possible standards in the way they packaged and presented their goods and services, especially when compared to the United States: "The UK was then light-years behind America, both in terms of aesthetic quality and functionality."

It was not that contemporary British packaging lacked these qualities *per se*; in fact it based itself on a long-standing history of packaging innovation and progress. Traditionally, retailers selling loose goods packaged these in envelopes or bags at the point of purchase, it was only in the nineteenth century, when manufacturers decided to adopt this process, that modern packaging was developed in the form of cartons, jars, tins and cans. Their aim was both to keep food fresh and protected, but also to enable a fixed price for standard sizes. Increasingly, manufacturers used advertising and early forms of branding to differentiate their products from those of competitors. This development stagnated slightly during and after the Second World War, when austerity led to a return of the plain brown paper bag.

After the war, confidence in British goods resumed and the development of convenience and prepared foods—along with an increase in affluence and leisure time—demanded new packaging strategies. Design consultancies such

as Tandy Halford Mills, Talmadge Drummond and Amos and Partners consistently focused on packaging with high quality results. Peters' main bone of contention, however, was the subtlety and underlying compliance of contemporary British packaging, the routinised application of formulas, which undermined its capacity to work as a potent selling force. Creating great packaging was therefore to be Michael Peters and Partners' unique selling point.

For Peters, packaging was more than merely a pretty wrapper or useful protective container. It was also more than simply a visual implementation of a company's corporate identity. Instead he emphasised that the full potential of packaging at the actual point of sale of a typical consumer product—the shelf or freezer in the supermarket—had not yet been fully exploited, and that it could play an even more important role in the marketing of both the product and the company behind it.

In order to maximise this potential, he employed both his business acumen and his design know-how. The overall aim was to generate original and brilliant ideas—the value of which he had come to appreciate during his stint at CBS in New York—and to have these executed with the highest design quality possible. Peters was certain that a package lacking a great idea, despite its aesthetic quality and practicality, would inevitably fail to sell the product.

Thus, his early notion of marrying art and commerce again grew more defined as he put into

Top: This packaging for Birds Eye's Hidden Centres was a real and tangible innovation in packaging. This frozen mousse had a small piece of fruit hidden inside the product. Michael Peters and Partners' idea was to invert the mousse packaging and create a pyramidic shape.

Bottom: These Cheesecake designs were an award-winning breakthrough in terms of product photography because Peters and his design team commissioned sport, fashion and still life photographers to bring their skill and expertise to food packaging.

practice his concept of utilising the highest order of creativity to achieve business objectives: of solving commercial problems with outstanding design. By prioritising design quality and marketing expertise equally, his newly founded company gained an important advantage over those company sales departments and advertising agencies which developed product packaging based solely on marketing criteria.

As a specialised, independent consultancy, Michael Peters and Partners was able to take on an advisory role by establishing a good working relationship with clients, furthering their trust in the possibility of employing design as a business tool. Here, Peters profited from the increased esteem granted by the industry to design, and let his eloquence and business astuteness do the rest to establish excellent and long-term designer-client

relationships. He learned to speak his clients' language, learned to empathise with them, and directly involved them in the design process. He thus found his clients more willing to accept radical departures from the status quo in order to differentiate their products. The final ingredient that distinguished Michael Peters and Partners from others was a generous dose of chutzpah: if Peters perceived a brief as inadequate, he would simply rewrite the brief and charge the client for the change.

Breakthroughs

One of Michael Peters and Partners' first regular clients was Birds Eye, a frozen foods manufacturer Peters had secured through his linkage with Collett, Dickenson, Pearce. Clients Tony Simmons-Gooding and Neil Ashley commissioned Peters to restructure the marketing of various food ranges and also to collaborate on the development of packaging for new products, with the overall aim of counteracting a gradual, but significant drop in sales. The job immediately provided Peters with the opportunity to practice what he preached, to prove that design could in fact solve a problem that was usually delegated to the marketing department.

Michael Peters and Partners conducted a comprehensive market study, which revealed that many consumers felt the representations on frozen

WINSOR & NEWTON
MADE IN ENGLAND
INK

food packages to be lifeless and unattractive. The design team therefore had to find a way to make the product look appetizing and nutritious, albeit within the limitations of the Trade Description Act. For an assortment of meat pies, Michael Peters and Partners decided to deviate from the norm by replacing the original photographs with illustrations by Tony Meeuwissen, adding warmth, character and appeal to the packaging.

The unpretentiousness and sense of homeliness evoked by the packaging for Birds Eye's Meat Pies and other ranges, revealed that the strength of Michael Peters and Partners' approach lay not only in using design to make a product more appealing, but also in being able to sense what the consumer—in those days, the housewife—wanted. The design change was rewarded by both an enormous increase in sales and by recognition amongst the design community. It received one of two D&AD silver awards in 1972 (the other being awarded to Doyle Dane Bernbach for a Volkswagen poster), and another silver for a range of cheesecakes in 1975. It was a long and fruitful working relationship for both companies, which lasted nearly a decade.

The work for Birds Eye and other early work reflected Peters' preference for a pictorial style over a more sober, modernist approach, and mirrored his early admiration for graphic movements emanating from the United States, such as the illustrative eclecticism of Milton Glaser's, Seymour Chwast's, Reynold Ruffins' and Edward Sorel's Push Pin Studio. It was an interesting choice for Peters to make, since his training at the London School of Printing had focused on lettering and typography rather than drawing and illustration—nevertheless, he knew exactly how to utilise an illustrative style for his purposes, and it came to characterise much of his subsequent work.

Michael Peters and Partners' designs for Winsor & Newton were a masterful example of using illustration to broaden the appeal of a product with maximum impact both on the world

of business and design. Winsor & Newton was a supplier of artists' materials with a 125 year old manufacturing tradition, serving a specialist market and selling its products in direct competition with rival products without advertisement. Peters recognised that he had to get more mileage out of the existing brand, and that a lack of supplementary advertising meant that the packaging itself would primarily have to sell the product.

Peters had always wanted to work for Winsor & Newton—he had encountered them during his apprenticeship with Rothholz, who had also designed for the company. His new business specialist Richard Beaumont therefore organised an initial meeting with the company over lunch. "We got off to a bad start, because I was flailing my arms about in excitement, and spilled wine all over the client's lap", Peters recalls. Impressed neither by Peters' antics nor his proposition of using design to aid sales, Winsor & Newton nevertheless suggested a follow-up boardroom lunch. "So Richard and I went for lunch with about six directors, and this took place in complete silence—like in a monastery. I decided to break the ice by asking whether we could now talk business. The chairman, however, only replied that I could have my moment over coffee. So in those 15 minutes, I had to sell to the chairman, a dour Scottish accountant, why I felt that design was so important to his company."

These 15 minutes sufficed for the board of Winsor & Newton to put their trust in Peters. "The chairman replied, 'I don't know anything about design, but I know how to make money for my business—if you succeed, I'm a client for life. If you fail, I'll fire you very quickly'", Peters recounts. The commission initially involved re-designing the packaging for a range of inks, which at the time were housed in standard bottles and plain cardboard boxes, as Peters recalls, "had very little shelf appeal. Most of its manufacturing costs actually went into the dropper stopper." His solution was to examine and re-distribute the manufacturing costs, a process which resulted

70

in a re-design of the shape of the ink bottle. To this purpose, he assembled over 20 illustrators to produce original and imaginative illustrations for the boxes around the theme of the ink colours. Each illustrator was to use the ink in a different way, in order to demonstrate the flexibility of the medium.

Among those commissioned were illustrators Tony Meeuwissen, Philip Castle, Nick Thirkell, John Gorham, Arthur Robins and designer Jeff Hockey of Michael Peters and Partners. An illustration of bluebirds signalled the blue ink, a sunburst suggested yellow ink, and the vermillion-coloured ink bottle was shielded by eighteenth century militiamen. "We... needed something which explained from the outside what the contents were all about", Peters told *The Times* in 1972, "a visual suggestion so that people who had never used drawing inks would be tempted to try."

The packaging for Winsor & Newton inks therefore acted not only as a protective and informative casing, but added value to the product by additionally addressing the dormant aspirations of artists and hobbyists. The hand-drawn illustrations also pointed towards the manual production process of the inks. And the synergy of various ink boxes stacked next to each other appealed to the collector's instinct. Peters'

approach was then commercially validated by an enormous increase in sales amounting to over 600 per cent over a two year period. Pleased, Winsor & Newton assigned Michael Peters and Partners to further products including poster colours, oil colours and alkyd paints. On the whole, the various ranges received four D&AD silver awards, as well as an Art Directors Club New York award.

For Winsor & Newton's alkyd colours, the original idea was slightly modified by featuring pastiche illustrations stylistically reminiscent of the work of famous painters. Bev Whitehead, who had joined Michael Peters and Partners as a typographer in 1975, and now teaches design, remembers how the designers had churned out concept after concept for the alkyds. "I knew what the solution should be and thought I would mention this to the designers, but I could already hear them say, 'Oh, the bloody typographer's telling us what to do.' So I went home and drew some things up. And the next day, I just slipped my things into the pile which was ready for presentation. Michael came back from the meeting, congratulating one of the student designers, Rod Weston, whose concept apparently had gone through. When he held it up, I saw that it wasn't Rod's, but mine."

With his work for the White Elephant Club, Peters took his signature style into the third dimension. The owner of the White Elephant Club and restaurant, Stella Richmond, had for charity purposes created a cook book in collaboration with showbiz and sports celebrities. The recipes were illustrated by well-known designers and artists, including Arnold Schwartzman (who had initiated the book), Saul Bass, Alan Fletcher, David Hillman, Lou Klein, John McConnell, and Marcello Minale. Peters was asked to design a page spread for the book, which was also turned into an invitation for the book launch. Rather than simply illustrating the recipe, he created a life-size pop-up sandwich—

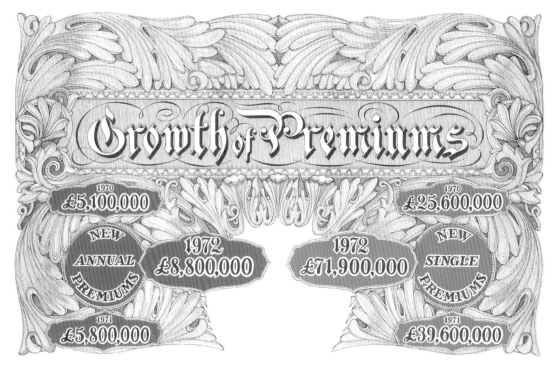

the invitation was even wrapped into a transparent 'sandwich' bag. Through this three-dimensional solution, he was once more able to combine his graphic training and passion for architecture.

A Second String to the Bow

Michael Peters and Partners' 1972 annual report for Abbey Life Assurance was a remarkable example of how Peters pushed the boundaries of what was considered acceptable for the genre. Obligatory facts and figures in this report were framed with ornate borders and illustrations based on European banknotes. Bev Whitehead, who had encountered the report before joining the company, recalls that it had "a very fiscal, rich look to it. It was terrifically pictorial and completely amazing because annual reports were often very drab and dull things."

It was to Peters' advantage that the design brief had called for a unique solution, and that Abbey Life left him a relatively large amount of freedom. He thus fully exploited the brief by bringing in no less than ten illustrators, Keith Bowen, Alan Manham, Robin Jacques, Peter Brookes, Jim Fitzpatrick, Giovanni Caselli, Ian Miller, Terence Daly, Rodney Shackell and David Rowe, to design pages in the report. The flamboyant solution did not fail to surprise and impress, and it was one of the 25 selected out of 16,000 reports in an American competition aiming to improve the quality of annual reports.

The success of the Abbey Life Annual Report led Michael Peters and Partners to register another company called Annual Reports Ltd, which would enable a specialisation in this field, but still maintain strong links with Michael Peters and Partners. The genre of annual reports was and still is an important factor in corporate communication, as they are the primary link with its existing and potential shareholders and the yardstick by which a company's success is measured. Peters found, however, that only a few annual reports reflected this importance in their treatment of visual and textual content.

Annual Reports Ltd was not the first company specialising in corporate financial communication, but Peters felt that there was room for improvement. Annual Reports Ltd therefore stressed its advisory role and the importance of exploiting annual reports as a selling tool, literally selling the company to the shareholders.

Furthermore, he knew that annual reports could grant direct access to company CEOs. "I liked the idea of working on annual reports because they were unusual things to work on. And I figured that if we could do something exciting with them, we would be working with

Top: The Michael Peters and Partners creative team at Pembridge Mews, around the infamous snooker table. From left to right, Gerry O'Dwyer, Madeleine Bennett, Vaughan Oliver, Paul Browton, Stuart Barron, Bev Whitehead, Pat Perchal, Claire Tuthill, Quentin Murley and Debbie Carter.

Bottom left: The Michael Peters and Partners' studio in Pembridge Mews, West London.

conceptualisation, strategic analysis, design and production management.

Although still feeding off the confidence of the 60s, the early 70s signalled a significant change of mood in politics, economics and the arts. The Conservative Party's Edward Heath had taken over the reins of Harold Wilson as prime minister in 1970. The old system of pounds, shillings and pence had been replaced by decimalised currency to aid an integration into the European Economic Community. And a more pensive outlook entered the arts through the increasing popularity of folk rock—Simon and Garfunkel's "Bridge Over Troubled Water"

the chairmen of the companies who may engage in further business with us. We then hired a marvellous man, Martin Stevens, who had come from competitor Lippincott and Margulies and had aspirations to become a member of parliament. He was extremely well connected, which very much helped."

Made managing director at Annual Reports Ltd in 1973, Martin Stevens was to further aid the establishment of a company that led the way with innovative, high quality work. It was important that Annual Reports Ltd concerned itself not only with the design, but also with an analysis of the company's requirements and corporate message. Through these services, Annual Reports Ltd was able to provide the client with a complete package of

Miners pay deadlock brings threat of a full confrontation

By Paul Routledge
Labour Correspondent

The miners' pay dispute moved into deadlock yesterday after unproductive talks lasting little more than an hour between the National Union of Mineworkers and the National Coal Board.

The Pay Board is being asked to rule on the principle of payment for "waiting time", but coal board's figures show that no more than 25 minutes of allowable overtime can be squeezed from the Phase Three

claim sinks into insignificance compared with the problem that faces the nation over the balance of payments."

At next week's executive meeting, it is almost certain that left-wing demands will be made to step up the industrial action, but the majority view still inclines towards continuation of the overtime ban, which has cut coal production by nearly a third.

The coal board statistics collected in a survey of 42 pits covering all coalfields and a

Spong was a
manufacturer of
kitchenware. The
company decided
to manufacture and
reintroduce into the
market the Traditional
Coffee Mill with
appropriate packaging
design to reflect the
origins of the product.

charted at No 1 in 1970—and through films such as Stanley Kubrick's *A Clockwork Orange* and John Schlesinger's *Sunday Bloody Sunday*.

By 1974, Britain had spiralled into an economic crisis, fuelled by a series of coal miners' strikes in response to the Industrial Relations Act. The energy shortage was aggravated when Middle Eastern hostilities resumed in the autumn of 1973, and Arab nations doubled the price of oil. The British government had no choice but to declare a state of emergency, which culminated in the so-called "three day week", a measure to conserve remaining energy sources. Britain's gross domestic product fell under that of the GDR, triggering both a high inflation rate and devastating economic recession, and leading Britain to be labelled the "sick man of Europe".

Things had been going remarkably well for both Michael Peters and Partners and Annual Reports Ltd until 1974, when several of its financial decisions collided with the economic recession and nearly proved fatal for the fledgling company. Michael Peters and Partners reached its financial limits by investing in property and setting up a Paris office, at the same time, both companies were hit by the bankruptcy of a client. Through Stevens, Annual Reports Ltd had been commissioned to design a visual identity and annual report for the financial planners Julian Gibbs Ltd, an enormously expensive undertaking shot by star photographer Barry Lategan.

Julian Gibbs Ltd however soon went into liquidation, owing Michael Peters and Partners tens of thousands of pounds. "I didn't really realise the

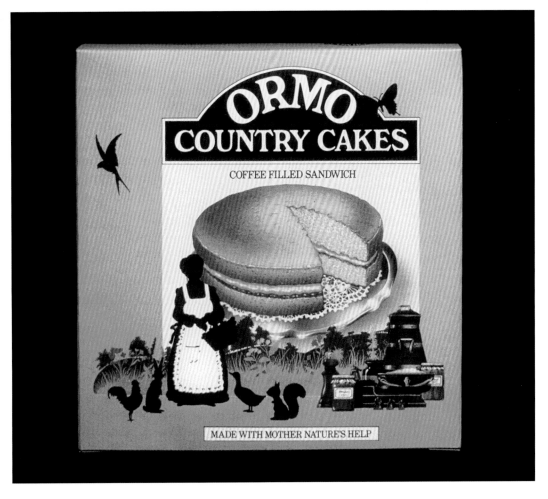

Ormo, a major bakery in Northern Ireland, wanted to be bold and different in a difficult market. The end result is imbued with beautiful illustrations depicting the handcrafted nature of its products.

facts of business life", Peters wrote in *Designer* in 1980. "I naively thought that I would sit in my office and produce beautiful designs, not appreciating that there are some people who want your wares, but aren't prepared to pay for them." He later adds that this episode taught him to ensure that the business was always in the black. "I demanded money up front across all phases of a project. This made real business sense and clients accepted it without question."

He was also fortunate to meet Simon Majaro at the time, an Israeli management consultant at the London Business School, who introduced Peters to a colleague of his, Robert Silver. Silver came into the business in 1974; with his help, Peters was able to pay off his debts and to recover his losses over the following 18 months. Stevens stayed with Annual Reports Ltd until he was made a member of parliament, and was replaced by Benjamin Rowntree.

Team Players

Right from the outset, Peters aimed to hire only the best young talent to work together in a setting which he describes as a "Kibbutz". Basically, this meant that the company structure was to be less hierarchical than at 'classic' design companies. He wanted a team that,

despite official job titles, worked on equal terms and with a collective responsibility towards the work produced. "It was my name on the door, but I made the tea", Peters illustrates.

The company name was a slight misnomer in the sense that Peters did not have another designer as partner. Instead, he surrounded himself with experts in other fields, such as Andrew McCall, who joined Annual Reports Ltd and became head of account management on its formation in 1971, and later became managing director of Michael Peters and Partners. Educated at Winchester, McCall had worked for Peters' former client Jaeger and had met Peters while working as an account executive at Collett, Dickenson, Pearce.

David Sowden, who was appointed production manager, was another early addition. "Andrew McCall was very public school", Bev Whitehead recalls, "very suave with the appropriate hairstyle and looking fashionably dishevelled, while David was more 'of the people', a kind of ducker and diver. Michael had a strange, very diverse mix of people—from the ethical Quaker to the tenacious Tory—all working together successfully."

On one occasion, Peters received a phone call from an ex-prisoner, Charlie Smith, who was looking for work, followed by a call from the BBC, which was working on a programme that accompanied people upon leaving prison. He agreed to let Smith join the studio, and after

Smith's placement had ended, the ex-prisoner expressed his gratitude by giving Peters invaluable security advice. "He said to Michael, 'Leave something on your office table, lock up the building, and I will produce it the next day.' He actually got in through the roof, and with that, he proved the office wasn't secure", Jo Peters recalls.

Michael Peters and Partners used the fact that it consisted of an array of people with different viewpoints to its fullest advantage. It resulted in a fantastic work atmosphere and cancelled out much of the elitism existent at other design companies. A democratic attitude also prevailed when it came to the acceptance of official design awards. When Winsor & Newton's alkyd colours were awarded in 1977, it was not Peters who received the D&AD pencil, but the responsible designer, Bev Whitehead. "He's a team worker", Whitehead confirms, "he strongly believes in teamwork and its results. And he was wise and generous enough to realise that we needed some of the glory as well."

Those who were only starting their career, coming fresh out of design school, benefited from the immense trust Peters put in them. He had a knack for spotting young talent, and generally put newcomers right into the thick of things. Debbie Carter (née Catford), who joined the company on a placement, recollects that the company was a superb training ground. "I learnt to do things quickly, because I had to do them myself, even client presentations. It was fantastic." Michael Peters and Partners was also an early career step for Vaughan Oliver, who later made a name for himself with album covers and poster designs for the music label 4AD. His leaving present in 1981 was a curious one. "He actually came in the night before and disassembled the desks, took down the mirrors, and hid everything", Debbie Carter recalls, "and when we came in the next morning, everything was gone...".

One of Peters' top priorities was establishing a productive and enjoyable work environment. On Valentine's Day, every female employee got a rose, a job well done earned a bottle of champagne with a handwritten note, and special events such as lectures and themed evenings supported the creation of a unique company culture. 1979 saw the creation of the 'Magical Mystery Tours', which were essentially trips to a secret location and another way for Peters to say thank you to his staff. The first tour consisted of a simple dinner in Paris and in following years, increasingly extravagant trips were made to various other British and European locations.

Michael Peters and Partners' first studio in London's Goodge Street was a 'prime location' for business but also in a more sinister sense. Northern Ireland's "Troubles" had in the 70s reached the capital through IRA bombings—and right outside of Goodge Street stood a lonely pillar-box. "It was a perfect place for hiding a bomb and just freaked everybody out", recalls Howard Milton, who had started as a young designer in autumn of 1974.

When the company gradually outgrew its premises in Goodge Street and moved to Pembridge Mews in London's Notting Hill area, Peters acquired the building housing his studio and tailored the work space to match an atmosphere of creativity. "You would come in through a plain white door into a very tight hall facing a bright yellow door", Bev Whitehead recalls. "It was entering through this door that, you immediately saw a 3/4 size snooker table, about

VIRGIN RECORDS

The Big Idea—this was never more appropriate than for these record bags produced for Virgin Records. Each bag illustrated a different letter of the Virgin retail brand.

ten to 12 desks with bright yellow frames, and then trendy blue denim chairs. Because this was the time when Volkswagen had introduced denim seats into the Beetle."

Peters' business ingenuity enabled him to effortlessly acquire new jobs, even those requiring specialisations the company did not possess... yet. "We were very adaptive", Whitehead confirms. This was possible because Michael Peters and Partners did not just employ "partners and pencil-sharpeners" (as a partner at a large design company once described its employment policy) but independent thinkers. Peters would listen to his designers if they had a better creative solution, if they did not, he followed a maxim he had learned from Lou Dorfsman, as he explained to *Creative Review* in 1981. "When I worked for CBS in New York I was always told, 'If you come up with a better idea we'll use it. If not then my idea will always go through.'"

Ultimately, Peters was in charge of the creative work produced, but gave designers a free hand to experiment and to explore. "If things grew a bit wobbly", Bev Whitehead recalls, "Michael would say, 'supposing you'd do this... and why don't you look at it that way...' allowing you to see a whole range of possibilities. We didn't need too much of his help, because we were just so inspired. We were trying hard to work towards the key points of the brief to generate various solutions. It was a challenge, but an enjoyable challenge."

An important factor was that Peters acted as a link between client and his designers by verbally providing a design-specific brief. Howard Milton, who had come to the company right after graduating from the London College of Printing, found himself in an environment where the design briefs very much supported independent thinking. "It wasn't so much saying 'Do what you want', but rather 'What can you do with this project?' So we were pushing ourselves instead of being pushed, and encouraged to give the client something that they wouldn't expect. It was incredibly stimulating."

Peters also knew how to bring his designers' ideas to fruition by even the simplest means, Howard Milton points out. "The magic that Michael had was that he would come by your desk and just glance over your shoulder and add something. When I was working for Johnson & Johnson, he took a red pencil and just added a single red dot. It was well laid out already, but he knew what he had to add to bring it to life. He's a master creative director."

Peters' art direction was also unique in the sense that he placed great emphasis on the production and presentation of as many ideas as possible. His accumulation and absorption of countless influences throughout his education had expanded his own visual repertoire, which he passed on to the designers working with him. Interestingly, creating a whole range of possible concepts was in a way running counter to the method of one of his greatest influences,

Paul Rand, who never presented more than one solution in the belief that anything more would undermine the designer's expertise.

Bev Whitehead had learned a similar way of thinking during his training, but was soon convinced by Peters' method. "Showing only one solution only invited criticism, because there were no alternatives. So it's either you like it or you don't. At Michael's, you always saw a whole range of ideas, regardless of whether it was a design for a shoebox, or for a paint tube. Honestly, I thought they were mad for a moment—you can't show these people so many ideas! Then I realised that it was the right way to do things, because the client must have been so fed up with seeing just one solution. By showing the client the other concepts you could also show them what didn't work."

The spectrum of concepts approach therefore also enabled client and designer to engage in a dialogue. Through it, Peters could guide the client through the complete design process towards a concept he felt was most suited. "I think that if a client commissions you, the design has to be explained if the client is less visual", he elucidates. "We would show the iterative sketches and the logic of how one design linked to another, for example, why we went from yellow to blue, why we used this or that typeface... We showed how the idea evolved, and the intelligence behind it."

It also reflected his belief that a design problem might have more than one solution. Howard Milton recollects how Michael Peters and Partners were commissioned to design a carrier bag for Virgin. They proposed a whole range of bags, with a different letter on the bag for each month,

each designed by a different illustrator, spelling out the company name. "It was a dream design brief", Milton says, "producing all these different visual concepts was great for us designers, because we could just get stuff out of our system".

When Milton, in 1980, founded his own company Smith & Milton with wife Jay Smith, whom he had met at Michael Peters and Partners (while working on Thresher and Kraft Cheese Slices), both preferred to be more selective when presenting solutions to clients. However, they had learnt to be prolific from the very competitive environment at their training ground. "When I had been there for about six months", Milton recalls, "and was hungry for every opportunity to design—as a junior I was mostly subservient to the senior designers—Michael came in with a fantastic brief for a skiing brochure. He said that the client was coming to see the designs in half an hour. So I went into overdrive and in half an hour, cranked out about ten solutions. That's almost unimaginable today."

Since the design process prior to production was at the time much less reliant on technology than it is today, and concepts were visualised on paper using coloured pencils and markers, Milton also learnt how to produce good solutions that would stand up for themselves, based simply on drawings. It encouraged one to think quickly. "You would think that with drawing, the output would be slower or more laborious", he explains, "but in fact it was much quicker. You couldn't change the colour back and forth as the computer now allows you to, but you already had made the decision simply by picking up a certain colour pencil." The results were always fresh and innovative.

The Outsider

It was the work environment and method, but also very much the type of clients and commissions, which distinguished Michael Peters and Partners from other design groups. It was one of the few design companies specialising in packaging, annual reports and later, new product development. And Peters saw no problem in working for mainstream brands and everyday shopping items. "I'm not the designer's designer", Peters states, "I love commerce, and I love creativity and the Big Idea. I never saw myself as a craftsman like Alan Fletcher or Milton Glaser. What I did see myself as being was a person who could create a whole new business out of one idea, and that was to bring art and commerce together, and making sure that the clients paid an appropriate fee."

While the major British design groups of the time, including Conran, Pentagram, Allied International Designers, Wolff Olins and Fitch (founded by Rodney Fitch in 1972), focused on securing illustrious clients, Peters, whilst effortlessly playing in their league, took a more 'American' approach by aiming to do the best work for all kinds of products or brands. This he achieved by working closely and on equal terms with clients, and aiming to make relevant to them his ambition of establishing design as a valuable marketing and sales tool.

"Michael could make fabric cleaning cloths seem good and look significant", Bev Whitehead states, "at Michael Peters and Partners there wasn't this snobbism about the brand. I think there were, and still are, many British designers who think it's demeaning to work for such a company,

which is nonsense, especially if you are designing something that is selling 12 million packs." David Hillman, who after working for *The Sunday Times Magazine* gained fame as art director of the celebrated magazine *Nova*, and joined Pentagram as a partner in the late 70s, adds that Peters "was there with the major design groups, but the thing that set him apart was his amazing business acumen. He managed to combine really good design with running a very successful business. We all have to do commercial work, and this is what brings in the money, but Michael was one of the few to admit it."

Peters' commercial take on design very quickly pushed him out of the inner design circle. "Because he was the smart-ass kid that made lots of money out of it, with an ability they hadn't encountered", Whitehead points out. Peters confirms that he never really felt comfortable in relationships with the contemporary design establishment. "I wasn't part of their circle, and I didn't want to be. For the Derek Birdsalls of this world, for the people who taught me at school, I was the commercial kid on the block."

Along with the mindset, it was Peters' stylistic approach that separated him from the rest, at a time when the clinical purism of Swiss typography was still the epitome of good design. "Michael Peters and Partners are not the prettiest designers around ... but it would take a lot to beat this company in terms of applying design to a selling situation", Peters wrote in *Designer* in 1980. He also had a knack for attracting publicity, which sometimes led to envy and resentment amongst fellow designers. The secret to getting media attention, however, was rather simple, as he explains. "I had a dear friend called Richard French

By appointment to
HRH The Duke of Edinburgh
Manufacturers of Toilet Requisites
Penhaligon's Limited, London.

PENHALIGON'S
41 WELLINGTON STREET
COVENT GARDEN
LONDON WC2
TELEPHONE: 01-836 2150

Perfumers Established 1870

who was in the advertising business. He told me that I only had to pick up the phone, speak to a journalist and say something controversial, so that's what I did."

However, Peters also had advocates in people like Alan Fletcher, who had supported his career from the very start. After Michael Peters and Partners had moved to Pembridge Mews, Fletcher would visit the studio every now and then, since he lived at the other end of the street. "He would have over designers from New York, such as Alan Peckolick, and would show them Michael's work", Bev Whitehead recalls, "at other times he'd amble around in the evening while Michael wasn't there and make suggestions to the designers. And the next day, Michael would come in and congratulate us on the hard work."

It was possibly Peters' diverse background and multiple interests, which had influenced his unusual approach to design, and established a link to Fletcher, who had been born in Kenya and had also attended Yale University. In contrast to those British designers who had made their career solely in Britain, Peters benefited from living in various cultures and countries, providing him with, as Bev Whitehead argues, "a multi-parochial viewpoint".

A less charming aspect of Peters' American background in particular, Whitehead continues, "was his litigiousness. If people crossed him or said something critical in a magazine, he'd immediately phone his lawyer." One of these situations occurred when Andrew McCall, David Sowden and Jane Seager (a senior designer) had decided to break away from the company. "They had a contract with the business not to take any of the clients", Peters explains, "they flouted the contract and started to approach both clients and staff. So I took legal action against them and won. It became very acrimonious, which was extremely upsetting for me, because, in a way, we were family. I firmly believe in the morality of being part of a business family. I don't like to be crossed."

Interpretations

Michael Peters and Partners continued acquiring an impressive list of clients throughout the 70s, and gradually emerged as one of the leaders in the field of packaging design. While Peters was unapologetic in working for everyday products, he also effortlessly crossed over into the area of luxury goods. One client in this area was Penhaligon's, an old established English perfumer. William Henry Penhaligon had been court barber to Queen Victoria from the 1870s onwards, and the original Penhaligon's shop in Jermyn Street sold perfumes, toilet water and pomades based on flower essences to the English gentry.

In 1975, the company was taken over by the Italian film director Franco Zeffirelli, who is best known for his film version of Shakespeare's *Romeo and Juliet*, 1968. Together with his former assistant Sheila Pickles, who had become managing director of Penhaligon's, Zeffirelli approached Michael Peters and Partners with the aim of recreating the atmosphere of the original shop. Guided and inspired by Zeffirelli's vision for the company, Peters and his design team attended to every aspect of Penhaligon's corporate communication, including stationery, packaging and a flagship store in Covent Garden.

Most importantly, the new identity and packaging programme was to capitalise on Penhaligon's esteemed heritage. This was achieved by incorporating original attributes, such the Duke of Edinburgh's crest, and materials, such as neck ribbons, into the new designs. The overriding image was one of luxury, supported by an elegant, richly detailed typography crafted by designer Madeleine Bennett, and revived Victorian imagery by Howard Milton and illustrator Harry Willock. Bennett had joined Michael Peters and Partners in 1976 after being educated at Ravensbourne College of Art and Design and working at Crosby/Fletcher/Forbes, the forerunner of Pentagram, where she learned and developed her craft.

Her attention to typographic detail signalled and enhanced the inherent qualities of Penhaligon's products throughout a period of commission spanning more than a decade. "The initial packaging had a mainly typographic solution which stemmed from the client's brief and a small amount of archive material remaining from the original business", she recalls. "The

packaging style then evolved over more than ten years introducing imagery as new perfume ranges were sold." The corporate identity programme and packaging ranges were remarkably successful, winning several awards including a Bronze Starpack Award in 1979 and a D&AD silver award in 1982.

The traditional English style revived by Michael Peters and Partners for Winsor & Newton and Penhaligon's was not merely a reproduction or plundering of bygone styles, but instead kept with the spirit of the times by nostalgically engaging with a newfound interest in tradition. Published in 1977, *The Country Diary of an Edwardian Lady* became immensely popular, as did the Art Deco revival by Biba boutiques and the Victoriana-inspired interiors of Laura Ashley. The nostalgic designs of Crabtree & Evelyn's toiletry ranges by Peter Windett had already, in 1972, started cashing in on associations with England's past. The concern of re-establishing and furthering a strong sense of heritage and thus, national identity, then maintained its currency throughout the 80s, when the Conservative government supported the development of a heritage industry on a national scale.

Michael Peters and Partners' design for a younger brand of Gauloises cigarettes was a marked departure from the usual conventions for cigarette pack design. The Blue Way brand featured various modes of transport from the 1930s, including a Berliet automobile and a streamlined train. Designed by Fred Fehlau and illustrated by David Penny, the packs nostalgically linked back to the original, 30s-style Gauloises packs, while simultaneously appealing to a younger generation through their fresh re-interpretation of the era.

*Opposite: A range of
the labels for Artus, a
German manufacturer
of high quality juices
and mineral waters.*

*Right: Old and new soup
packaging for Batchelors
Food. The company
needed to reflect the
quality of its products
with illustrations of the
ingredients painted
on the rim of the
soup bowls.*

A nostalgic, primarily typographic solution
was chosen for the packaging of Michael Peters
and Partners' clients Lacroix Soups. The intricate
design and lettering by typographer and designer
Klaus Schultheis suggested a premium product,
and was awarded an Art Directors Club of Germany
medal in 1979. Schultheis had joined shortly
after 1975, and was responsible for several
other significant projects, such as packaging
and identity work for Heldenbräu and Arienheller.
When Schultheis left, he commemorated his time
at Michael Peters and Partners by staging an
impromptu re-enactment of Hitchcock's *Psycho*
in the studio. "He rang up three actors through
The Sunday Times", Bev Whitehead recalls with
a laugh, "it was dark and everyone was just
scared out of their wits."

Other work also demonstrated that
Michael Peters and Partners never aspired to a
one-style-fits-all solution, but that every design
solution was led by the generation and high quality
execution of an excellent idea. A range of aerosols
and sprays for Aerosols International in 1979 led
to the creation of the Yellow Can Company, a
generic name representing products filling the gap
between branded goods and own-label aerosols
by supermarket chains. The design solution by Bev
Whitehead consisted of coloured cans combined
with bold, eye-catching typography, which instantly
communicated the function of the content.

The menswear outfitter Michael Barrie in
contrast was interested in making his carrier bags
and stationery, both being part of the corporate
communication of the store, conspicuous amongst
those of other retailers. The Big Idea, art directed
by Peters and Madeleine Bennett, and illustrated
by Gerry O'Dwyer, was to devise a specific bag
for each garment, again clearly communicated by
straightforward, colourful graphic representations,
and to adapt this theme to the stationery. Little
did the client and the consultancy anticipate that
the carrier bags would end up in a museum: they
were selected as exemplary pieces by the Cooper-
Hewitt Museum in New York.

Innovations

A key element of the thinking at Michael
Peters and Partners was innovation. The
consultancy explicitly aimed to be one of the
most creative and innovative companies in
the design industry, and clients soon bought
into the difference, realising that it was beneficial to

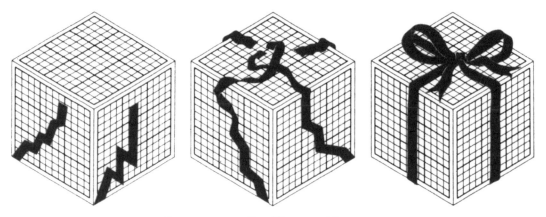

Packaged for Success

Top: The logo for
Packaged for Success.
Peters' desire to show
that great design can
improve the quality of
its clients' earnings
resulted in an exhibition
at a major London art
gallery. The exhibition
(opposite) showcased
the work of clients and
the financial results
thereof. This show
(opened by a senior
government Minister)
was a huge success.

Bottom: Peters teamed
up with a doctor friend
to produce a book of
50 of the most common
medical complaints so
as to help patients more
simply understand the
nature of their problems.

try something new rather than to simply emulate their competitors. Being innovative was something Michael Peters and Partners became well known for, and an important part of the services it could offer to clients.

Producing innovative, original solutions did not only concern the graphics and typography of packaging and corporate communication, but also extended to materials, production methods and brand strategy. For AF Cricketer's Gin, a premium gin developed for Seagram, the design brief called for a brand identity, which could do without heavy advertising. The spirit was to literally sell itself off the shelf through a concept that was truly groundbreaking at the time, and which entailed the simultaneous development of the product name, the shape of the bottle, the pack structure and graphics.

Howard Milton, who together with Peters was in charge of the design, recalls coming up with the name AF Cricketer's because "cricket is quintessentially English. We went into the design and I suggested shaping the bottle as a cricket bat." This idea then involved experimenting with innovative glass moulding techniques to attain the desired shape. The packaging graphics in turn were devised as an optical illusion. Illustrated by Jooce Garrett, a cricketer was printed on the back of the bottle, while the ball was printed on the front. A person who walked past the product sitting on the supermarket shelf then would perceive the ball as travelling through the bottle. "It was a very cool, very genteel product", Milton says.

The aim to innovate also led Peters to create for his company a new field of activity by registering Logoptics Ltd in 1974. The brand name Logoptics, derived from the Greek words for seeing and studying, stood for the use of illustrations and pictograms to encode complicated verbal and textual messages. Logoptics was to solve communication problems on an international level, to function as a sort of visual Esperanto. In terms of basing itself on the notion of a universal language functioning without words, Logoptics was quite similar to Otto Neurath's Isotype System, developed in the 1920s, and Otl Aicher's pictograms for the Munich Olympics in 1972. In contrast to the former, Peters' Logoptics was, however, not limited to pictograms, but could incorporate any type of graphic mode.

One possible area identified for the application of Logoptics was medicine labelling. A simple label containing symbols and a time grid to be ticked and annotated by the pharmacist would make vital information accessible to the illiterate or those who do not speak the language. Logoptics was also to aid the translatability of information in multi-lingual contexts, finding use in manuals, recipes and instructions. Both areas of application, however, also made clear that the concept of Logoptics could only work if it was assured that visual conventions were also universally understood.

In 1978, *Design* aimed to put the idea behind Logoptics to the test by asking Michael Peters and Partners to re-design an instruction manual for a complex machine (a sewing machine) to aid inexperienced users (men). As a first measure, the project design team, which consisted of Bev Whitehead, Gerry O'Dwyer and expert interpreter Rita Pyzdrowski, cut unnecessary information in the manual, and numbered each instruction to correspond with an illustration. "Then we came up with the idea of putting lines on the machine to show how to thread it", Whitehead recalls, " so we took a basic Singer, spray painted it cream and applied colour-coded paths directly on the machine.

THRESHER

In 1978, Thresher were facing growing competition from other off-licences. Their shops had the anonymity of links in a vast chain, and it seemed that there was no particular reason to buy in a Thresher store rather than any other.

Our aim was to give the Thresher family of shops the warm and glowing feeling of a local pub. Although the budget was relatively low, only natural materials were used, wherever possible, avoiding the unfriendly aluminium/plastic syndrome.

Rigid standardisation as applied to the fitting out of chain stores can often have a dehumanising effect on the people who work in them. With our flexible system, each store manager can feel almost that the shop is his, and play the satisfying role of genial host.

The shop signs were an important part of the new graphic personality, and we decided to use stove enamelled plaques, enhanced by the use of warm colours and lighting, to announce the Thresher name. By standardising the plaque sizes, we effected considerable savings.

Inside, as much of the stock as possible was put on display, in order to create a busy, friendly feeling. The natural materials used included solid wooden shelving systems and earthenware floor tiles. Enamelled advertising plaques introduced the further necessary touches of colour, and advertisers were happy to meet production costs.

Keeping well away from the chain store image, individual architectural features were carefully accentuated in each shop. Occasionally, this had a stunning effect, as in the Hampstead branch, where sales last year increased by 30%. To emphasise the local image, a sign hangs under the fascia, with the name of the particular branch underneath.

Delivery vans carry the new Thresher image throughout the country. Painted rich burgundy, the name panels, with their evocative "drink" symbols, were super-imposed in blue and yellow. The result is conspicuous and memorable.

Research carried out in the six pilot shops after refitting showed a sharp increase in sales, and the client decided to spend a considerable sum on developing the new image.

We have now produced a Thresher design manual, and are now applying its principles to the rest of the 400 off-licences in the Thresher empire.

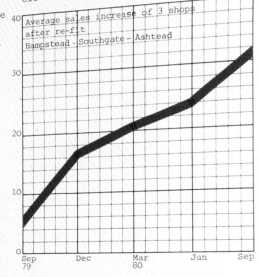

Average sales increase of 3 shops after re-fit
Hampstead - Southgate - Ashtead

"With a little time and effort, it is possible to have a chain of shops that are individual, relate to their environment, and yet suggest they have the buying clout of a large organisation."
quoted in DESIGN Magazine November 1978 by Michael Peters.

It came in second in a five machine test: only because one other machine's male participant had previously used a machine, skewing the results." Logoptics Ltd, despite collaborations with Johnson & Johnson, never really took off. "I just didn't have the time to further pursue it", Peters laments.

In 1980, Michael Peters and Partners celebrated its ten year existence by staging a controversial exhibition in London's Poland Street. Entitled Packaged for Success, the exhibition was promoted as "an optimistic look at the future of British Industry, and at the fund of talent which lies at the very heart of our nation". Britain was at the time still suffering from economic difficulties, thus Peters' angle was to show how design could increase the profitability of a wide range of goods and services. It was planned like a major art exhibition, and was to emphasise that design was a better investment than advertising, which Peters believed could only achieve short term goals. It attracted nearly 5,000 visitors.

To visually demonstrate their expertise in both design and marketing, Michael Peters and Partners suspended gigantic, three-dimensional reproductions of packaging from the ceiling, accompanied by client descriptions of how design had proved beneficial to their product. A re-design for the packaging of Batchelors Soups, for example, led its deliveries to retail outlets to rise by 32 per cent. Miners cosmetics, after a packaging re-launch, was more than pleased that sales leapt by 32 per cent within a year.

Crocodillo, a new product development for Seagram, only a few months after its launch reported conquering a staggering 49 per cent of the market. It was conceived as a sparkling wine alternative to Allied Breweries' Babycham; both were targeted at young female pub goers. The name was intended to have a continental ring to it, while still being pronounceable by the average Briton, and to be linked to a likeable character.

The Crocodillo bottle, designed by Jim Groark, was extraordinary in representing only the top third of a champagne bottle, and therefore functioning as a single-serve flask. However, despite its innovative and high-quality design, the initial success did not last. Allied Breweries quickly responded with a similar product—and in the end edged Crocodillo out of the market. It was thus defeated by the very rival it sought to surpass.

Designing a Company

Since its inception in 1970, Michael Peters and Partners had through its commercial success steadily grown by adding more and more people to its design teams. At the same time, individual teams with specialist knowledge were assigned to specific areas such as corporate literature, new product development and brand identity, as well as environmental and retail design.

Along with Annual Reports Ltd and Logoptics Ltd, Michael Peters and Partners spawned Hawkeye Studios Ltd, an artwork studio which also worked for external designers under the direction of Aubrey Hastings-Smith and Lynette Grass, and Brand New (Product Origination) Ltd, a design-led new product development company headed by Pamela Conway, which was located in Roseheart Mews.

The strategy underlying an increased specialisation by registering new companies and appointing a managing director for each, was to avoid Michael Peters and Partners growing beyond a manageable size. The aptly named off-shoots also attracted specific commissions, became profit centres in their own right, and could directly respond to the growing diversification of the market in the late 70s and early 80s.

In 1970, Michael Peters and Partners had started off with roughly six or seven designers, after one year, already 15 people were working on creative solutions, while other work was given to external experts. By 1980, the company's turnover in fees had reached the one million pound mark, and its staff totalled 25. At this point, Peters had no intentions of expanding the company any further; only three years later however, Michael Peters and Partners had grown to 40 people.

Peters' change of mind had come with the consultation of Robert Silver, whom he had brought into the company when experiencing hard times due to the bankruptcy of one of its clients. The plan was to devise a structure which would guard the company against similar problems, and maximise its business potential. Michael Peters and Partners was thriving as a design firm, but there was room for improvement in terms of how the company was run. "Bob Silver said I needed business people to run the business, to take some of the weight off my shoulders", Peters recalls.

He could instead focus on attracting larger and more illustrious clients by building a larger company. "Bob asked me what my dream would be. I wanted to build the biggest design company in the world, an international, multi-disciplinary business focusing on packaging, graphic design, three-dimensional work, innovation and so on. Because I had come from nothing, and wanted to leave a mark that had its roots in quality and creativity."

He found that the time was right to fully realise his plans of creating a "commercial Bauhaus", an ambition he had already partly put into practice by diversifying via subsidiaries, and producing work which offered several integrated services to clients. For the off-license chain Thresher, Michael Peters and Partners had devised an identity comprising a logo, stationery, enamel advertising plaques, shop signs, a modular system of versatile stickers, carrier bags, delivery vans and the shops themselves. The company's work for the promotion fund of the International Coffee Organization encompassed designs for a symbol—based on the contrasting swirls of cream in coffee, stationery, promotional

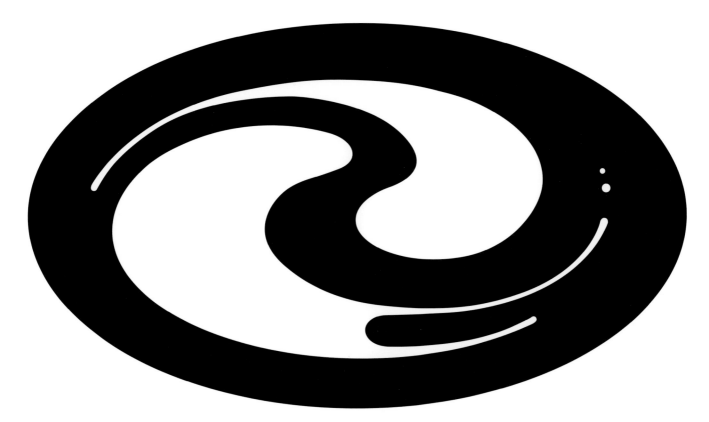

Logo for the International Coffee Organization Innovation Centre in London.

items and an award-winning information centre in London's Berners Street.

The multi-disciplinary, collaborative aspect of his ambition Peters also shared with other important design companies, such as Conran, Pentagram and Allied International Designers—however, in contrast, Peters wanted to make his a mainly commercial enterprise. The key question was how he would achieve growing such a large company. "Bob Silver then said that if I wanted to do that I was going to have to leave others some of my responsibilities, because I would have to think about expanding the business. We then discussed becoming a public company as one option", Peters states. "Taking the company on to the stock market would give us enough money to realise our aspirations. We then spent a great deal of time debating the pros and cons and eventually decided to take the plunge."

Peters' plans of realising his vision of a large, multi-disciplinary company coincided with significant changes in the political and cultural climate of Britain. The Royal Family had provided causes for national celebration with the Queen's Silver Jubilee in 1977 and the wedding of Prince Charles and Lady Diana Spencer in 1981. The Sex Pistols and The Clash played their first spectacular gigs in 1976. Racial tensions sparked riots in Notting Hill, Brixton and other areas of London during the late 70s and early 80s.

As the decade came to an end, industrial action by lorry drivers, ambulance staff and dustmen, again paralysed Britain, culminating in the "winter of discontent". The vote of no confidence in the Labour government under James Callaghan in the spring of 1979 then forced a

general election, won by Conservative party leader Margaret Thatcher with a majority of 43 seats. To counter a deepening of the still prevalent recession, the Thatcher government over the next years developed and implemented a rigid programme of privatisation and de-regulation. Luckily for Peters, it also supported business expansion and a greater awareness of design by the industry.

The project for Adams Childrenswear (a chain of clothing shops for children) was a designer's dream. Michael Adams, the owner, wanted to create a shopping 'haven' for parents and their children. The idea was to create a wonderland for the shopper and particularly their children to experience a play environment. The interiors were very bright and colourful with a large abacus for children to climb and play on, large rulers for them to measure themselves against and discover objects or animals that are the same size as themselves. Large meccano-type structures displayed clothing and accessories, while the lighting was designed to create an atmosphere of calm. The colourful exterior displayed a stove-enamelled 'layered' Adams logo. All the graphics reflected the energy of a retailer who wanted to ensure his customers a unique shopping experience.

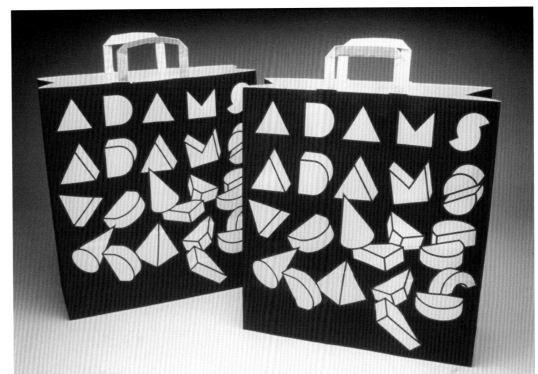

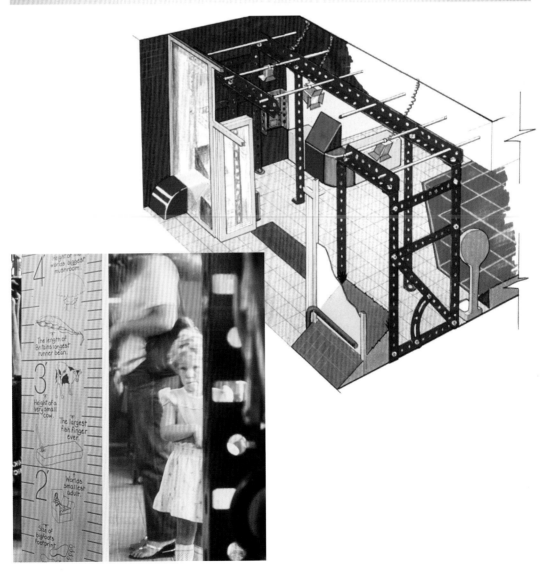

HAYTER

*Opposite: Logo
for Post International
Productions.*

*Top: Logo for Hayter,
a manufacturer of
lawnmowers and
gardening equipment.*

*Middle: Logo for
Creative Excellence in
Newspaper Advertising,
The Annual Award.*

*Bottom: Logo for
CC Soft Drinks Ltd,
a manufacturer of
carbonated beverages.*

DAILIES

L'EXCELLENCE EN CREATION PUBLICITAIRE DANS LES QUOTIDIENS
CREATIVE EXCELLENCE IN NEWSPAPER ADVERTISING

CC•SOFT•DRINKS

An identity for
Snopake—a typo-
correction fluid product
that puts the delete
symbol at the heart
of its name.

bake

Chesterfield
CHAUSSETTES LONGUES
Chesterfield
CHAUSSETTES LONGUES

Left: Sock packaging for
Chesterfield Socks, a
French manufacturer of
hosiery. The socks were
displayed on cardboard
cut-out trouser legs,
each range with its own
patterns and colours.

Above: Swimwear
packaging for Louis
Féraud—a distinguished
French couturier, who
designed a unique
range of swimwear for
both men and women.
The packaging was
designed to look like the
canvas from deckchairs.

Elsenham Jams and Preserves Limited has been manufacturing jams and condiments for over 100 years. The brief was to reflect the reputation of a firm that made its products with love, care and attention, reflecting the tiled kitchens in which Elsenham first created its products.

*Opposite: Pipers
Scotch Whisky—one of
the brands designed for
Seagram, a Canadian
beverage company.*

*Above: Over five years
Michael Peters and
Partners designed
all the private label
packaging for Fine
Fare. This award-
winning packaging
is one example.*

Taylors of Harrogate was established in 1886 and is still an independent family business. The company commissioned Michael Peters and Partners to design the packaging (old packaging opposite bottom) for a range of quality teas and coffees. Yorkshire Tea is a major bestseller in the competitive tea market and this packaging is still around today after being designed over 25 years ago.

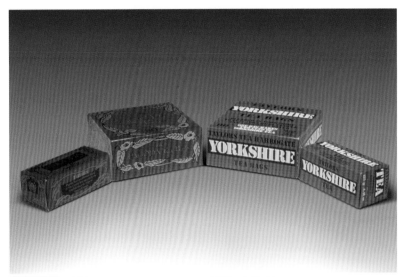

Old and new packaging for Winsor & Newton's ink range. The work for Winsor & Newton is a major commercial and creative success. Over an eight year period, Michael Peters and Partners designed numerous ranges of packaging and continued its role as brand guardians for the whole Winsor & Newton brand. The Big Idea was to show, via the packaging, the flexibility of Winsor & Newton's products by commissioning illustrators, designers, and artists to demonstrate how their products could be used. This project, first commissioned in 1971, has now become an icon in the sector and is displayed in museums of packaging all over the world as an example of total innovation in packaging design.

Numerous illustrators and designers were commissioned for these inks. They include: Tony Meeuwissen, Philip Castle, John Gorham, Nick Thirkell, Arthur Robbins, Alan Manham, Barry Craddock, and children from local schools.

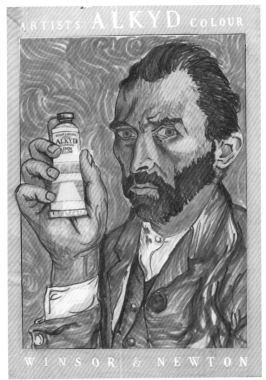

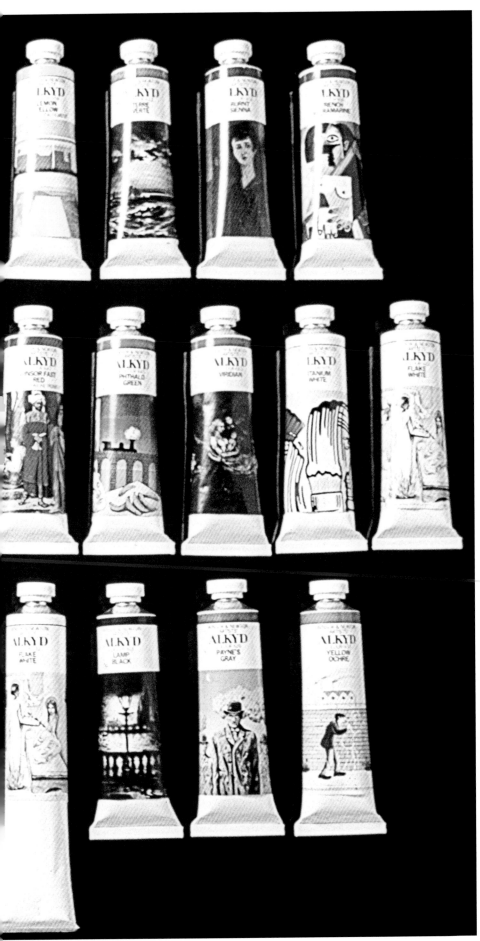

These Alkyd colours were designed to pay homage to great artists and painters. From Magritte to Lichtenstein, from Rousseau to Stella, and from Turner to Stubbs. All posters and promotional materials were developed in the same genre. Some of the illustrators include: Guy Beggs, Ginetto Coppola, Bill Dare, John Davies, Roy Ellsworth, John Gorham, John Rose, Colin Salter, David Sharp and Jan Stringer.

This calendar was designed as a catalogue for Winsor & Newton's retail customers. The illustrations by artist/ designer Jan Stringer displayed the wide use of artist materials, along with the birth dates of famous artists and designers.

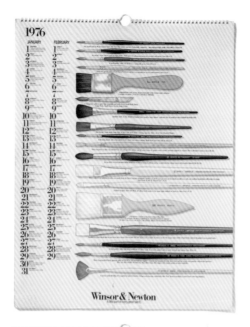

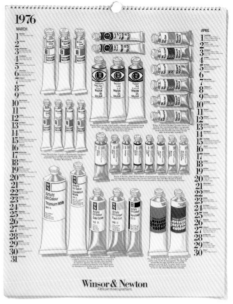

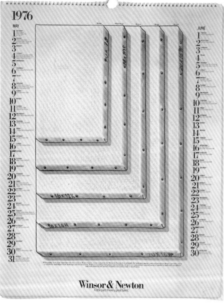

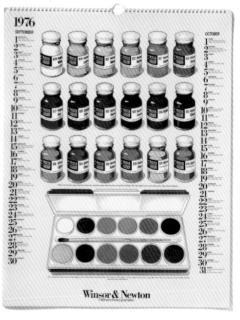

108

1976

NOVEMBER

1 MONDAY
Laurence Stephen Lowry b 1887

2 TUESDAY
Jean Baptiste Simeon Chardin b 1699

3 WEDNESDAY
Annibale Carracci b 1560

4 THURSDAY
Guido Reni b 1575

5 FRIDAY
Raymond Duchamp-Villon b 1876

6 SATURDAY
George Howland Beaumont b 1753

7 SUNDAY

8 MONDAY
Charles Demuth b 1883

9 TUESDAY
Adolf Dietrich b 1877

10 WEDNESDAY
William Hogarth b 1697
El Lissitsky b 1890

11 THURSDAY
Paul Signac b 1863
Edouard Vuillard b 1868

12 FRIDAY

13 SATURDAY

14 SUNDAY
Claude Monet b 1840

15 MONDAY
Cornelius Bega b 1620

16 TUESDAY
Francis Danby b 1793

17 WEDNESDAY
Charles Lock Eastlake b 1793
Pierre Mignard b 1612

18 THURSDAY
Wyndham Lewis b 1882
David Wilkie b 1785

19 FRIDAY
Louis Tocque b 1696

20 SATURDAY

21 SUNDAY
Graham Bell b 1910
James Clarke Hook b 1819
René Magritte b 1898

22 MONDAY

23 TUESDAY
Romain de Tirtoff Erté b 1892
Jose Clemente Orozco b 1883

24 WEDNESDAY
Toulouse Lautrec b 1864

25 THURSDAY
Maurice Denis b 1870

26 FRIDAY
William Sydney Mount b 1807

27 SATURDAY
Tsuguharu Foujita b 1886
William Orpen b 1878

28 SUNDAY
William Blake b 1757

29 MONDAY
James Rosenquist b 1933

30 TUESDAY
Winston Churchill b 1874

DECEMBER

1 WEDNESDAY

2 THURSDAY
Georges Seurat b 1859

3 FRIDAY
Julius Bissier b 1893
Victor Pasmore b 1908
Gilbert Stuart b 1755

4 SATURDAY
Thomas Good b 1789
Vassily Kandinsky b 1866

5 SUNDAY
David Bomberg b 1890

6 MONDAY

7 TUESDAY
Bernini b 1598

8 WEDNESDAY
Aristide Maillol b 1861
Diego Rivera b 1886

9 THURSDAY
John Macallan Swan b 1847

10 FRIDAY
Renato Birolli b 1906

11 SATURDAY
Mark Tobey b 1890

12 SUNDAY
Pierre Andrien b 1821
Helen Frankenthaler b 1928
Edvard Munch b 1863

13 MONDAY
John Piper b 1903

14 TUESDAY
François Hubert Drouais b 1727
Roger Fry b 1866

15 WEDNESDAY
George Fennel Robson b 1788
George Romney b 1734

16 THURSDAY
John Charles Robinson b 1824

17 FRIDAY
George Houston Thomas b 1824

18 SATURDAY
Ludolf Bakhuizen b 1631
Paul Klee b 1879

19 SUNDAY

20 MONDAY
Martin Archer Shee b 1769

21 TUESDAY
Thomas Couture b 1815
San Giovanni Masaccio b 1401

22 WEDNESDAY
John Crome b 1768

23 THURSDAY
Antonio Tapies b 1923

24 FRIDAY
Pierre Soulages b 1919

25 SATURDAY
Christopher Clavaria Sanders b 1905

26 SUNDAY
George John Pinwell b 1842
Maurice Utrillo b 1883

27 MONDAY

28 TUESDAY
P Wilson Steer b 1860

29 WEDNESDAY
Julius Caesar Ibbetson b 1759

30 THURSDAY
Alfred Stevens b 1817

31 FRIDAY
Henri Matisse b 1869

Nacryl. An acrylic medium which may be mixed with any water-based colour to produce a versatile paint which is waterproof when dry.

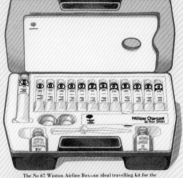

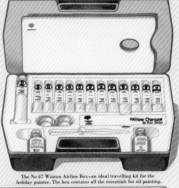

The No 67 Winton Airline Box—an ideal travelling kit for the holiday painter. The box contains all the essentials for oil painting.

One of three beginners' outfits with vacuum formed polystyrene tray for pots which doubles as a mixing tray when the pots are removed.

One of a range of Mixing Trays from Winsor & Newton in porcelain or plastic.

Winsor & Newton supply all oils, painting media and varnishes.

Winsor & Newton manufacture a wide range of canvases and easels at prices and sizes suitable for all types of artists.

The double tin dipper—just one of a wide range of accessories available from Winsor & Newton for the oil painter.

Various painting and palette knives are available, some of the latter with stainless steel blades, of particular interest to acrylic painters.

One of a range of reasonably priced water colour boxes.

Charcoal Pencils. Winsor & Newton although not manufacturers of drawing pencils, hold stocks of leading makes together with other drawing accessories.

Winsor & Newton's famous mahogany palette comes in 3 shapes and various sizes. Palettes for left handed painters are available to special order.

Winsor & Newton WP20 Water Colour Pad
20 sheets, Bockingford Paper 70lbs per ream. 14 x 10" Size.

One of a wide range of specially selected drawing pads available from Winsor & Newton.

Winsor & Newton
A little part of every great talent.

Printed by Perivan, Williams Lea Group on Everovde White Offset Twin Wire S/O 250gsm; manufactured by John Dickinson & Company Limited, at Croxley Mills, Warford, Hertfordshire.

These Winsor & Newton poster colours are designed as a homage to some of the most famous poster artists in the world. All were done with the permission of the estates or of the artists, with the designers showcasing these Winsor & Newton colours as a poster medium. Illustrations are by Anthony Reid Partnership.

Who would have had t

1. Jean Arp?
Robert Desnos?
Meret Oppenheim?

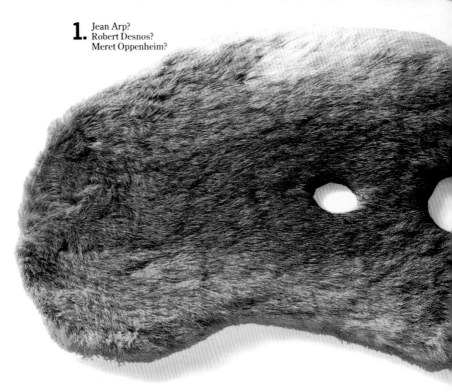

4. Roland Penrose?
Kurt Schwitters?
Yves Tanguy?

5. Salvador Dali?
Max Ernst?
Maurice Henry?

nerve to treat our products like this?

2. Marcel Duchamp?
Léonor Fini?
Francis Picabia?

3. Georges Malkine?
André Masson?
Man Ray?

6. Paul Delvaux?
René Magritte?
Dorothea Tanning?

Before we get to some likely answers (which are at the foot of this page) we should admit that when artists' materials were first subjected to this kind of treatment, we were as shocked as everybody else.

After all, we had been accustomed to seeing our materials used for graceful landscapes and genteel portraits. So when the Dadaists appeared, with their irreverent notions about art, no one knew quite what to think. At first the way they used colour made a lot of people see red. But at the same time they opened our eyes to a world of new possibilities. In the end they stretched our imaginations as much as our canvas. And taught us all a thing or two about art.

Which brings us back to the quiz.

If you got three right then you know something about Dada and Surrealism. You can learn more from the exhibition at London's Hayward Gallery: 11th January – 27th March 1978.

If you got less than three right then you should <u>definitely</u> go.

You'll get quite an education.

WINSOR & NEWTON
A little part of every great talent

1. Meret Oppenheim. 2. Marcel Duchamp. 3. Man Ray. 4. Kurt Schwitters. 5. Maurice Henry. 6. René Magritte.

113

Above: Old packaging.

Right: Brocks for many years has been a pioneer of innovative fireworks. They were keen to create a brand image that reflected the excitement and energy associated with the world of pyrotechnics. This was, therefore a golden opportunity to reflect the 'pzazz' of the products through the visual language associated with firework display.

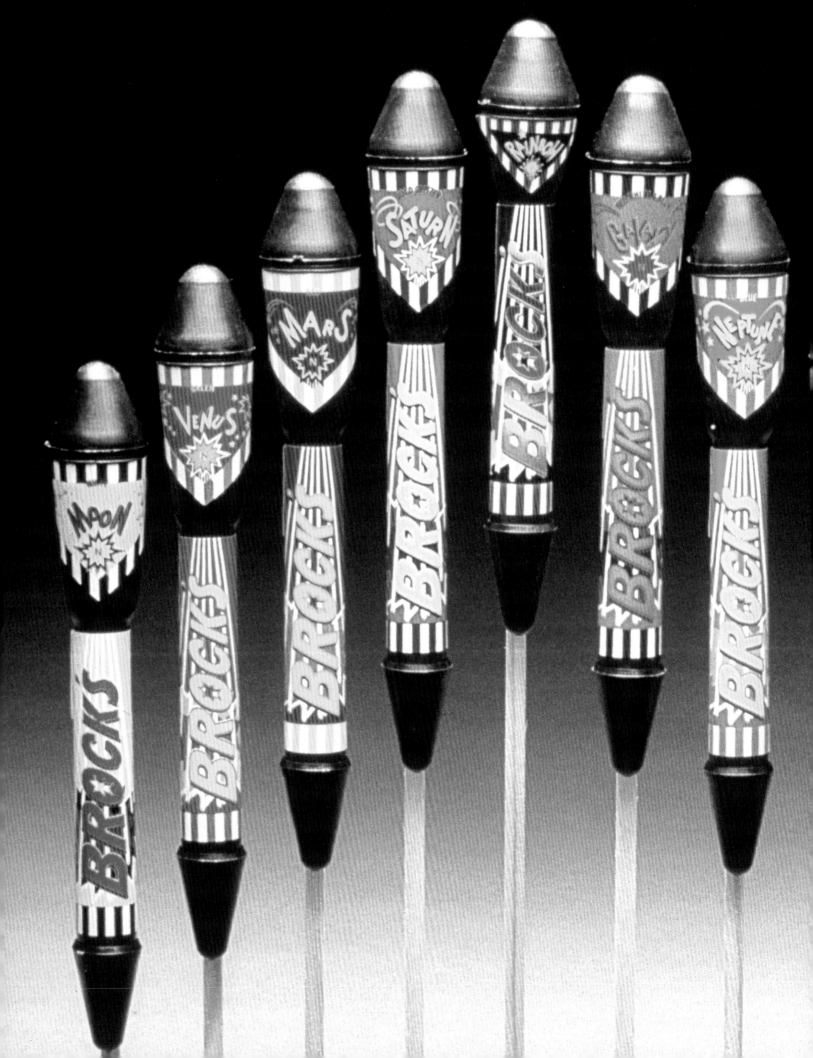

Every part of the new Brocks brand was designed and implemented, across rockets (left), gift packaging (above), point of sale, and the total brand image.

Penhaligon's is one
of the few English
perfume houses in
the world today.
Although the Penhaligon
family had created 'fine
perfumes' over 100
years ago it was not
until Franco Zeffirelli
bought the business
in the early 1970s
that there existed an
opportunity to take
the brand out of its
historic shadows into
the competitive world of
perfumery. The key and
secret of its success
was to lovingly re-craft
the look and feel of the
'brand' through its retail
presence, its packaging
and all of its marketing
collateral material.
The detailing of the
typography, the beauty
of the illustrations and
the support of a strong
client makes this project
one of the most revered
in the history of Michael
Peters and Partners.

Every part of the Penhaligon's brand was examined and developed in minute detail, especially in the design and production of the packaging. The budgets were relatively small for the bottles and outer packaging, and it was the skills and commitment of the client, designers and production teams that created this beautiful end result.

Promotion was key to the commercial success of this brand, with the client and design teams working in tandem to achieve this, especially through direct mail communications.

McKnight Kauffer, the celebrated American poster designer, once said that "posters should be read as you run". The packaging of the carrier bags was designed to create a 'walking poster', which immediately endorsed the excellence and originality of the seasonal range of clothes throughout Michael Barrie's UK Menswear chain.

MICHAEL B

MICHAEL
BARRIE

White cans make
ironing EASIER.

Brown cans WAX
wood furniture.

Orange cans
CLEAN ovens.

FRESHEN air.

This packaging, for the Yellow Can Company, an own-label aerosol manufacturer was designed to create a stand-alone brand to compete with private label supermarket products. This is one of the most famous award-winning projects produced by Michael Peters and Partners.

Michael Peters Group had a very long relationship with Seagram—the Canadian distillers and worked on nearly all of its brands over 25 years. The relationship with this client enabled Michael Peters and his team to create and develop a number of new products. One such idea was the creation of a premium Gin—AF Cricketer's. The uniqueness of the cricket bat-shaped bottle, the illustrations of the bowler, batsman and wicket keeper on the reverse of the bottle (an idea now emulated by other brands) and the silkscreen cricket ball on the front of the pack (giving the illusion of the ball travelling through the bottle) was all part of the brand personality. This is a brilliant example of a Big Idea, beautifully designed and well executed down to the minutest detail.

DISTILLED FROM 100% PURE GRAIN SPIRIT

A·F
CRICKETER'S

A·F·CRICKETER & SONS · LONDON SW11 0DC · ENGLAND

SPECIAL RESERVE
GIN

PRODUCED AND DISTILLED IN
THE UNITED KINGDOM

75 cl   40% vol

DISTILLED FROM 100% PURE GRAIN SPIRIT

A·F
CRICKETER'S

A·F·CRICKETER & SONS · LONDON SW11 0DC · ENGLAND

SPECIAL RESERVE
GIN

PRODUCED AND DISTILLED IN
THE UNITED KINGDOM

75 cl   40% vol

Crocodillo—a new product to compete in the 'sparkling perry' sector of alcoholic beverages was the brainchild of the Seagram/Michael Peters and Partners team. The idea was to create 'a half champagne bottle' as the packaging idea. The creation of a name and the unique crocodile character soon became the icon for the brand and the main presenter on all communications, including point of sale for all pubs, clubs and hotels.

HOW TO CREATE THE PERFECT CUP OF COFFEE

THE LONDON COFFEE INFORMATION CENTRE.
POUR IN AND FIND OUT EVERYTHING YOU NEED TO KNOW.

THE LONDON
COFFEE INFORMATION CENTRE

Michael Peters
and Partners were
commissioned by
the International
Coffee Organization in
1981/1982 to create
a home for innovation
in London's West End.
Apart from the iconic
logo, the application of
a big brand idea was
applied as a total identity
programme. A flexible
exhibition area was also
invented to showcase
innovation and creativity
as part of the promotion
of coffee.

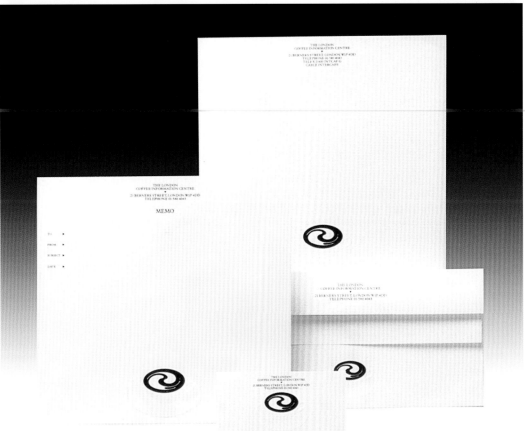

Thresher is a chain of wine and beverage shops, once owned by Whitbread. Michael Peters and Partners were commissioned in 1978, in partnership with FCO (French, Cruttenden, Osborne—an award-winning advertising agency), to create a new brand look and feel for all of the retail outlets and advertising communications. The design team designed a totally fresh image for the chain that allowed for all outlets to have the flexibility to promote themselves as a 'local shop' with their own personality e.g. Thresher in Fulham, Thresher in Luton, etc.. In addition, flexible window alphabets were produced for the managers to create their own promotional messages. The signage, both internally and externally, were stove enamelled letters with appropriate 'beverage' symbols as part and parcel of the identity, with all the brand labels enlarged and produced in stove enamel as part of the internal point of sale display.

136

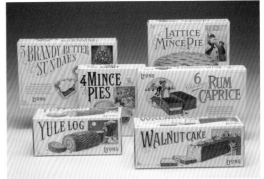

A total brand revamp for Lyons the bakers. Apart from the re-design of the original packaging (bottom) to the new packaging (left) there was an opportunity to create and design seasonal Christmas packaging that would change every year (top).

Fürstenberg—showing the label design for the German beer—imported and distributed by Guinness. The labels were designed and printed in different layers of silver inks and foil to create a luminescent glow at point of sale.

IMPORTED
Fürstenberg
BREWED AND BOTTLED IN GERMANY
Fürstenberg
GERMAN BEER
DONAUESCHINGEN, BLACK FOREST
WEST GERMANY

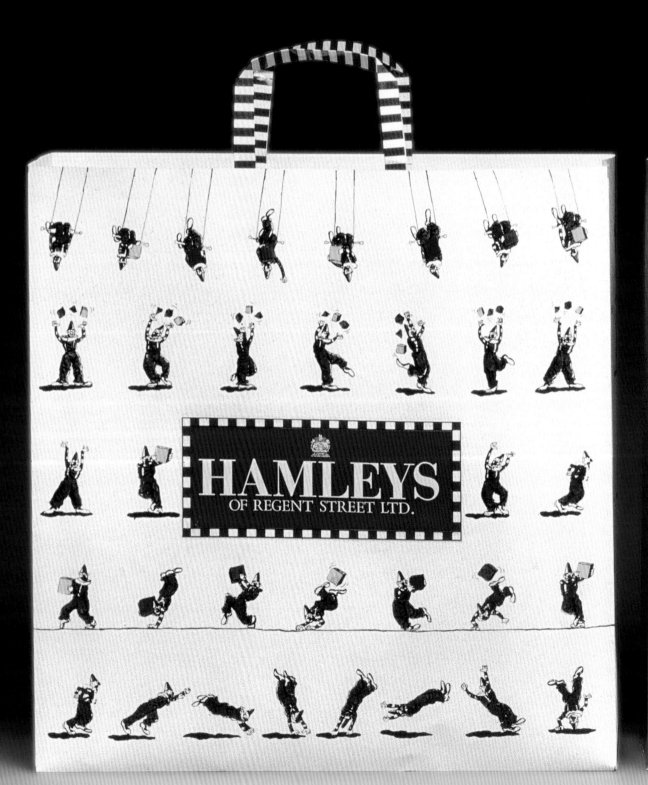

Promotional carrier bags for Hamleys of Regent Street, one of the greatest toy shops in the world. Beautifully illustrated clowns were created as part of a high energy, in-store promotional campaign.

THE

**Flotations
1983–1990**

Glenn Tutssel

In a truly world-changing decade, a period that was defined by Thatcher and the fall of Communism, an era that brought us Madonna and Boy George, there was also a complete change in the UK industrial landscape. Businesses that had previously been in a stranglehold to the unions were now being celebrated for their entrepreneurship and Michael Peters and Partners were at the forefront of that change.

When you look through the D&AD annuals of the time you will see work that tried to be bold and stand out from the crowd—it was the work of Michael Peters and Partners. Packaging that consumers not only bought, but collected, in a way that had never happened before. The work for clients such as Winsor & Newton inks and Penhaligon's perfumes were iconic pieces of design that defined an era and have stood the test of time. These were built on big ideas, beautifully crafted and they flew off the shelves. The work was ahead of its time, mould breaking, and innovative.

Packaging design had turned into a profession that had gone from creating a commodity to creating a lifestyle choice. In effect, modern packaging design was born. Until now packs showed serving suggestions, describing the content in a bland apologetic way to appease trading standards officers. We changed all this by applying Michael's mantra of "good is not enough, it has to be great, be new, and different". We created 'appetite appeal', with stunning art direction, innovative use of illustration, hand drawn typography and dynamic photography.

We were a team of mavericks, who went out on a limb when our competitors were playing safe. Michael knew that by being bold and breaking new ground we could win the respect of our competitors and clients alike. We dramatically increased profitability for our clients by using our creativity, adding seriously to their bottom line. This resulted in raising the value of what designers produced, and enabled us to charge clients accordingly.

Businesses could for the first time see the added value design brought to the marketing process.

Michael, established as a packaging expert, also applied this rigorous creative process to annual reports, retail interiors, corporate identity and, of course, product design. The Ross Radio, along with 3-D packs for Shell and BP took structural design to a new level. Whenever a client's production team said that something could not be made, Michael found a way to do it. As with our group's 'pop up' Annual Report, or the Sweet Factory, or Cricketer's Gin, there was a fresh and innovative approach, pushing the boundaries of creativity, challenging the brief and exceeding expectations.

By doing the best design work, Peters knew that we could attract the very best talent and the commitment from the team gave us the energy to produce outstanding work. There were plenty of late nights and long weekends working, but that's what it took to be the best. We broke the rules and created new ones; designers and clients regarded us as innovators, changing perceptions wherever we worked.

There was a work hard, play hard culture, and definitely a culture of winning. But Michael also invested in up and coming young talent. Just to be invited for an interview was a privilege and Fiona Gilmore called it the "University of Design". Every year we took on four or five young stars of the future, who were nurtured and mentored and given the best environment for their ideas to flourish. We were in our metier surrounded by creativity— pottery, sculpture and paintings in the spacious Olaf Street studio.

By investing in young creative talent Michael has become a "founding father" of the design industry. In addition, his desire to make design a powerful driver of international business has been realised. Each of these achievements is supported by his enthusiasm, passion and energy to leave his mark in the world of design. I'm sure he has succeeded!

	1983	**1984**	**1985**	**1986**	**1987**	**1988**
Politics	• Iranian forces invade Iraq • Thatcher celebrates a landslide	• Mrs Ghandi shot dead • Gas leak at Bhopal • Riot police battle miners at Orgreave • Indian troops storm Sikh Golden Temple • IRA bomb blast at Tory Conference • China and UK agree on Hong Kong deal	• Pound falls to lowest value ever • Mikhail Gorbachev new Soviet leader • Ethiopia famine • Greenpeace Rainbow Warrior damaged in Auckland harbour	• Chernobyl Nuclear Disaster • Biggest ever health campaign in Britain: AIDS "Don't die of ignorance" • Kurt Waldheim elected Austrian president • Chinese democracy demonstrations in Shanghai	• Thatcher elected for third term • Ordination of women priests by the Church of England • Klaus Barbie given life imprisonment • Storm of the century lashes England • King's Cross fire	• Moscow agrees to withdraw Soviet forces from Afghanistan • French voters re-elect President Mitterand to a seven year term
Music	• Michael Jackson's *Thriller* • Muddy Waters dies	• Count Basie dies • Bob Geldof and Band Aid release the single "Do They Know It's Christmas"	• Compact Discs start to gain popularity • Madonna "Like a virgin" • Live Aid at Wembley	• Raymond Burke dies • First induction into the Rock and Roll Hall of Fame	• Acid house • Aretha Franklin first woman inducted into the Rock and Roll Hall of Fame • Nirvana formed • Fred Astaire dies	• Chet Baker dies • Roy Orbison performs last concert • Michael Jackson *Bad*
Art	• Kenneth Clark (*Civilisation*) dies • David Niven dies • Christo's *Wrapper*	• Richard Burton dies • Truffaut dies • *Amadeus* by Milos Forman • Neville Brody art directs *The Face* • Sir John Betjeman dies	• Orson Welles dies • Marc Chagall dies • The Turner Prize is awarded for the first time	• Henry Moore dies • Georgia O'Keeffe dies • Simone de Beauvoir dies • *Nature Study* by Louise Bourgeois	• Andy Warhol dies • *Spycatcher* banned in the UK	• Freeze, Surrey Docks, London • *The Last Emperor* wins nine Oscars • Tony Cragg wins Turner Prize
Design / Architecture	• Trump Tower, New York • Royal Gold Medal to Norman Foster • Eton Center, Toronto • Buckminster Fuller dies • Michael Graves Alessi kettle • Audi Quattro Sport	• The Prince of Wales denounces a proposed modernist extension to the National Gallery • York Minster set ablaze • Renault Espace • Apple Logo	• Seattle Art Museum is completed by architect Robert Venturi • Stuttgart's brightly coloured Neue Staatsgalerie is completed by James Stirling • Pippa folding chair and desk by Rena Dumas and Peter Coles	• Royal Gold Medal to Arata Isozaki • The Lipstick Building in New York City is completed • The Lloyds Building in London, designed by Richard Rogers is completed	• Ernö Goldfinger dies • Stade Olympique and La Tour de Montréal in Montréal completed • Frank Gehry 'Little Beaver' armchair • Norman Foster's Nomos Desk	• The Seikan Tunnel in Japan is completed • Torre Picasso, in Madrid, Spain is completed • Pritzker Prize to Oscar Niemeyer and Gordon Bunshaft • 'Fat Chance' off-road racer introduced
Innovation	• Freddy Laker Skytrain • Braun Multi-practice electric mixer • Swatch watches	• First untethered Space Walk • BMX-mania hits Britain • First Apple Mac introduced	• CD-Rom introduced • Sinclair C5 is introduced • New Coke is introduced • Sony HandyCam	• Nissan open UK car factory • Space Shuttle explodes on take off • Dyson Dual Cyclone introduced • Amstrad PC 1512 by Alan Sugar is launched	• Adobe Systems introduces Adobe Illustrator	• Very first Fair Trade label launched in The Netherlands
Fashion	• Annie Lennox—Gender-bending • Vivienne Westwood's Witches Collection	• New Romantics	• Laura Ashley dies • Madonna's trash style miniskirts, lacy tights and layered clothes	• Nike and Adidas inform Hip Hop fashion	• Dior's new look celebrates 40 years on at Paris fashion show	• Barbour jackets • Car accessories—furry dice • Billy Idol introduces fingerless gloves
Sport	• Tom Watson wins fifth British Open • Daley Thompson wins Gold in World Athletic Championships	• Navratilova wins a fifth Wimbledon • Torvill and Dean win Olympic Gold • Soviets boycott Los Angeles Olympics	• Boris Becker wins Wimbledon age 17 • 41 killed as Liverpool fans are crushed at Heysel in Brussells • Bradford City Football grounds inferno—40 die	• Mike Tyson is youngest Heavyweight Champion • Argentina win victory in World Cup—Diego Maradona's 'Hand of God' goal	• Australia win World Cup for the first time	• Enzo Ferrari dies • Olympic Games held in Seoul, South Korea
Projects			**DAR SALONS**			**CONSERVATIVE**

1989

- Revolutions of 1989 across Eastern and Central Europe
- Tiananmen Square protests
- Fall of the Berlin Wall
- George Bush 41st president of USA

- Kylie Minogue and Jason Donovan
- The Bangles "Eternal flame"
- James Brown sentenced to six years imprisonment

- Eisenstein: His Life and Work, MOMA touring exhibiton
- The Keith Haring Foundation is established

- *Magiciens de la terre* at Centre Georges Pompidou
- Robert Mapplethorpe dies
- Vitra Design Museum in Weil am Rhein, Germany by Frank Gehry is completed
- Louvre Pyramid is completed

- Ron Arad's Three Thirds of a Table
- Harley Davidson Tour Glide Classic introduced
- Nintendo begins selling the Game Boy in Japan
- Fluocaril toothbrush

- Lambada look
- Nike Air

- Sugar Ray Robinson, American boxing champion dies
- Steffi Graff is female athlete of the year

1990

- Apartheid ends in South Africa
- Nelson Mandela freed from jail
- Margaret Thatcher resigns

- The Three Tenors sing together for the first time
- MC Hammer
- Madonna's Blonde Ambition Tour

- Robert Mapplethorpe *The Perfect Moment*
- Rushdie threatened with death sentence for his work *The Satanic Verses*

- Leaning tower of Pisa closed to the public
- Bank of China, Hong Kong

- World Wide Web introduced

- Supermodels
- Vogueing
- Madonna's cone brassiere designed by Jean-Paul Gaultier

- West Germany wins World Cup

Joining the Club

Peters took the first step towards bringing to fruition his vision of a multi-disciplinary design company in 1981, when the Michael Peters Group was formed as a holding company for Michael Peters and Partners and its satellites Annual Reports Ltd, The Hawkeye Studios Ltd, Brand New (Product Origination) Ltd and a newly acquired promotion company called The Idea Works Ltd, which was based in Wiltshire. The flotation of the company, the keystone of its aspired multi-dimensional structure, was then prepared over the next two years through regular meetings with the City of London.

With Robert Silver masterminding the process (he later became deputy chairman of the company), the Michael Peters Group was quoted on the Unlisted Securities Market (USM) in 1983. It was one of the first design groups in Britain to go public—while the advertising industry had been on the stock market for several years, only a few design companies had dared take this step (Allied International Designers were the first in 1980). The flotation brought the Michael Peters Group directly to the forefront of the design industry.

"On the day we floated", Peters remembers, "I took my mother-in-law and my family to the stock exchange and there we were, up in lights: Michael Peters Group. My mother-in-law told me that she didn't think our share price was high enough, so our broker, Brian Winterflood, asked her how much she wanted the share price to be. She said, 'At least another ten pence.' So Winterflood smiled, saying that he would see what he could do." The group, valued at £4.8 million, joined the USM at 85p per share, and was accompanied by a clever PR operation that included both a radio and television campaign (written by Tony Hertz) and an extraordinary origami prospectus that literally metamorphosed in the hands of the shareholders. Written by the *Daily Mirror* columnist Donald Zec, the prospectus contained four pieces of coloured paper, which could be folded into the shapes of a box, a book, a bottle and a shop—each representing a specialist field in which the Michael Peters Group operated.

The obligatory half-year reports followed a similarly Big Idea. They were not merely printed on sheets of paper, but consisted of signed limited editions of artwork produced by young artists, designers and photographers, which carried the financial results on their reverse sides. Thus every shareholder was additionally rewarded with their own work of art.

HOW TO MAKE THE SHOP
PLEASE SEE THE GENERAL INSTRUCTIONS
PRINTED INSIDE THE ORIGAMI FOLDER

FOLD AND RETURN

MICHAEL PETERS GROUP PLC
AN INSIGHT INTO THE CREATIVE PROCESS (USING BOTH HANDS)

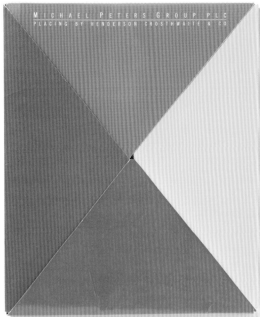

The Michael Peters Group documented its flotation one year later in the country's first pop-up annual report. As with the Abbey Life Annual Report a decade earlier, Peters broke one of the fundamental rules of the genre that demanded factual information to be depicted in tables. Instead, he gave facts, figures and information a playful, three-dimensional form. The corporate literature accompanying the launch and the pop-up annual report were the brainchild of Jackie Vicary (who was joint managing and creative director of Annual Reports) and designer Peter Chodel, and soon became sought-after collectors' items. Their popularity verified that more and more shareholders were willing to buy into Peters' unconventional thinking. "We broke new ground with the whole thing", he asserts, "it was all a big razzmatazz to demonstrate our power as designers."

Despite suddenly finding himself amongst "red braces, pin-striped suits and designer shoes that talked ROI (return on investment) and leverage", he gradually felt right at home. "I loved being on the stock market... it was very exciting." The media attention was indeed mind boggling. A poll conducted by the independent UK research organisation MORI (Market & Opinion Research International), and commissioned by Peters in the year of the flotation revealed that Michael Peters and Partners was the best-known design group in the country. A plethora of articles featuring the launch and its PR coup followed; the magazine *Designer* in its December issue of 1983 even placed Peters on its cover, clutching the origami prospectus, standing amidst the buzz of the Stock Exchange.

Opposite and top: The Michael Peters Group prospectus (the mandatory flotation document) was a 'tour de force' in the dull world of city flotations. The prospectus was designed to not only include financial information but also depict the nature of the group's activities via origami. Each prospectus contained different coloured pieces of paper that, when folded, made a shop, representing retail design activities; a brochure—annual report and literature side of the business; a bottle, representing the packaging and brand identity activities. This prospectus together with ingenious radio and TV 'commercials' created by Tony Hertz, made a sensation that enabled the share price to get off to a momentous start.

Bottom: Designer magazine showing Michael Peters on the trading floor of the Stock Exchange on the first day of trading.

Right: 3 Olaf Street, was the new location for the Michael Peters Group. Troughton McAslan were commissioned as the architects to design the interiors of the warehouse along with all furniture and lighting. Michael Peters has had a long friendship with Takenobu Igarashi— the famous Japanese designer and artist who was commissioned to create the number 3 to be housed on the outside of the building. Igarashi came to England to work with Ralph Selby in his workshop in Matlock, in Derbyshire, to fabricate and install this beautiful sculpture.

Opposite: In the new Olaf Street offices, the environment was designed to reflect the creativity of the company and, above all, the quest to produce the best work on behalf of its clients. However, Peters and his team recognised the importance and influence of many of his peers all over the world and wanted, in some way, to acknowledge their talents too. The first thing on entering the reception of the company was a sculpture of a man dressed in a white overall with his head in a red bucket of sand—a fitting reflection, said Peters, of British business' attitude to design.

Apart from instant fame, being publicly quoted provided the company with the means to achieve its objectives of financing a larger building, pursuing plans of extending its disciplines and global expansion, taking advantage of the latest developments in technology, and rewarding its staff with shares in the company. "Many were able to put a deposit on a house, a boat or a car. It was a thank you for contributing to the company's success", Peters explains. Joining the USM furthermore publicly demonstrated that design was no longer a cottage industry, but efficiently successful to warrant being a part of the Stock Exchange. As design luminary David Pocknell attests, "it was a brave move and an important step for design and design awareness in the country".

During the years that followed, the Michael Peters Group expanded steadily, and set sights on moving to a larger office. Peters found a building in the West of London, close to Westbourne Grove. However, as he recalls, "I happened to mention it to Alan Fletcher at a conference, and Alan, bless his heart, was nimble afoot and convinced his partners at Pentagram to buy it behind my back." Bev Whitehead, who had already left Michael Peters and Partners before it went public, adds, "It was an ex-dairy and had a huge old wire-mesh sided elevator, which gave it a sort of New York loft feel. But it needed a lot of money put in and took Pentagram years to fix up."

While Pentagram's acquisition was disappointing for Peters, it accelerated the search and soon, an ideal building was found in Olaf Street by Bruce Green, Peters' property developer friend. "It was a coachbuilder's premises in Shepherd's Bush, which was used as a warehouse by an importer", he says. With the help of architects

Troughton McAslan, the warehouse was rebuilt and restructured to feature open-plan floors, naturally lit atriums and a central staircase, which like a marketplace, fostered interaction and communication. It housed model-making and workshop facilities, a library, a photographic studio and restaurant. On its exterior, the building was marked by a stunning sculpture of the number "3", its house number, by the Japanese artist and life-long friend of Peters, Takenobu Igarashi.

It was important for Peters to also create a beautiful and pleasant atmosphere by meticulously designing the interiors of the building. Desks and lights were especially designed to accommodate the needs of each member of the staff. The newest technology entered the building in the form of a telex machine, large colour photocopiers and one of the first available computer models, which, as he recalls, "took up half a room and cost nearly a quarter of a million pounds". This was years before the Apple Macintosh, introduced in 1984, was established as the tool of the trade. A statue by the artist Ian English, positioned at the reception signalled that visitors were dealing with a company with humour: it was a sculpture of a man with white overalls, his head in a bucket of sand. "The man, of course, represented the British industry", Peters laughs.

While designing the building he furthermore wished to pay homage to "the greats of graphic design", to his early design heroes and esteemed contemporaries. Each conference room was named after a typeface, including Baskerville, Bodoni and Futura. "One was very light, so we called it Gill Light, and one was rather dark, so it was called Gill Bold", Peters illustrates. Then, he commissioned 57 international designers to create signs for various rooms and doors of the building.

The list of contributors read like a Who's Who of graphic design and the fine arts—amongst the contributors were Alan Fletcher (reception), Saul Bass (main studio), Sam Antupit (shower), Herbert Spencer (print room), Art Paul (general store), Ivan Chermayeff (cleaner's room), Henry Wolf (photographic studio), Seymour Chwast (another main studio), Arnold Schwartzman (electrical services), FHK Henrion (a third main studio), Colin Forbes (conference room), April Greiman (archives), David Pocknell (stairs), David Davies (PMT room), Wim Crouwel (electrical services), Massimo Vignelli (restaurant), John McConnell (dry transfer room), Marcello Minale (kitchen), Brian Tattersfield (archives), Lynn Trickett (gentleman's toilet), David Hillman (communications room), Avi Eisenstein (kitchen) and even Tom Eckersley (retail).

In 1985, the group moved to Olaf Street. The structure housed the offices of nearly 200 people and was thus able to integrate subsidiaries that had formerly resided in other locations. There followed a spectacular opening ceremony, to which the group had invited all of its suppliers— from taxi services to typesetters—and clients, cabinet ministers and the mayor of London. Peters also embraced the opportunity to invite those who

*Following pages:
Perhaps the most
impressive thing, in
addition to the new
building, were the
signs on all the doors.
Peters commissioned
designers from all
over the world to
each create a sign
reflecting the use of
the door and the room
behind it—e.g. toilet,
mail room, archives,
etc.. The result was a
homage to this great
body of designers, with
a collection of stove
enamelled signs, fitting
of a museum display.
Designers included:
Henry Wolf, Mervyn
Kurlansky, David
Hillman, David Pocknell,
Saul Bass, Colin Porter,
Seymour Chwast, Peter
Rauch, Alan Fletcher,
Alan Peckolick,
Herbert Spencer,
Arnold Schwartzman,
Henry Steiner,
Fernando Medina, Ivan
Chermayelf, Marcello
Minale, Wim Crouwel,
April Greiman, Peter
Windett, Massimo
Vignelli, Lynn Trickett,
Brian Webb, Barry
Tucker, Howard Milton,
Yarom Vardimon, Art
Paul, Sam Antupit,
Mike Dempsey,
Bruno Oldani, Fritz
Gottschalk, Jerry
Rosentsweig, David
Davies, John Rushton,
Brian Tattersfield,
Jim Cross, Rudi
Ruegg, David Stuart,
Ralph Steadman,
Stafford Cliff, Deborah
Sussman, Michael
Manwaring, Ken Cato,
Michael Vanderbyl,
Tom Eckersley, Avi
Eisenstein, and a
sign also designed
by Peters.*

had taught and supported him in the past, such as his former master Arnold Rothholz. "He and his wife were very proud of me, they looked around with such pride that their protégé had become so successful. Even a number of Mr Chattell's family came and reported back with pride to my benefactor."

And while Lord David Young, at the time Secretary of State for Employment, was busy cutting the ribbon, Peters' opening speech gave a foretaste of his plans for the Michael Peters Group in particular and design in general. "Design is all around us, and it is now recognised as a very important part of the marketing of a service, a product or an idea in a unique and powerful way. The building where we are standing was once a derelict factory, but now, through design, it will, we believe, contribute to the betterment of the local community. Like the proverbial snowball, design is gathering momentum. More and more is being talked about it, and it is, perhaps, the United Kingdom's untapped source of future prosperity."

153

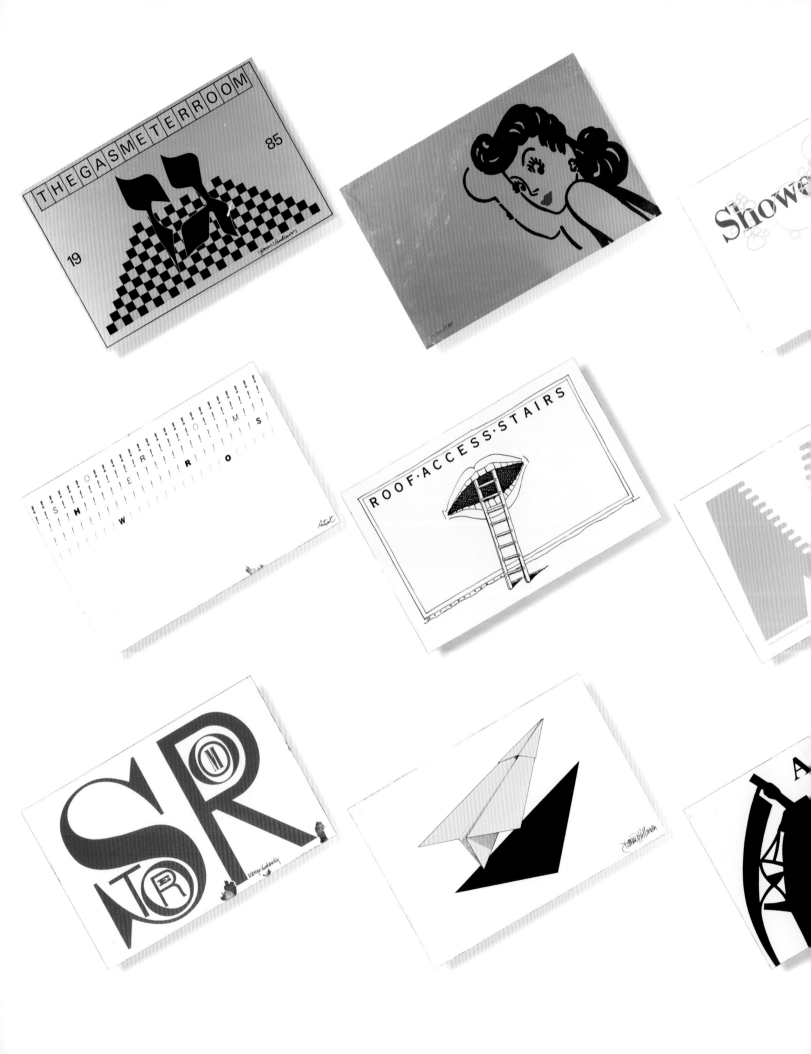

oom

To the
SPRAY room.

Photo
Graphic
Studio
and
Dark
Room

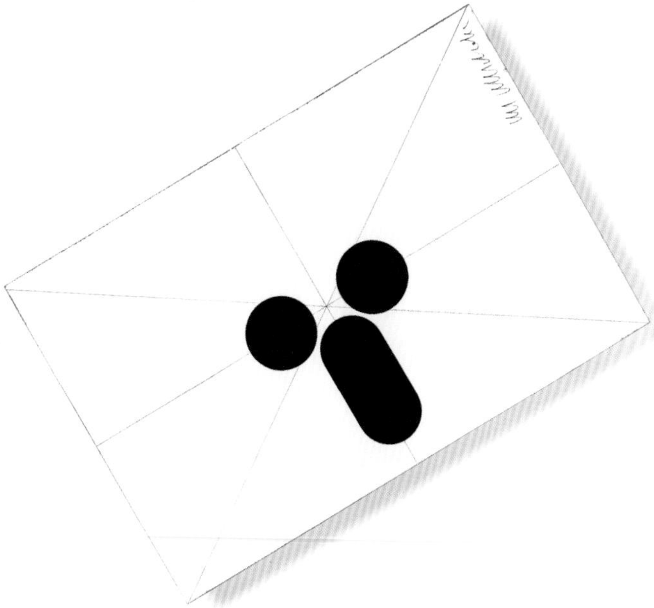

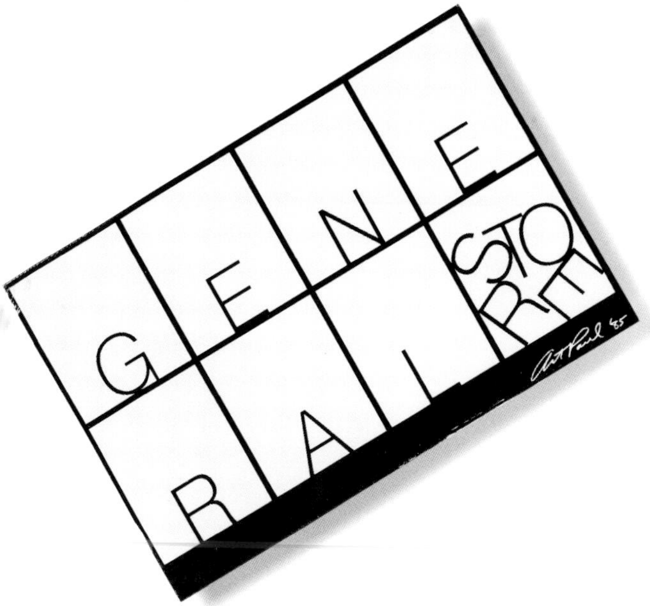
GENE
RAL

IVES
Brian Tattersfield '85

BOILER
ROOM

SOUTH
ESCAPE
STAIRS

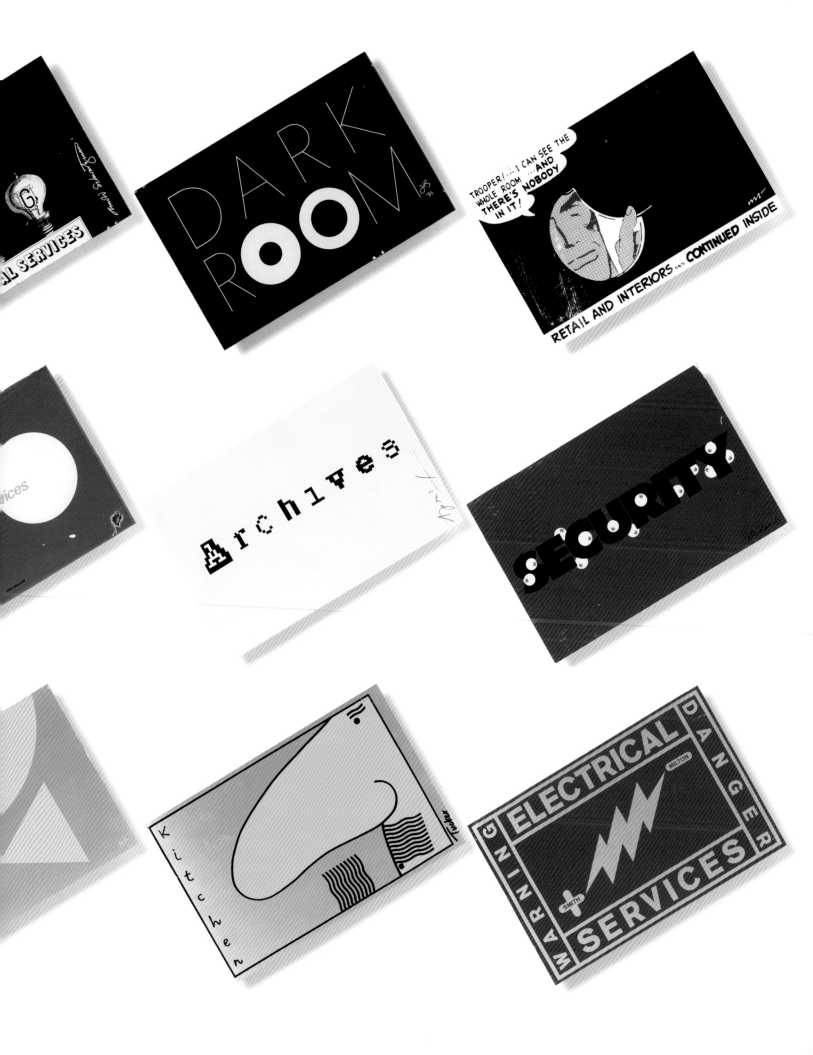

Main Studio

E S C A P E S / S T A I R S

T T

Reception: Alan Fletcher

A C

"PMT Room No 1"   David Stuart

FIRST AID

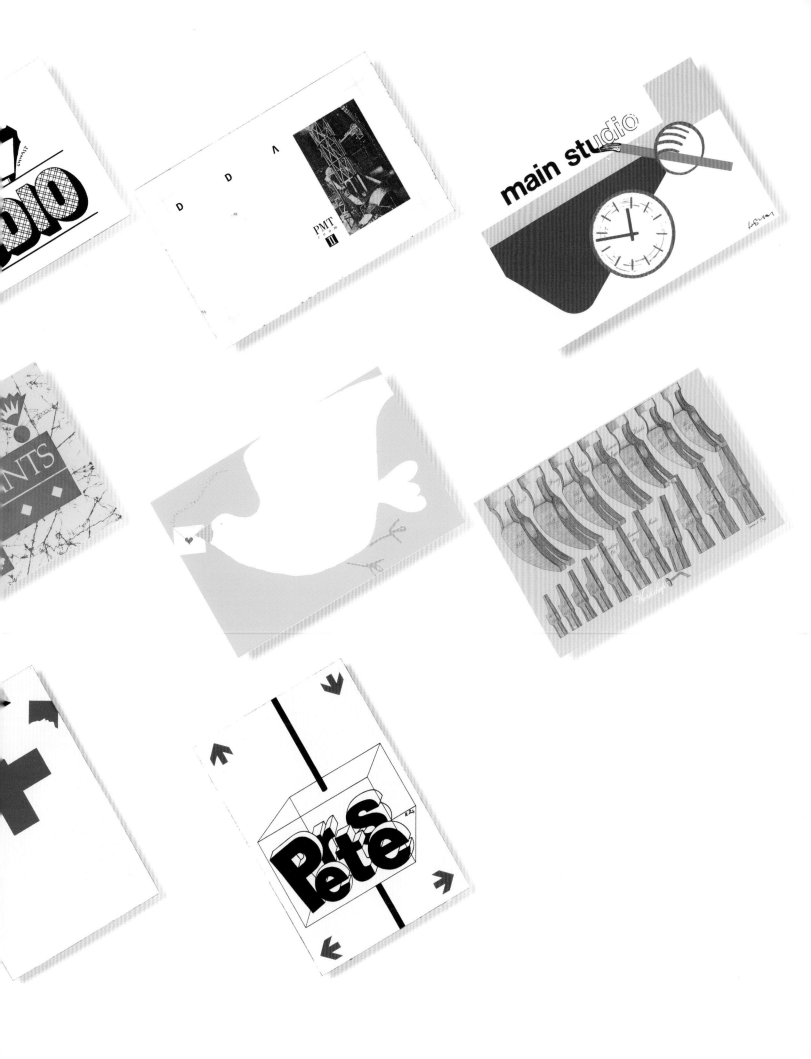

Right: Illustration, by Peter Brookes, of the miners strike in 1984–1985. Courtesy Peter Brookes and The Times.

Opposite: The Magical Mystery Tours were the highlight of the year for all employees, where everyone was taken away to a secret destination for 24 hours. Organised by Virginia Alexander and Michael Peters, false clues were leaked as to the much anticipated location.

A University of Design

For the Michael Peters Group, excellent design had already become a reliable source of prosperity. By the time of its move to Olaf Street in 1985, the group was achieving a turnover of £6 million and a profit of nearly £1 million a year. Its commercial success, coupled with its reputation for high-quality design and stock-market fame, now more than ever made it *the* place to work, both for those with experience who came from other design groups and agencies, and for those straight out of college.

Karen Welman, who had joined as a designer in 1983, recalls first encountering the group at art college. "There was this brochure handed around the studio, and I thought it would be the best possible place to work, everybody was aspiring to it. I managed to secure two interviews after I left college, one with Jo, Michael's wife, and the other with the production manager, Aubrey Hastings-Smith. The same day I got a phone call from both, offering me a job, and I remember Aubrey saying 'Let's talk about the salary', and me thinking 'What, you want to pay me, too?' I was so happy I would have worked for nothing."

The group's success, to put it simply, was down to a lot of hard work. "You worked evenings, all-nighters, weekends—sometimes for days on end to get things done", Welman says, "it was especially hard in the morning if Michael walked up and said, 'It's shit, luvvey, start again.' But you knew he was right." Jonathan Ford, who came to the company as a designer a year after Karen Welman, confirms that such criticism was hard to swallow. "But Michael would demonstrate that he was right. He would take a little scrap paper and scribble something on it, and explain to you what

it was, and it would all make sense. And you'd go and work through the night, acting on this sketch, and you'd come up with something brilliant. And you felt like you were walking on air—partly because you were delirious because you'd been up all night."

Glenn Tutssel, Michael Peters and Partners' creative director, who was headhunted by Peters while working at the design consultancy Lock Pettersen, agrees that Peters was tough to work with. "But I never ever came out of a briefing or conversation with Michael where I felt that he was being tough for the sake of being tough. It was being tough to push you further than you ever believed that you would go. One of the jobs I'll never forget was when I was working with Mark Pearce, and we were designing packaging for a range of saws and tools for Sandvik, a Scandinavian company. And we worked all night and presented to Michael, and there was this long silence after the presentation. Then he asked, 'What does this saw do?' And we answered, 'Well, it can cut through wood, plastic, metal, cardboard, all sorts of....' And Michael replied, 'This saw, luvvey, can cut a bloody house in half. Go back and do it again!' By the end of that same day, the packaging we turned out was ten times better than the one we had presented in the morning."

Such an all-night work culture would nowadays most likely be seen as an enormous exception, and even at the time, it was an aspect that distinguished the Michael Peters Group from others. Jonathan Ford recalls one designer leaving and joining Minale Tattersfield. "At Minale, they would ring a bell at 5:30 pm and you would have to be out the studio by six. Marcello being Italian probably was a lover of life and food, and expected his employees to appreciate such things as well.

But at Michael Peters there were BMWs parked outside and all-nighters to be done and D&AD awards to win. It was a completely different company culture."

It wasn't that Peters demanded his staff to work non-stop, it was rather the employees who wanted to prove themselves by giving the best they could. Peter Chodel, who joined the group's corporate communications division in 1983, recalls that the work ethic permeated all of the company. Paul Langsford came to the group in 1986 and was later made joint managing director of Michael Peters Literature. He agrees that the difference to other groups "lay in the expectation that everyone who joined had to perform. Everybody was challenged and rose to the occasion."

Peters stressed the importance of producing high-quality work, and that this standard had to be achieved regardless of the task. "Even if we did a letterhead, it was an award-winning letterhead", Glenn Tutssel points out. Peters' mantra was that "good work sells", which meant that the company had to maintain the highest standards of excellence, in all areas. "Everything we did, down to serving the tea, was done in excellence. You knew you were in a design office,

because our office manager Virginia Alexander ran things to perfection. Everybody had extraordinary talent and skill, from the secretary to receptionist to the designers and creative directors. April Greiman even came from California to spend a sabbatical month at our company."

Although the high standards of the work required toughness and stringency, Peters gave his designers license to experiment, and also, to fail, resulting in an atmosphere which encouraged independent learning and a sense of trust. "Nobody worried that you were going to experiment all day and that it wouldn't work out", Jonathan Ford recalls. "So you could just do anything you wanted to do, really. And that meant you grew in confidence and experience. Nowadays, everyone who has a computer can be a packaging designer, which is why the most important thing we learnt was the quality of thinking and ideas." Part of the company's learning culture was the initiation of lectures, for which designers such as Paul Smith, competitors such as Martin Lambie-Nairn, entrepreneurs such as Anita Roddick, surgeons such as Jeff Glazer, filmmakers, artists and even the head of the Metropolitan Police were brought in.

The hard work and dedication was, of course, generously rewarded. Peters continued his habit of writing individual thank you notes for jobs well done. Every employee's birthday was celebrated. Peter Chodel recalls that Peters also honoured good work by running up and down the stairs at Olaf Street, and showing the work around. "He would shout, 'Come and see this! Look at this!' He was so excited when people did great work."

Right and opposite: These charts from one of Michael Peters Group's Annual Reports show the size of the Group, its diversity and geographic spread.

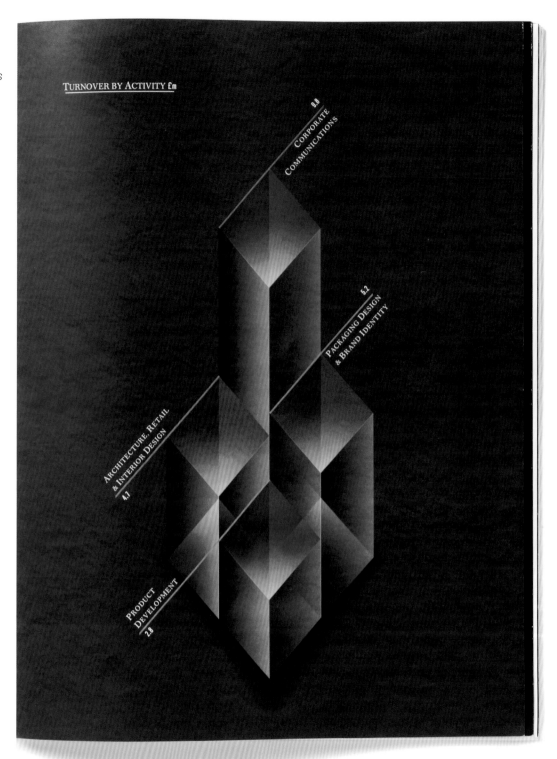

TURNOVER BY ACTIVITY £m

9.8
CORPORATE COMMUNICATIONS

5.2
PACKAGING DESIGN & BRAND IDENTITY

ARCHITECTURE, RETAIL & INTERIOR DESIGN
4.7

PRODUCT DEVELOPMENT
2.8

Peters managed to pass on his boundless enthusiasm and energy to work colleagues. His personal assistant and 'right arm' for more than seven years, Di Picard, remembers having to keep up with his frenetic pace all day long. "He never stopped for a minute, his red Economist Diary was full all day from 8:00 am. Juggling his diary was probably the worst nightmare of my working life. And there was always another project, always a new idea. But Michael was incredibly kind and generous, he would always find time to write a personal note or send flowers to show his appreciation. We all worked hard, and we loved what we did."

The working environment at the Michael Peters Group was industrious and intense, but also very sociable, generating a sense of kinship amongst its staff. It was important for Peters to foster the team spirit, and to make sure that his staff never felt like assembly line workers. There was, as Karen Welman describes it, "an absolutely magical atmosphere. We worked hard, but we also played hard." Pranks and practical jokes were a constant, phones were wired up to

162

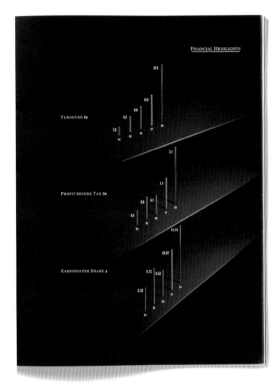

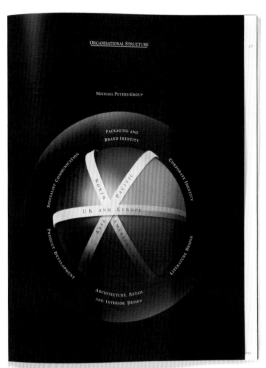

transmit electric shocks, earpieces were prepared with superglue, "and the naughtiest thing we ever did", she admits, "was when we used the colour photocopier to make false five-pound notes. We stuck them to the ceiling so people would get ladders to pick them up. Glenn got back at me by bringing in a policeman, and I panicked, thinking I was going to get jailed, and hid in the loo. It turned out that he was a stripper gram."

The company culture was further cultivated with the continuation of the Magical Mystery Tours, the company field trips which had started in 1979 with a dinner in Paris. Peters would keep the destination secret until the last minute, merely giving his colleagues clues, which often turned out to be red herrings. After the Paris dinner followed an excursion to Dromoland Castle in Ireland in 1980, and subsequent years saw trips to Rheims, Jersey, Scotland, Canterbury, Austria and Stevenage.

"On these tours", Karen Welman says, "you could guarantee that 75 per cent of the people weren't in the correct bedrooms, for one reason or another." These romances sometimes even ended in partnerships and marriage, Peters points out. "Bev Whitehead and Claire Tuthill, Howard Milton and Jay Smith, Jonathan Ford and Karen Welman all met each other at my company. Seeing the children of these relationships, or the companies that developed out of these partnerships, makes me terribly proud."

Throughout the years, the Magical Mystery Tours became increasingly extravagant. At the 1985 outing to Stevenage, which had an Indian motto, Peters made a grand entrance on an elephant; in Austria, he arrived on a sled, dressed as Santa Claus. "Michael was a showman and we loved that", Jonathan Ford recalls. "I remember a presentation for a retail project, for which a

giant clock with revolving hands was made. We didn't really know what it was for. During the presentation, Michael then said, 'Watch this!' He clapped his hands and the clock started spinning, and when he clapped his hands again, it stopped. And the clients were just amazed. Afterwards we discovered that there was just someone standing inside it. That was true showmanship at work."

Peters certainly never let the traditional rituals of business meetings hinder him from inserting some sort of theatrical element into his presentations. One occasion he still recalls was a pitch for Foster's Menswear. For the initial meeting, the design team mocked up the front page of a future issue of the *Financial Times* with a headline reporting the resultant success of the company, after having engaged the services of the consultancy. They had also bought some of Foster's clothing, which Peters and his colleagues wore to the meeting. However, upon being presented with the *Financial Times* cover, the client was not amused. "They found it extremely arrogant, and criticised us for not even being able to dress properly. And then we opened up our jackets and showed the labels that said 'Foster's Menswear'", Peters laughs. The whole team was thrown out of the office, and needless to say, did not win the pitch.

The combination of a sociable work environment, the company's commercial success, and the racking up of important national and international design awards contributed to a feeling of great confidence for the staff. "There was a sort of arrogance and swagger—we just knew we were good", Peter Chodel recalls. Fiona Gilmore, who had come to the group from Benton and Bowles, and who was in 1987 appointed managing director of Michael Peters and Partners Ltd, found that

The logo for Hawkeye Studios—the artwork and production arm of the Group.

(criticised by some as vicious self-centredness) was a catalyst for the creation of new jobs and large personal fortunes.

Thatcherism and Reaganomics (as it was called in the United States), then gave rise to the yuppie, the status-obsessed young urban professional most memorably exemplified by Tom Wolfe's Sherman McCoy, a stockbroker with a Park Avenue lifestyle consisting entirely of brand names and credit card statements. "I remember reading *The Bonfire of the Vanities*", Jonathan Ford states, "and how the bankers feel they are the masters of the universe. And I thought, that's a bit like us, because we felt we were the best! We truly felt invincible."

Rubik's-Cube

While Michael Peters and Partners had already started diversifying into various specialised areas in the 70s, the 80s provided Peters with the chance to further develop an integrated design solution in his company. He felt that this type of branching out was required to respond to the increased specialisation within design consultancies. While smaller consultancies often chose to concentrate on particular areas, larger ones preferred to expand in order to offer a wide range of expertise.

His vision was for the Michael Peters Group to grow into a multi-disciplinary design consultancy, comprising several smaller operating units within a shared management structure. Uniting these teams under one roof would solve the problem of communication difficulties within disciplines, and provide the group with an unrivalled breadth of knowledge and incentive. With this structure, Peters would be able to fully implement his aim of establishing a "commercial Bauhaus", a consultancy in which experts of various design fields worked together to achieve a common goal.

The Michael Peters Group therefore started a programme of organic growth and strategic acquisition by spinning off further subsidiaries and buying various independent but complementary companies, adding them to the group. By 1987, the Michael Peters Group operated with a total of ten divisions, of which four, Michael Peters and Partners Ltd, The Hawkeye Studios Ltd, Brand New (Product Origination) Ltd and Annual Reports Ltd, had already existed prior to the group joining the Unlisted Securities Market.

Some of these companies had since then undergone significant changes. Brand New, under its new managing director Dorothy McKenzie, further developed initial links with the Generics Group, a company based in Cambridge and led by Dr Gordon Edge, with the aim to synergise science and design to aid the creation of new products. Annual Reports Ltd had been halved in 1985, forming Michael Peters Corporate Literature, led by Paul Langsford and Jackie Vicary, and Michael

"passion permeated the company, whether they were creative people or an account person in a suit. We were young, had a lot of energy, and were carried away by the exciting climate of the time. And Michael was just at the right moment in his own career, where he was supremely confident. He had already built a successful business, and so the timing was perfect."

The external circumstances were also ideal. Although dampened by the recession in the early 80s, and by a 12 months miners' strike and ensuing civil unrest in 1984, Britain by the mid-80s was experiencing a period of exponential growth and wealth, supported by the economic politics of the Thatcher government. Thatcher's programme of privatisation and de-regulation of major, publicly owned industries, combined with the neo-liberalist value of a radical, consumption-led individualism

Isabel Bird was one of the most successful recruitment consultancies in the UK. The idea of the birds of prey (printed on the reverse of the stationery) was simply a visual pun to reflect the enormous effort the recruitment team went to in order to find the right talent for its clients.

Peters Financial Communications, which operated in its own offices in the City.

Michael Peters Retail Ltd was in 1985 established as a separate company to converge those activities in retail design that had previously been performed under the mantle of Michael Peters and Partners; the unit was led by managing director Rob Davie and creative director Paul Mullins. The group's market research activities were similarly fused with the setting up of Diagnostics Market Research, an autonomous market research company also serving external consultancies and companies, in the same year.

In 1984, the Michael Peters Group acquired Cockade Ltd, one of Britain's leading exhibition design companies. Another major acquisition was then made in 1986, when the group sold its promotion company Idea Works and bought the industrial design and new product development company PA Design in a deal valuing it at £1.3 million.

PA Design, headed by its founder Roy Gray, benefited from the arrangement by being able to orientate itself away from technology and towards design and marketing. The Michael Peters Group could in turn utilise for itself PA Design's product development, technology and computer-aided skills. Based in Holland Park and Cambridge, PA Design in 1987 spun off a second company, PA Design Corporate Identity, under the direction of Peter Sampson. This division was placed with the rest of the group in Olaf Street and carried out all of its corporate identity work.

As the group expanded, Peters was cast into a different role, one which involved a much greater amount of time sitting in boardrooms and

selling the business, and moving further away from the design studio. While the managing directors each ran their own companies, Peters' duty as the chairman, managing director and creative director of the whole group was to find clients which required the multiple skills of the company, and to co-ordinate and interconnect the various disciplines. He did not much miss putting pencil to paper. "At meetings I would design in my head and give a clear steer on what I wanted to have done. I don't have the skills of a Paul Rand or Alan Fletcher, but I do have the ability to solve a problem, and I can visualise the solution in my head. That's why I am probably a better art director than designer."

Through its organic expansion, the Michael Peters Group, unlike other multi-disciplinary design consultancies such as Wolff Olins and Pentagram, turned, literally, into a one-stop shop. In 1988, the group introduced matrix management to advance and secure this development. The matrix was basically a mesh consisting of six core design services offered by the group (packaging, brand identity, corporate identity, literature design, retail and interior design and specialist communication), and its three core geographic regions of operation (North America, Europe and the Pacific Basin).

The result was a strategic formation to which the group could apply consistent standards, implement strong, local management and assess future business prospects. It made possible a flexible service that, in theory, could be adapted to suit every client need. "I thought of it as a Rubik's-Cube", Peters explains, "the cube is defined by a shape, but within the shape are a number of configurations. If a client had a problem concerning several different fields of design,

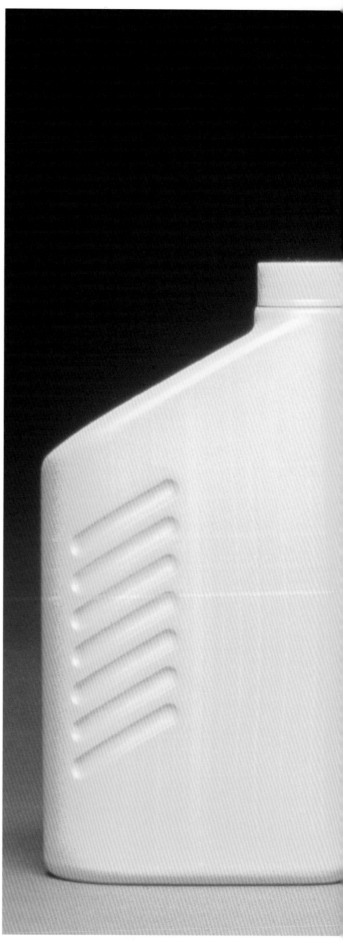

Below and right: Michael Peters Group worked with both Shell and BP, to create oil containers for the international market. Utilising the skills of the product and packaging design teams, along with expertise from the Generics Group in Cambridge (science and materials technology), the end result was a unique range of oil packages that were cheaper to produce and technologically superior to their competitors. Projects like these take between three to four years before entry into world markets, largely because of regulatory and complex production issues.

the cube turned its face according to the client's requirements."

The Michael Peters Group also provided Peters with the opportunity to further develop and implement principles that later resounded throughout the British design industry. For instance, since he had briefly worked in advertising, he knew of the disproportionate budgets of client companies that still were, more often than not, in favour of advertising. He therefore emphasised to clients the synergy that was possible between advertising and design, and persuaded young talent from advertising agencies to cross the floors.

One such talent was Mike Branson, who joined the Michael Peters Group as an account director. For Branson, coming into the design industry was a breath of fresh air. "Advertising and account management are both well structured in hierarchies of three, four, five people. And in the design industry, there was this tremendous sense of freedom. There weren't all these rules and guidelines and remedies in terms of what we could or couldn't do."

Skill bases such as consumer research, strategic planning and brand strategy had formerly been the terrain of advertising agencies. By introducing these into the design process, the Michael Peters Group was able to capitalise on a wealth of valuable information, and to provide its designers with inspiring briefs. Strategic planning, especially, was a new language for design consultancies, explains Fiona Gilmore. "Historically, the design industry was a craft industry and quite dependent on the intuitive understanding of the creative director. Michael's intuitive understanding was extraordinary—this was why even without consumer research he would arrive at something very clever and successful.

The Burton Group Annual Report is now regarded as a classic of its time. This famous fashion retailer, led by its eponymous chairman, invited Michael Peters Group's Annual Report team to create the first Annual Report (designed as a fashion magazine) to have full page advertising as part of its presentation to shareholders. The report is the recipient of numerous awards worldwide.

The reason why we brought in strategic planning was to ensure that not only the intuitive understanding would be fantastic, but that we also knew the way the consumers thought about things."

A keystone of Peters' principles was the notion of ROI, or "return on innovation", a spin on the business term "return on investment". The rephrasing emphasised that both terms were intrinsically linked, that clients could expect enormous returns not only upon investment, but also upon innovation with the help of designers. He disseminated principles and views by giving lectures worldwide, and setting a good example through his use of innovative presentation devices such as film clips and animations. Giving speeches

was an alternative way of getting the message across; in addition, it was an excellent means of reaching major league clients.

The Midas Touch

As in the Pembridge Mews days of Michael Peters and Partners, Peters' reputation and astute salesmanship—"He can sell oil to the Arabs", David Hillman asserts—continued bringing in work for high profile clients such as Seagram, Fine Fare, Unilever, the BBC and British Airways. He could also rely on the skills of his colleagues, including Pamela Conway, who

after heading Brand New and Michael Peters and Partners, had taken on the role of group marketing and executive director, and helped the group develop foreign markets, eg. Japan and the Far East, and build client relationships. "Whether it was retail or new products or communications or packaging, everything we touched, turned out to be a big success", Peters says.

The company's working relationship with Seagram commenced when a good friend of Peters married the marketing manager of Seagram, Stuart Kershaw. As it turned out, Peters had in fact first met Kershaw as a young boy at summer camp. Their collaboration started with the repackaging of Seagram's Hundred Pipers Whisky by Madeleine Bennett, and went on for several years thereafter. A notable, subsequent commission from Seagram was the overhaul of its Sandeman Port range which called for an expression of distinguished heritage. Designers Pat Perchal (who had already joined Peters in Pembridge Mews days) and John Rushworth decided to retain the unique bottle shape and the silhouette of the Sandeman 'Don',

and to enhance these with elegant and skillfully designed labels. To emphasise the refinement and uniqueness of the "Founder's Reserve" Port, the Sandeman bottle was dipped in acid to produce a matt, greenish-black tone, onto which the Don was silk screened in gold. In the three years following the repackaging, Sandeman's market share doubled.

During the economic recession of the 70s, supermarket chains decided to sell products under their own label to compete with manufacturers' branded goods. To enable a competitive, often much lower price, the packaging or marketing of own-label products received little or no budget. Own-label packaging was therefore often bland, unappealing or shamelessly copying the market leader. Peters decided to take matters in his hands by contacting the supermarket Fine Fare, which together with Tesco was one of the earliest advocates of own-label. He had an idea: to take the own-label concept one stage further and to provide Fine Fare with packaging that rivalled the high quality of a manufacturer's brand, but could still be sold for the own-label price. Marketing manager Mike Flanagan was soon convinced, and thus, the foundations for a fruitful business relationship were established.

Fine Fare's Dark Rum came to be particularly successful after its re-design. In order to create a distinctive brand identity, and because rum seemed to evoke a traditional, nautical theme, the bottle carried semaphore flags and a fully-rigged sailing ship (it was designed by Glenn Tutssel and illustrated by Rory Kee). It won a D&AD silver in 1987. After Fine Fare was taken over by Safeway, Peters worked with its managing director Alistair Grant to employ a similar approach with Safeway's own-label goods.

Cordon Bleu, the second largest frozen food retailer in Britain headed by Brian Bayliss, was another client seeking to revamp its own-label range. "Michael came in one day", Glenn Tutssel recalls", and went, 'I've got a brief! For a frozen food company. Who wants it?' And designers are quite prissy, they'd rather design something like Penhaligon's, so I said, 'I'll do that. But I've never designed a frozen food pack in my life.' Michael answered, 'Ok, well you were great at literature. Design me a brochure and stick it on the pack.' So together with Carolyn Reed, I designed a cook book that sat on the pack."

The unconventional use of editorial copy that provided added value (through recipes, serving suggestions and further information), coupled with a highly illustrative depiction of the contents and their origin made for a style unique to Cordon Bleu. The designs raked up several awards, including D&AD silver and a Starpack Award in 1984, a Clio Award in 1985, and three Communication Arts Awards of Excellence. "It was a breakthrough in terms of packaging", Tutssel adds, "because Michael could see that you could transfer skills from one discipline to another by looking at the problem in a very different way. It was one of the first packs we copyrighted."

Also to be found in the supermarket was Showerings' K-Cider, a new, extra-strong cider packaged by Michael Peters and Partners. "It was a typical Michael Peters approach to the project", says Jonathan Ford, who worked on the packaging with Glenn Tutssel. "The thinking that went into it was very solid, we did all kinds of evaluations of what was going on in terms of cider at the time. And we knew we had to do something

groundbreaking with the design. So we did five to six concepts and the night before the presentation, we discovered that the visualiser had left us an extra black bottle. We thought it would be a shame to waste it, so we threw together a design in about ten minutes using the spare. We produced a really simple, minimalist label with a small red K on it. It just happened. We took the train to Somerset and the client said, 'That's the one I want.' Nobody else had done a black cider bottle; they were all clear. It was revolutionary, years ahead of its time."

A project that very much reflected the period was the creation of an identity for Joseph Ettedgui, an established fashion designer who wanted to introduce an exclusive, feminine fragrance named "*Parfum de Jour*" in 1985. The design brief presented to Madeleine Bennett, who had become a creative director in 1980, required the identity to keep with the style of the Joseph shops, which were monochromatic and architecturally minimal. Since Joseph chose not to invest in the creation of his own bottle shape, Bennett decided to make the most of the stainless steel flask used. "It was a chance to do something contemporary and innovative, which is the sort of work I most like to do", she states, "it had an open brief and a very receptive client." The result was an extraordinary bottle with a black label and beautifully crafted typography. It was at once both masculine and feminine, reflecting the contemporaneous cultural fascination with androgynous film stars and musicians such as Grace Jones, Boy George and Eurythmics' Annie Lennox.

Through matrix management and its provision of an integrated design solution, the group also attracted projects that defied categorisation,

170

K-Cider—new packaging design for Showerings, a cider manufacturer in the west of England.

incorporating, for example, aspects of both packaging and product design. In the early 80s, Shell International commissioned Michael Peters and Partners to create five sizes of oil containers that employed innovative structures. The packs featured built-in tamper evident caps and ergonomic grips systems; more importantly, the wedge-shaped packs could be bundled to eliminate the space between the cans. It saved Shell a six-figure amount in distribution costs.

Glenn Tutssel, who designed the Shell Helix pack together with Brand New's industrial design director Graham Thomson, recalls that the project also provided him with a valuable business lesson. "We were in the cab going to the meeting, and Michael said, 'Glenn, I want you to look me in the eyes and repeat after me: 100 thousand pounds.' I hadn't a clue what he was talking about. So I go, '100 thousand pounds.'—'No, luvvey, say it again, but with conviction, I want you to look me in the eyes and say 100 thousand pounds.' So I do it again. I still hadn't a clue what he was getting at. We went to the presentation, won the pitch, and when the client asked, 'What will it cost to develop the project?' I was able to reply, '100 thousand pounds', without blinking. I learned for the first time in my life that design has a value and that you should never be ashamed of asking for that value."

Those commissions that called for pure product design were predominantly handled by the Michael Peters Group subsidiaries Brand New (Product Origination) Ltd and PA Design Ltd, which later merged to form Brand New Product Development Ltd. In 1983, the British company Ross Electronics, helmed by Ross Marks, approached Brand New for a re-design

of some of its products, in order to compete in a market saturated with Far Eastern products. Brand New's first task was to re-design its cordless headphones system, so that these could be quickly and cheaply assembled in Britain. The answer lay in a simple ball-and-socket joint, which alleviated the manufacturing process, and kept down costs. Then followed the Ross Radio, the first radio to be manufactured in Britain for several decades (although its parts were imported). Its designer Graham Thomson opted for a design with a softly rounded styling reminiscent of the 50s, which appealed to all age groups and enabled a reasonable price of £30. The success of both products later enabled Ross Electronics to become a publicly quoted company.

For the European confectionary manufacturer Sweet Factory, the Michael Peters Group serviced three main areas: packaging and brand identity, product development and retail design (it had in fact started with a simple request for a re-packaging). Michael Peters Retail, under the art direction of Rob Davie, Paul Mullins and Bill Carden-Horton, initiated a complete retail design programme and visual merchandising system, based on industrial and funfair imagery. It resulted in Sweet Factory being able to open 22 new shops all over Europe.

On the corporate identity side, the Michael Peters Group won the BBC as a client in 1986. The task comprised the design of a new livery and logo to reflect a more modern and high technology image of the company, with the difficulty of it being able to adapt to various BBC activities and regions. The new logo, designed by Glenn Tutssel and Mark Pearce, retained some of the aspects of the original

Top: The Heads and Senior Personnel of all the businesses within the Michael Peters Group at an Annual Senior Management Conference in the UK in 1988.

Bottom: Alliance and Leicester is the result of two building societies merging their interests. Michael Peters Group were responsible for Alliance and Leicester's total brand and communications programme.

one by housing each letter in a separate box, the boxes were however slanted and the green colour substituted by a sleek grey. Coloured bars beneath the boxes signalled BBC regions: green for Northern Ireland, blue for Scotland and red for Wales. A visual audit, initiated to explore the company in terms of its visual identity, part of which included vehicles, then alighted on the fantastic advertising opportunity the lorries represented. After all, they were often parked at highly publicised events. "But they were the dreariest, dullest vehicles you can imagine", Fiona Gilmore recalls, "they certainly didn't promote the BBC." The solution was to expand the visual identity system to include three poster spaces on the vehicles, which advertised upcoming BBC radio and television programmes.

Apart from massive, prestigious clients like the BBC, the group also took on small gems such as the letterhead for the recruitment agency Isabel Bird. Paul Browton, who had joined the company in 1979, had the delightful idea of covering the letterhead verso with illustrations of various types of birds, some of which were birds of prey. His identity work on behalf of the Alliance and Leicester Building Societies, which after a merger in 1985 necessitated a new identity, was equally inventive. Browton's solution, which he recalls scribbling on a piece of paper while visiting his grandmother over Christmas, was a "Golden Plus",

which symbolised both the merger and the added value that Alliance and Leicester provided with its products and services.

Michael Peters Literature meanwhile continued the Annual Reports Ltd tradition of creating breakthrough corporate communication, and questioning the staid conventions of the genre. A remarkable example of this was the 1986 annual report for the fashion retailer The Burton Group. Conceived as a glossy fashion magazine by Peters and designed by David Stocks, it replaced financial tables with stylish typography and high-class fashion photography by *Vogue*'s John Swannell. It was the first annual to be covered in the news pages of the *Financial Times*.

The account however was not an easy one to acquire, Peters recalls. "I really wanted to work for The Burton Group, but its chairman Sir Ralph Halpern—a very successful retailer—was just impossible to meet." Since Halpern frequently flew abroad, Peters mobilised a friend at British Airways to conveniently place him next to the Burton boss on his next flight. "The flight was overbooked, and they constantly upgraded Halpern until he was put on the Concorde. So even though we couldn't really afford it, I thought, 'Screw it!' and bought a ticket. On the flight, Halpern took out his eye mask and announced that he never talked to people on flights. So I said, 'You bloody well listen to me!' and told

him the whole story. He shrieked with laughter, and after that, we worked together for eight years. That kind of 'hunt' was for me an exciting part of the business."

As the 80s drew to a close, Michael Peters and Partners was asked to design its first set of stamps for the UK Post Office. Intended for cheerful occasions, the stamps assembled a variety of classic smiles, from Stan Laurel's smirk to the Cheshire cat's broad grin. Similar to the Winsor & Newton inks packaging almost 20 years prior, the stamps, which were designed by Mark Pearce, came to life through the interplay of various illustrative styles, combining commissioned illustrations with iconic images. The set, which was sold in its own die-cut folder, and accompanied by special message labels, was honoured with a D&AD silver award in 1990, and won the BBC National Design Awards in the same year.

A Designer Decade

The 80s were a decade in which the Thatcher government actively nurtured business expansion through various governmental support schemes, in particular, it had recognised the benefits that the British economy and industry could derive by aiding and encouraging a further growth of the design industry. This insight was brought to the attention of the Department of Trade and Industry (DTI), which developed several design-specific initiatives.

Prime Minister Thatcher furthermore appointed John Butcher as Minister of Design and Technology, and in 1982, initiated a seminar at 10 Downing Street to consult established designers, amongst them Peters, about issues related to design.

Peters' involvement with the Conservative Party had commenced through his professional links with Lord Basil Feldman, whom he had met through his identity work for the Better Made in Britain exhibition in 1983, and who was a key fundraiser for the Party. (Peters must have kept mum about the fact that he had in the late 60s, together with David Kingsley of Kingsley Manton and Palmer, designed posters for the Labour government). Feldman introduced Peters to Thatcher: "She had heard about me through Feldman, and I got to know her quite well. I suggested a re-design of the Conservative Party logo, which I thought was old-fashioned." A re-design of the Tory torch had also been prompted by the creation of the Labour Party Red Rose by Michael Wolff in 1986, and by preparations for the upcoming general election.

Fiona Gilmore, who together with Peters, Glenn Tutssel and Jonathan Ford, oversaw the project, recalls that there initially had been some confusion over who had actually been commissioned with the re-design: "I was pregnant at the time, and remember an advisor saying to Margaret Thatcher, 'You should be using somebody really good like Michael Peters and instead you're using this pregnant woman.' He came back later after a bit of research, saying

'Actually, you are using Michael Peters!'" The project itself was classified as strictly confidential, causing journalists to scale the pipes of the Olaf Street building in order to catch a glimpse, and finally unveiled in September 1989.

Since the torch already existed as an identity element, the design team had faced the question of how to make it more dynamic and modern, but also gentler and more human. The solution was to add to it a sense of forward movement, similar to an Olympic flame. A hand was also added. "When I introduced the logo, Margaret Thatcher looked at the rather masculine hand on the torch and asked whether I would make it a little bit more feminine, to suggest that she was holding the torch", Peters recalls. By working for the Conservative Party, the Michael Peters Group confirmed its place in the era, as well as allowing those involved a more personal political statement. "I'm very proud of it, since I'm a great supporter of the Conservative Party and what it's done for our industry", Peters told *Design* in 1989.

State intervention in the name of design was, however, not exactly new under Thatcher. Already in 1944, the Council of Industrial Design (CoID) had been established in Britain for the purpose of furthering the opportunities of design in industry and to educate manufacturers and the general public in the principles of "good design" through initiatives such as the Britain Can Make It exhibition in 1946. 40 years later, the Conservative government was able to build upon the pioneering work of the Council, which had been similarly active throughout the years, and to aim to foster the attention given to design by the British industry.

Businesses slowly but surely began discovering the importance of design for the marketability of products, and increasingly granted design a key role in the areas of marketing and advertising, and later, in the strategic development of products and brands. The 80s then saw the design industry gather momentum; its key figures included Peters, Terence Conran, Wally Olins and Rodney Fitch. Likewise, small start-ups became a force to be reckoned with. The boom was accompanied by a surge in high-street spending, property prices and corporate mergers and acquisitions. "Overnight, the rules of business changed", Peters says, "it was no longer all about plant, capital, equipment. The most valuable resources were ideas, people and creativity."

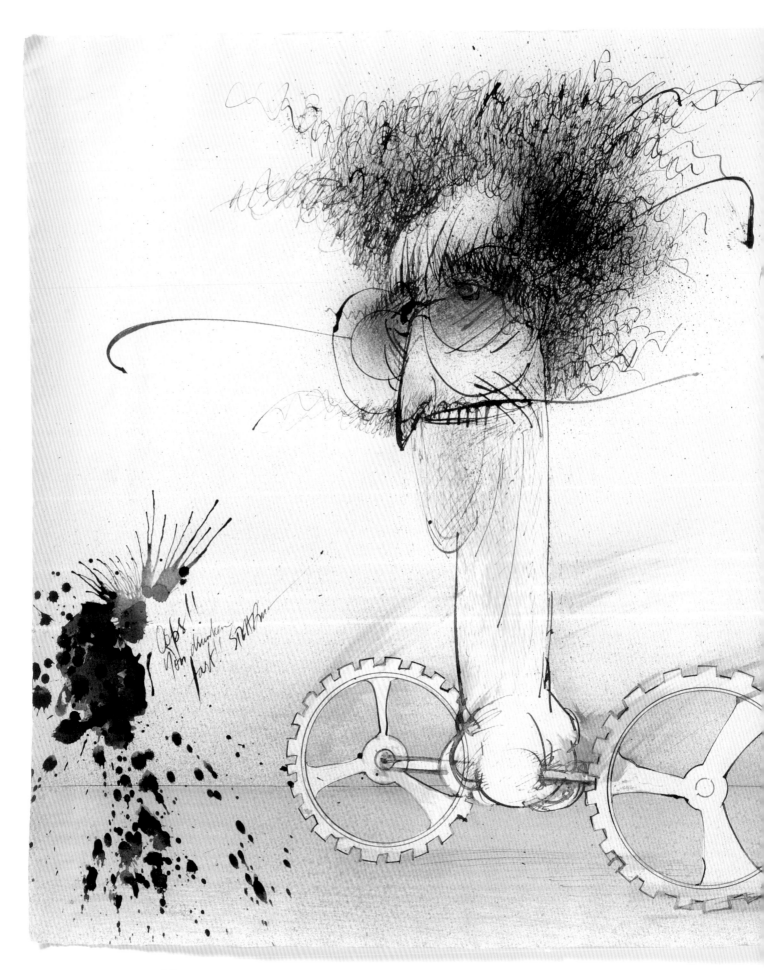

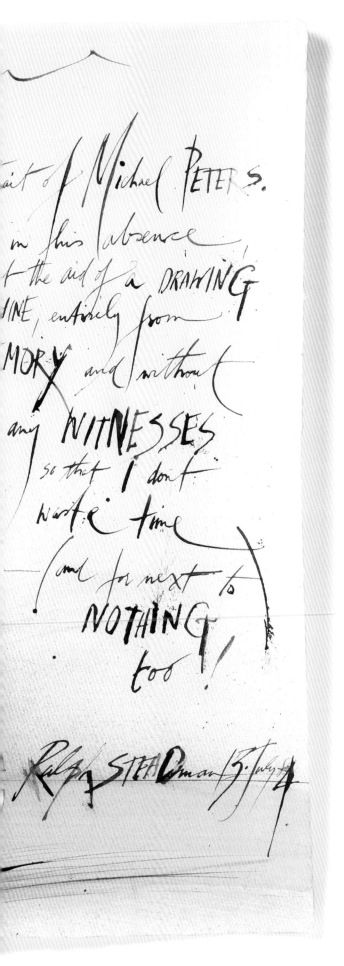

ait of Michael PETERS.
in this absence
t the aid of a DRAWING
HINE, entirely from
MORY and without
any WITNESSES
so that I don't
waste time
(and for next to
NOTHING
too!

Ralph STEADman 13. July 4

Design issues were now regularly featured in the media, in programmes such as the Channel 4 documentary *Design Matters* and in newspapers and specialist literature such as the newly launched *DesignWeek* and *Blueprint*. The establishment of the National Design Awards by the BBC and the Design Museum in London furthered a public recognition of design and an increase in consumer awareness. Design grew in importance in the construction of lifestyles and identity, leading consumers to pay a premium for designed products (even if the signature on the designer jeans was merely fake).

Initiatives and Innovation

Having developed enough clout on behalf of the design industry to exert influence on national government policy on design, and utilising its expert knowledge and increasing prosperity, the Michael Peters Group set upon improving the perception of design through various initiatives.

One scheme that was operated by the Design Council, funded by the DTI and developed by Peters was "Support for Design/Design for Profit". It entailed that small manufacturers (with less than 500 employees) could apply for government sponsorship to take up 15 days of design consultancy with fees reduced to 25 per cent, the balance being borne by the DTI. This was a golden opportunity for the Michael Peters Group to encourage manufacturers to hire design expertise and to get them to understand the potential of design. Over 2,500 firms, including Ross Electronics, took advantage of the offer.

In 1986, concerned by the high unemployment in the heavy industries, and convinced that strategic consultancy could provide a way out, Peters persuaded the DTI to make funds available for a pilot programme titled "Design for Recovery" in the industrialised city of Middlesborough. Here, a design squad assisted small manufacturing companies in new product development with such success that the programme was later run on a national scale by the Design Council.

"What I realised then was that there was no collective voice for the design industry", Peters says. He thus set upon developing plans for a trade association for designers, which would represent UK design consultancies and provide mutual support and professional advice. "So I wrote to every designer in the country I could think of, about 600 to 700 people, and said that I wanted to host an evening to see whether we could form an association. The idea was that we would all pay a sum of money according to our size, but would all get the same legal and financial advice. Big groups therefore supported smaller groups. And people said, 'This is one of Michael Peters' stunts again. What's in it for him?' But they came, and in 1986, the DBA was born."

*The new logo to herald
the birth of the Design
Business Group,
originated by Peters
and Michael Wolff.*

DESIGN BUSINESS GROUP

The founders of the Design Business Association (DBA) in a further effort to communicate and demonstrate the value of design, then set up the Design Effectiveness Awards. This was an annual award assessing the commercial performance of design rather than its aesthetic aspects (as did the D&AD awards), with a panel of judges from client companies. The scheme also recognised that effective design relied on the equal contribution of both consultancy and client, thus the award itself (which had been designed by ex-Michael Peters and Partners employees Barbara Lewis, Gerry O'Dwyer and Bev Whitehead) comprised two connecting parts.

"The entries were evaluated based on how solid each case was argued", recalls Fiona Gilmore, who was appointed chairman of the Design Effectiveness Awards in 1987. Paul Southgate, design planning director at the Michael Peters Group, in 1989 made a particularly convincing case for Highland Spring Mineral Water, which the group had re-designed to create a stronger and more distinctive brand emphasising its "Scottishness". It soon was able to establish itself as the number two brand to Perrier. Most importantly, the outstanding results could be directly traced back to the packaging, as the company had not run any advertisement.

By the mid-1980s, a new-found ecological awareness gained increasing currency among the general public, which had developed out of the eco-movements of the previous decade and was further triggered by environmental disasters such as Chernobyl in 1986. The Michael Peters Group was one of the first large-scale design consultancies to recognise that the "Green issue" necessitated new solutions by manufacturers and designers, including reducing unnecessary packaging, using water-soluble inks, saving energy and improving the re-cyclability of materials. The group further commissioned a report on eco-friendly packaging, finding that consumers preferred green products and environment-friendly companies if given the choice, but that British companies were too passive in responding to environmental concerns.

"We as a public design company cared about the environment, also for the shareholders' interest", Peters states, "and it was especially Dorothy McKenzie at Brand New who took the mantle of bringing ecological issues to the attention of all our clients. She provided a link to the Generics Group, with which we developed many ideas. One of the visions we had was a bottle made from the fibre of maize and sunflowers, as a packaging for oil. Once you finished the oil, the inner membrane of the bottle would dry out and you could put it down the waste disposal unit."

Peters during this time had also come to a point where he wished to give something back to the wider community. An advocate of raising the standards of design education, and along with John Hegarty and Lindsay Masters of Haymarket Publishing, he endlessly campaigned for and financially supported the founding of the highly influential School of Communication Arts. This was a private design and advertising school led by John Gillard, which spawned many talents working in the creative industries today. According to Peters, the school, however, unfortunately failed when Gillard died in 2000.

The philanthropic idea of supporting and encouraging young talent likewise led to the setting up of the Hyman Peters Foundation, a contemporary applied arts collection in memory of Peters' father. Only several years prior, father and son had been reunited with each other through sheer coincidence. "One of my sisters married a man who had a market stall in South London, and the stall next to his was owned by a woman who was my father's second wife. Meeting him was very emotional and difficult, because I had been manipulated by my mother to hate him, but I found out that he was the most remarkable man. Although we were quite poor he had throughout the years secretly supported young, talented musicians and artists. I set up the foundation after he died so that in the collection, I could see my father every day."

The Hyman Peters Foundation was established as an independent charitable trust, aiming to establish a deeper and better appreciation of the applied arts. Liz Lydiate, who worked at the Crafts Council and was introduced to Peters through a mutual friend, left the Council to head the foundation at Olaf Street. "The collection focused on contemporary British work because the United Kingdom had a long and distinguished tradition of craftsmanship in the applied arts. Michael also wanted to give the sector a bit of status; in a way it needed an important patron. The foundation was very effective in recognising and celebrating talent, which was, in a sense, also going on in the company."

New Territories

During the late 80s, the Michael Peters Group continued its programme of expansion and acquisition, which had commenced with the takeover of Cockade Ltd and PA Design, as a route into international operations. The support of design in industry by the Thatcher government prompted not only the Michael Peters Group, but also several other large, contemporary design groups such as Addison and Fitch-RS, and marketing services groups such as Saatchi & Saatchi and the WPP Group, to go on an international acquisition spree. Between 1987 and 1988, all groups combined spent roughly £60 million on takeovers of American companies.

In 1987, the Michael Peters Group opened offices in New York and Toronto (spearheaded by Robin Budish and Duncan Bruce) to prepare for its entry into North America. Peters spent more and more time jetting across the Atlantic. "It was a very exciting but also lonely time in my life", Peters says, "at the weekend I'd be with the family, and over the week I'd fly to New York and be on my own." The group's New York studio was led by Karen Welman and Jonathan Ford, who aimed to cultivate a similar cultural feel to the one in London. "One of the ways to establish that was by sending over people from the London studio and blending them with people we recruited in New York. It started to take on its own character, and was very successful. By 1990, we were about 20 people and were doing $5 million a year."

After setting up North American offices, Peters decided to go for the big time, with the objective to "form the world's leading independent design and communications business with an extended range of creative services and wide geographic coverage". The group in February 1988 acquired the retail design and architectural practice Hambrecht Terrell International, which designed department stores for Macy's, Bloomingdale's

and Saks Fifth Avenue, for £5.7 million, as well as Spectrum Communications, a leading Anglo-German conference specialist. Eight months later the group bought the Canadian corporate communications company Communiqué and the management psychology consultancy John Nicholson Associates.

By 1989, the Michael Peters Group operated with offices in London, Los Angeles, Toronto, New York, Madrid, Milan, Berlin, Helsinki and Tokyo, and roughly 700 employees, of which 300 were qualified designers. In addition, it boasted an impressive £45 million annual turnover and had an enormous track record of more than 800 clients in 21 countries. Its economic growth was accompanied by a rise in reputation. A 1988 client survey conducted by *DesignWeek* crowned the Michael Peters Group the best-known group in the areas of product and graphic design, and Peters as the best-known individual designer.

The company's purchases reached a high point with the acquisition of the Minneapolis-based Duffy Design Group in 1989 in a £3.6 million performance-related deal. Duffy Design, whose clients at the time included Lee Jeans, Porsche North America and Ralph Lauren, had been set up in 1984 by Joe Duffy, a trained designer and illustrator who had a background in advertising with the successful American advertising agency Fallon McElligot. Peters came to know Duffy through his director of business in New York, Jimmy Benson (formerly the vice chairman of the Ogilvy Group), who introduced Peters to Pat Fallon of Fallon McElligot, who in turn acquainted Peters with Duffy.

"I went to meet him and we just fell in love", Peters recalls, "of all the acquisitions we made, the personal relationship with Joe was the strongest. It's very rare in the United States to find somebody of the quality in both work and character like Joe, he had created a look and feel that set a trend in the States. The intention was that Joe would act as creative director overseeing all of the design business in America, and we would take care of the European side." Joe Duffy recalls his "utmost respect and admiration" for Peters during his early years in the design business. "I looked upon the work that was done from his office and from London in general during that period, as being the absolute best when it came to package design and brand identity. So it was with some surprise and much excitement that I learned Michael was interested in my little design office joining his rapidly expanding global group. I was ready to expand our business and become part of something bigger. Fortunately, my partners agreed and were willing to be bought out."

Duffy and Peters decided to create an inaugural book showing a view of America through the eyes of the Michael Peters Group, and a view of England through the eyes of the Duffy Design Group. The book, written by Chuck Carlson, could be read from both sides, and was skillfully designed by Glenn Tutssel, Joe Duffy, Garrick Hamm, Sharon Werner and Haley Johnson. It featured a delightful

How odd to find amongst
the savage and blood-
spilling American West
a more civil way to con-
duct The Hunt. The way
things are now, the poor
fox gets run ragged only
to meet a bloody end. So
let's call off the dogs
please and give the fox a
sporting chance. With
practice and a strong
grip, any bloke can stay
atop a horse. But it
takes true skill to han-
dle a lariat. And once
caught, the fox could be
released. After all, no
more fox; no more hunt.

The Peters/Duffy book was produced to celebrate the two companies coming together. When both teams met they joked about each other's national idiosyncrasies and felt the best way to express this was through a witty, intelligent and engaging piece of print. Each team submitted ideas of how the Brits would change America and vice versa. The whole idea was to get both teams working together to demonstrate their joint skills—the reason for a unique and attractive partnership.

mixture of differences in language and culture, including a baseball bat in the shape of a cricket bat, the Statue of Liberty conquering Trafalgar Square, and a Greyhound double-decker bus. "We did a spoof", Tutssel recalls, "and hired a Queen look-alike, dressed her up and got her to eat beef burgers in a burger bar on the King's Road. The audience outside stopped the traffic, people were looking in, thinking it was the real Queen."

On the day the partnership between the Michael Peters Group and the Duffy Design Group officially commenced, Duffy and Peters took out a full page advertisement in the *Wall Street Journal* and the *Minneapolis Star Tribune*, which read: "How two guys with art degrees can do more for your business than a conference room full of MBAs." Written by Pat Fallon, one of the senior writers at Fallon McElligott, the ad was to let American corporations know how both groups felt about the pursuit of design excellence in the world of commerce. "Good design, we believe, can be the most profitable way to spend a marketing budget. It can be the quickest way to build a new brand. Or save an old one." Once more, the ensuing attention was overwhelming, Peters recalls. "It brought us $5 million of fee income in the first month, a cover page in the *Wall Street Journal*, and six minutes of prime time on NBC. It was the Brits moving into America all over again."

While many American designers admired Peters' and Duffy's courageous self-promotional work, the foray into American territory was also met with hostility. At the 1989 "Dangerous Ideas" conference given by the American Institute of Graphic Arts (AIGA), hosts Tibor Kalman of M&Co and the eminent Milton Glaser took the opportunity to publicly criticise the *Wall Street Journal* advertisement, arguing that it supported the trivialisation of graphic design in the name of commerce, and that Duffy and Peters had succumbed to the rules of corporate capitalism.

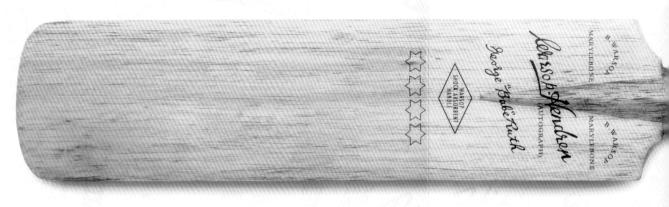

One visit to Southern California has convinced

place in Britain rises so high or stoop

does Hollywood | except maybe

We must have it here. Ar

the entire lot c

and que

Earthwide Champion-
ships, the PLA-BOL
games, will match each
league's winning team
in a best of 3 series to
be played in the middle
of the Atlantic aboard
the QE 2 one year and
on a U.S. aircraft carri-
er the alternate year.

MODEL: BUX SCOTT PHOTOGRAPHY KIM FORRETT

asy;
erhood
e need only
nd a national
sour and stardom.
ough we lack a balmy
climate, we can raise local
temperatures as they do in
Hollywood, by gushing
personal warmth at each
other from our first
waking hour.

Now that knighthood has crossed the boundary into Hollywood, i.e. Ronald Reagan's historic knighting, how about restoring a little dignity to the honor. Mr. President refused to bend a knee or even stoop to being called Sir. Let's put knighthood back on royal footing with the knighting of not just a president, but The King. After all, if The Queen is going to pass these medals out to masters of image, ought not the recognition go to a genuine artist? If he didn't show for the ceremony, then we'd know he's really dead.

American fast food often refers to itself in regal terms but we doubt that royalty would ever stoop to Majesty Queen Elizabeth II could be persuaded to sit down to a double cheeseburger, large order Perhaps that would induce the franchiser of the queen's choice to make the meal healthier, mor china. And what an advertising claim they would have in offering not just french fries, but "The

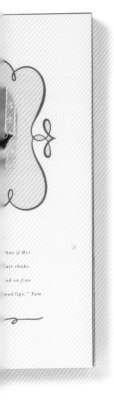

It was a rather rude attack led mainly by Kalman, who was well-known for his anti-commercialist crusade and the statement "Designers: stay away from corporations that want you to lie for them."

After Kalman's accusation, Peters decided to bide his time until he was invited to give a keynote speech at the 1991 AIGA conference with the appropriate title "Love, Money and Power" in Chicago. "I was to speak in front of 1,500 people. And this was my chance to get back at them. So I told them that they were just jealous because we Brits loved both creative and financial success. I explained that we were not knocking other designers with our ad, but actually aiming at the client, who needed to reassess the design contribution. We wanted to expand and improve the market for design, not raid clients from our colleagues. Halfway through the speech, a prominent member of the design community came on to the stage and publicly apologised. Tibor also later wrote a letter of apology. That was very grown up."

Fall from Grace

1987 was a fateful year, which saw Britain's most devastating post-war civil disaster at sea, the capsize of a Townsend Thorenson ferry, and the King's Cross tube station fire in London, in which 31 people were killed. When the American stock market collapsed on "Black Monday" in October 1987, a worldwide economic recession kicked in, followed by years of high unemployment rates and unprecedented governmental and corporate deficits.

Businesses that had previously eagerly expanded were now forced to drastically cut their expenses, and first and foremost, advertising and design budgets. Financed largely by debt, and facing a problematic situation aggravated by the fact that the British government raised the lending prices, design empires began to crumble. Addison, which in 1984 had bought Allied International Designers, Conran, WPP and similarly large design consultancies were forced to make jobs redundant; Fitch-RS axed roughly half of its staff in the years between 1987 and 1991.

Although the Michael Peters Group rode out the initial wave of the recession, it was soon hit by problems occurring with its subsidiary Hambrecht Terrell International, which suffered severely in the ensuing US retail slump. The situation grew worse when it was made public that one of the founding partners of Hambrecht Terrell International had fallen ill. The acquisition quickly turned from being an opportunity into a massive burden. The group had to make all efforts to keep its shareholders and the market from panicking, and much hope was put in the acquisition of the Duffy Design Group. However in 1989, the year in which the Berlin Wall fell, the group failed to reach its goal in terms of pre-tax profits, and was forced to make 33 of its London staff redundant.

How two guys with art degrees can do more for your business than a conference room full of MBAs.

With all due respect to the business acumen of your company's employees, we can solve some business problems with a Crayon that your brightest MBA couldn't solve with a Cray.

THE SECRET INGREDIENT CLASSICO USED TO GAIN NATIONAL DISTRIBUTION FOR THEIR PASTA SAUCES IS PRINTED RIGHT THERE, ALL OVER THE LABEL.

Because we specialize in a marketing skill they don't teach you in business school— the power of design.

It's a marketing skill that most CEOs think of using only to make their company's annual report look better. But a smart few are using design to make their annual profits look better, too. Which is the whole idea behind the

BY MAKING ROSS RADIOS LOOK AS GOOD AS THEY SOUND, WE BOOSTED THEIR MARKET SHARE, SELLING 10,000 UNITS A MONTH IN JAPAN ALONE.

Duffy Design Group joining the world's largest independent design firm, the Michael Peters Group.

Good design, we believe, can be the most profitable way to spend a marketing budget. It can be the quickest way to build a new brand. Or to save an old one. It can make your

WHEN WE DELIVERED THIS DESIGN FOR RALPH LAUREN'S CHAPS CLOTHING, THE CLIENT HAD ONLY ONE PROBLEM WITH IT: "WE'RE WORRIED ABOUT HAVING ENOUGH PRODUCT TO MEET THE DEMAND."

product disappear off the shelf, instead of disappearing into it. And as more and more competitive products become more and more alike, a good package can become a packaged good's best if not only point of difference.

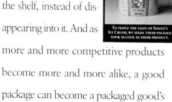

TO TRIPLE THE SALES OF SONNY'S ICE CREAM, WE MADE THEIR PACKAGE LOOK AS COOL AS THEIR PRODUCT.

SEAGRAM'S COMPETITION GULPED WHEN THE DISTINCTIVE IMAGE WE GAVE SANDEMAN'S PORT HELPED DOUBLE SALES WORLDWIDE IN JUST THREE YEARS.

Mr. JOSEPH DUFFY, CHAIRMAN OF THE DUFFY DESIGN GROUP
Mr. MICHAEL PETERS, CHAIRMAN OF THE MICHAEL PETERS GROUP

The good news is that you don't have to give a fig about "understanding the design process" to appreciate the beauty of its results.

WITH OUR DESIGN ON THE POCKET, LEE JEANS PUT EVEN MORE IN THEIR POCKET THAN THEY'D PROJECTED SALES FOR.

As these case histories show, beautiful design is simply one of the best ways to get ugly with the competition.

To see exactly how ugly we've helped our clients get with their competition, call us and ask for one of our detailed case histories. We have them in a wide range of product categories as well as in a wide range of services—from retail design to product development, corporate identities to packaging, and annual reports to special event presentations.

WE HELPED CAMPBELL'S V-8 JUICE GAIN HEALTHIER SALES AND DISTRIBUTION IN THE U.K. BY ADDING BETTER TASTE TO THE OUTSIDE OF THE CONTAINERS.

Or talk to one of our CEOs: in New York, call the Michael Peters Group at 212-371-1919. And in Minneapolis, call the Duffy Design Group at 612-339-3247.

THIS SLICK OIL CONTAINER WE DEVELOPED FOR SHELL WORLDWIDE GREASED THEIR PALM BY CUTTING MANUFACTURING AND DISTRIBUTION COSTS AND AIDING A BRAND IMAGE LIKE NO OTHER COMPETITOR'S CONTAINER.

The Michael Peters/ Duffy Design Groups

THE DUFFY DESIGN GROUP: 701 FOURTH AVENUE SOUTH, MINNEAPOLIS, MN 55415 FAX: 612 339 1121.
MICHAEL PETERS GROUP: 800 THIRD AVENUE, NEW YORK, NY 10022 FAX: 212-735-8008.
LONDON • TORONTO • MADRID • HELSINKI • MILANO

The downward spiral continued when by the end of 1989, the group experienced losses of roughly £3 million, coupled with a drastic increase in debts. In order to avert the worst, Spectrum Communications, Cockade Ltd and the ailing Hambrecht Terrell International were thrown overboard and sold in 1990. The Michael Peters Group, however, could not foresee the fatal decision by one of its (as Peters says, "so-called friendly") American bankers to withdraw all its financial support. After the bank pulled the plug, the whole group literally collapsed overnight, with share prices dropping from 287p to 5p and finally being suspended on 22 August. "It was the first of many similar collapses of large creative companies", Liz Lydiate explains. "I think it's absolutely logical that we were the first because we were probably the biggest and the best. Unfortunately, we left an enormous crater, which other companies fell into."

The next day, Arthur Andersen & Co came in as administrative receivers. "The receivership was one of the most shocking experiences of my life", Peters says, "they tried to carve up the business like butchers. My car keys were taken away from me, my credit cards taken away from me, and I was literally thrown out into the street. I phoned Jo and my mother-in-law while walking and crying all the way home. I had suspected that like all good things, this had to come to an end."

It was a traumatic experience for many in the company. "After the collapse", Paul Langsford recalls, "the administrators came to me and said we had to get rid of 30 per cent of the staff, and we were sitting there, trying to reach a decision. Afterwards I drove home utterly depressed, thinking, 'these are my kids'—that's how it felt, it was family." "I remember going into Michael's office and that we were both very upset, because genuinely, we loved that business", Glenn Tutssel adds, "the day that Michael left was a very sad day for me, I felt quite isolated, because it was fun working with this bloke."

A crucial turning point for Peters then came with the phone call of Brook Land, a senior partner of a major law firm. "He phoned me up at home, since I had been dismissed from the company, and said, 'I've always admired your company, and I heard what happened. Do you need help?' And I really did need his help, and asked what was in it for him. He answered, 'It's not what's in it for me, it's what I can do to help you.'" Land then achieved Peters' reinstatement as a chairman of the company by proving that the receivers had committed a "legal faux-pas".

"When the company went under, it was tough", Joe Duffy remembers. "I was literally faced with closing down my company in Minneapolis or going through bankruptcy proceedings in London, which could have dragged out for years. I chose the former, paid everybody off, shut the doors and started a new design company with my old friends at Fallon McElligott. I was bitter at first, since it was hard to see the positive side of the experience after giving so much time and effort, but with 20/20 hindsight, it was a good and important period in my life."

Over the long bank holiday weekend following the receivership, several companies expressed their interest in taking over the group. The bid was accepted by Craton Lodge and Knight, later the Princedale Group, which was backed by the venture capital company Hillsdown Holdings. 48 hours after the crash, Craton Lodge and Knight acquired the Michael Peters Group core companies dealing with brand development, literature and corporate identity, and formed Michael Peters Ltd. Diagnostics Market Research and Michael Peters Retail (which from 1990 onwards operated as the breakaway XMPR under Rob Davie) were sold to their management. Peters continued at Michael Peters Ltd, heading the company together with senior managers from Craton Lodge and Knight. The company was left only with a small team, and operated at about 15 per cent of the size of the original group.

The design industry received the news of the collapse with mixed feelings. "There were many who were envious of our success", Peters states. "Which meant that a lot of people clapped when we collapsed. It's called the tall poppy syndrome. Rather than support one another, they cut you off when you grow too tall. But many others were there for me. David Hillman phoned on the day of the crash, saying, 'I don't care what you are doing, we are going out tonight to get pissed.'" He also received letters of support from other key figures of the design community, including his perennial competitors Wally Olins of Wolff Olins and Mary Lewis of Lewis Moberly, who wrote, "We know for sure that very soon you'll be back at the top where you belong."

Uncannily coinciding with the downfall of Prime Minister Thatcher, who resigned in November 1990 to be followed by John Major, the collapse caused Peters to reconsider past decisions. Hambrecht Terrell International had turned out to be the group's Achilles' heel, but Peters knew that it was also the rationale behind the acquisitions which had led to an unfortunate ending. The Michael Peters Group had acquired businesses that complemented its own area of activities, but did not expand its core area of expertise. As he told *The Independent* in 1991, "trying to make our management team, which had been used to working in the brand and corporate identity business, manage activities it wasn't familiar with was a recipe for disaster".

With the benefit of hindsight, Peters acknowledges that he had also been somewhat egged on by the City to expand at a rate that could not be sustained in commercial terms. "The company had become a bit of a monster", Jo Peters agrees, "if they didn't grow and acquire businesses, the share price went down. Acquiring businesses seemed like a good idea at the time, but no one had any idea of what that was actually going to mean. It was a bit like being on a treadmill, having to pedal faster and faster." And it might have been that Peters also simply let himself get carried away. "There I was, a high-flyer, my name was in the press every day, flying to New York by Concorde. I thought I could walk on water. But of course I couldn't. They say that he who lives by the sword dies by the sword."

Mike Branson remembers feeling that the company had indeed overreached itself. "In a way, we had our fingers burnt, but that meant nothing worse could happen. Like the 80s, it was a company of extremes, both highs and lows." Joe Duffy says that he "learned much in that year about all aspects of business—the good, the bad, and the downright ugly. What I learned, above all else, is never to put growth and the desire to make more money above the simple joy of doing creative work. From my limited vantage point, it became obvious very early on in our relationship, that Michael had gone from being a creative genius to a man determined to grow an empire and serve shareholders. But part of me also suspects that his timing was wrong and the world wasn't ready to buy into his vision on a global scale."

After the storm had cleared, it was time for the Michael Peters Group staff to move on. Those whose jobs had been made redundant left to find other employment, "but most of us got jobs very quickly, because we were highly regarded, and even though there was a massive recession going on", Liz Lydiate recalls. For instance, Paul Langsford and Peter Chodel were headhunted by Addison as managing director and creative director, respectively.

Others decided to set up their own companies, joining early breakaways such as Smith & Milton and Wickens Tutt Southgate (formed by Mark Wickens, Paul Southgate and Simon Rhind-Tutt, and now called Brandhouse WTS). The New York studio under Karen Welman and Jonathan Ford, working with Simon Williams, became Sterling Design, and both later returned to London to set up the design consultancy Pearlfisher with Mike Branson.

Fiona Gilmore and Mark Pearce, joined Lewis Moberly, and in 1991 started the international brand and corporate identity consultancy Springpoint. After selling it to IPG in 2001, Gilmore set up Acanchi in 2003, a consultancy which specialises in developing brand strategies for countries, cities and regions. Paul Langsford started his own consultancy named Langsford. His colleagues at Michael Peters Literature, David Stocks, Nick Austin and Jeremy Sice, had set up Stocks Austin Sice in 1989, while key staff at Brand New (Product Development), Dorothy McKenzie and Jane Mann, had teamed up with former Michael Peters Group chief executive Ian Farnfield, Debbie Carter and Pat Perchal to form Dragon International. By artificially dispersing into other companies and forming their own start-ups, the former Michael Peters Group staff thus percolated and

impacted upon the design industry, while the shared experience allowed the network of people associated with the group to grow.

Private label packaging for Cordon Bleu. The client and CEO, Brian Bayliss, had created a chain of frozen food stores and asked Michael Peters and Partners to create unique private label packaging. The Big Idea (the recipient of many international awards), was to take a page from a cook book, blending fine illustrations and text to describe the origination of the products, its ingredients, and how they were harvested and prepared for the table, as well as recipes for suggested use.

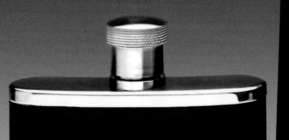

Opposite: Joseph Perfumes was the brainchild of Joseph Ettedgui who had created a very exclusive chain of womenswear and menswear shops worldwide. To create a special bottle would have been too expensive and the idea was to use an existing whisky flask as the perfume container. Covered in silk finished printed paper labels, the overall design complemented the soft lines of the flask.

Top: Törq was a chain of jewellery stores. The name, and the Big Idea was to challenge the 'norm' in this sector. The end result was a subtle and elegant example of how to display small items of beautifully designed jewellery, making them look extraordinary within specially designed fixtures.

Bottom: Perfume packaging for Susie Faux, owner of Wardrobe, a women's fashion shop in London's West End.

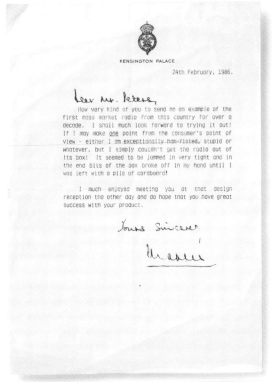

Left: This Radio, commissioned by Ross Electronics, was the first radio to be manufactured in the UK for many years. The product design attracted much applause and became a great commercial success.

Top: Ross Electronics produced and manufactured headphones for the international market. The company became a client of the Group in 1984. Ross Marks, Chairman and CEO, worked with all the design teams in the Michael Peters Group on all products, packaging and communication for his newly floated business.

Bottom: Letter from HRH Prince Charles.

Sweet Factory, a name created by the Michael Peters retail team, was created in 1986 as a chain of franchised confectionary stores and kiosks. The idea of the Michael Peters Group Retail design team was to eliminate the stock room for the retail outlets and create the first gravity-fed confectionery displays in order that customers could fill one bag with a variety of different sweets for one price. This chain is now a huge international success and much emulated by competitors.

All aspects of the projects, from the creation of the idea and implementation, down to the last detail, was the result of a brilliant collaboration between the designers and client. Each retail outlet, regardless of its location—i.e. high-street, railway stations, etc.—all 'housed' an individually designed 'robot' as part of its presentation.

Packaging design for the Leopardi Family, one of the best 'ice cream makers' in the UK.

These stamps for
the Royal Mail (now
the Post Office) were
designed to bring
famous smiles to the
recipient of the letter.
The end result being a
huge commercial and
creative success.

GIORGIO ARMANI
OCCHIALI

GIORGIO
OCCHI

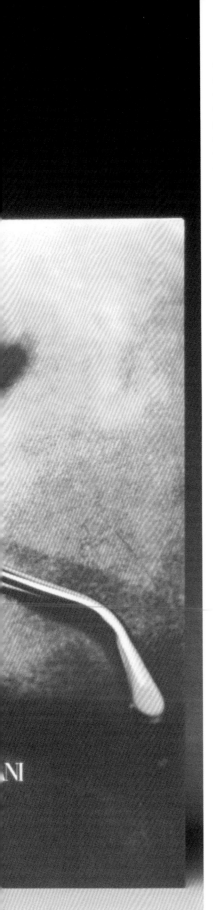

Michael Peters and his team worked with Armani on a whole range of fashion related products. This included packaging, point of sale, sales presenters and literature for Occhiali (eyewear), hosiery and other products.

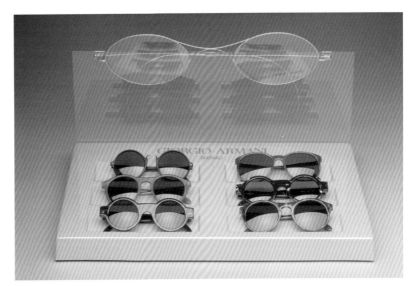

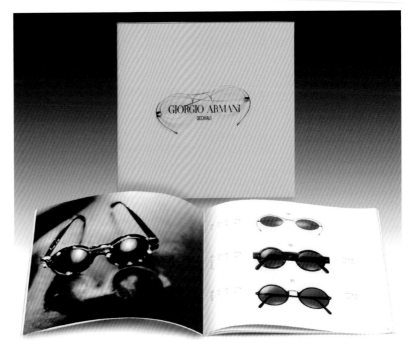

Right: Vodkas are best drunk ice-cold from the freezer. It was, therefore, the creation of a frosted bottle with an area 'wiped' away from the frost surface (revealing a label at the back of the bottle) that was the inspiration for this new product, Tsaritska, designed for the US market.

Opposite: For the launch of this premier strength lager for Carling, the intention was to create packaging, that through shape and design, reflected the high quality of their new product innovation. Carling were one of the first brewers to engage with the idea of creating a completely new shaped can. Both the shape and the layered foil and ink technology were breakthroughs in this somewhat conservative market.

CARLING
Extra Dry

PREMIUM
STRENGTH

*A unique beer
from Carling,
brewed with a fuller
fermentation to give a
distinctively strong,
fully refreshing
taste.*

fully fermented

AGED **12** YEARS

INCHGOWE

▸ SINGLE HIGHLAND MAL

DISTILLED *and*
Matured at the
Inchgower
distillery in Buckie, Banffshire.
Built in 1824 at the mouth of the
Spey, the distillery was moved
to its present site nearby
in 1871. One of *Bell's* most
famous Highland Distilleries.

SCOTCH WHISKY

75cl

DISTILLED AND BOTTLED IN SCOTLAND BY

Arthur Bell & Sons plc

PERTH SCOTLAND

40%vol

Over many years the Michael Peters design team worked with Arthur Bell & Sons, on the evolution of existing malt whiskies and the development of new products requiring new and innovative packaging. The skill to evolve the look and feel for any brand is sometimes more difficult than starting with a clean sheet of paper. The malt whisky packaging was the first step of the re-design of the range that would also include blended whiskies. Packaging innovation and technology is key to the success of any brand—not least of all with this 21-year old rare Scotch Whisky, and the production of its laser-etched bottle (overleaf).

BELL'S

REGD

Old Scotch Whisky

75 cl

100% SCOTCH WHISKIES
DISTILLED BLENDED AND
BOTTLED IN SCOTLAND

40% vol

Arthur Bell & Sons plc

PERTH SCOTLAND

EXTRA SPECIAL

ESTABLISHED 1825

When Michael Peters Group was commissioned to work with Seagram on the acquisition of the Martell brand, a great deal of work was swiftly produced to show Seagram what a revamp of the brand would look like in the future. In addition, a study into how packaging costs might be reduced as part of their bid was initiated. Seagram were successful with the Martell acquisition and the Michael Peters Group were rewarded by working on a worldwide packaging programme across the entire product range. As part of this, the Michael Peters Group identified gaps in the market for a beautifully designed premium duty free cognac. The current L'Or bottle (at the time, the brand was called Extra) is a masterpiece of 'glass architecture' and became one of the most profitable and prestigious products within the Martell range.

Henry Clarke, the US entrepreneur, had built a reputation for creating new brands and sparking life into older products. With the acquisition of Lyons Maid ice creams, Clarke invited the Michael Peters team to work with him to revitalise and upgrade this famous brand. In addition, the Clarke family wished to create high quality premium ice creams under the Clarke's name—the result being this beautifully crafted montage of elements reminiscent of the old days of ice cream parlours.

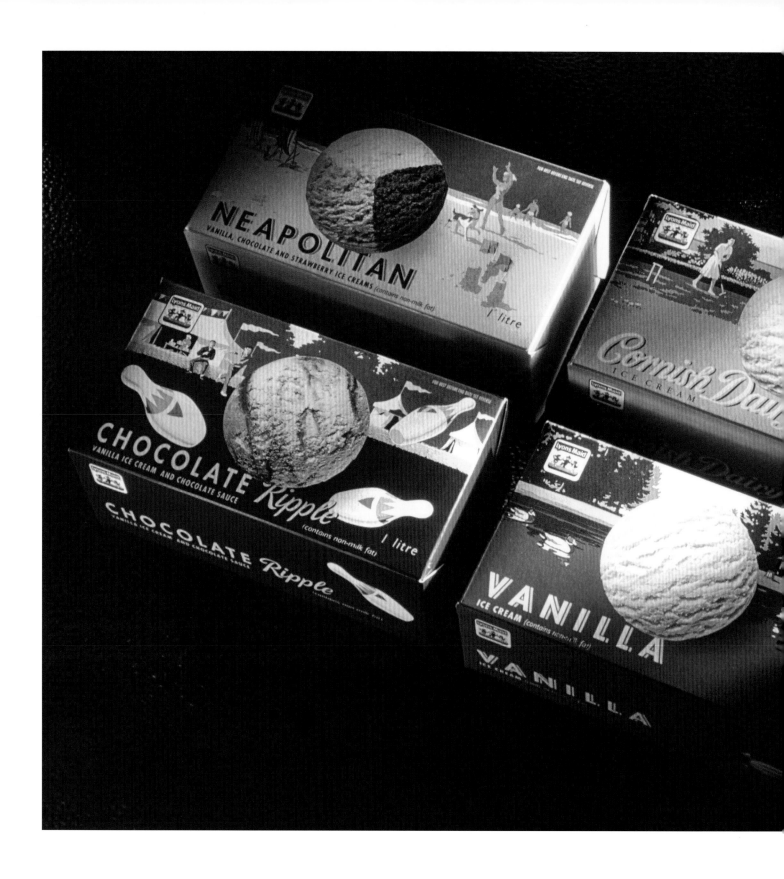

Whilst Lyons Maid in its day was a famous ice cream brand it had fallen behind its competitors because of lack of investment. As part of his commitment to re-energising this famous name, Henry Clarke was committed to total packaging design innovation while still retaining the memories of what "great ice cream was all about". Clarke insisted on a different approach, hence these very successful and innovative packaging designs.

Based on their success of other private label brands—Michael Peters and Partners were commissioned to design over 200 products as part of a private label range for Consilia in Italy.

A range of logos and brand identities for a variety of clients.

First row, left to right:
• A New Zealand wool carpet manufacturer.
• Brand identity for the British Museum.
• ESRB (Foundation for Education Business Partnerships).
• The new identity for Powergen, formally the Central Electricity Generating Board.
• Logo for National Children's Bureau.

Second row, left to right:
• New Symbol for Danisco—a Danish holding company.
• The identity for a small family fishing business in Scotland.
• Identity for TV production company, The Entertainment Network.
• New identity for a major Oxford Street department store.
• Identity for a new transport terminal.

First row, left to right:
- *A new identity for an insurance business.*
- *The new brand identity for The Danish Dairy Cooperative.*
- *A logo for a fashionable London hairdresser.*
- *The identity for a charitable worldwide bike ride.*
- *A logo for the Victoria & Albert Museum's Enterprises.*

Second row, left to right:
- *The identity for a small retailer selling high quality British souvenirs.*
- *The new identity for a London Fund Management Company.*
- *A new brand identity for body, a Japanese cereal bar.*
- *The new brand identity for the BBC.*
- *Logo for ATS—a tyre and exhaust repair chain.*

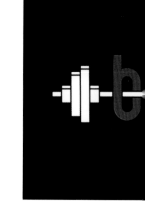

NARD

FOUR CORNERS

WORLD BIKE RIDE

ENTERPRISES

Michael Peters Group Annual Reports. Both the Annual reports and the half yearly figures were publications eagerly anticipated by investors. Each Annual was carefully crafted to portray the work produced by the Group for that year, especially when good results were delivered to its investors. The Pop-up Annual Report (the first Annual Report for the Group) was viewed as a classic of its time and, along with the flotation prospectus, is now a collector's item.

VINYL MATT

SEALER FOR WALLS AND CEILING

BRILLIANT WHITE

Another product from the new "Home Quatro" range.

Brand New (Product Organisation) Limited
When Brand New created "Quatro" for CC Soft Drinks Limited (a subsidiary of the Coca Cola Company), modern graphics were combined with original and striking packaging to allow the product to compete highly successfully in the fastest growing section of the soft drinks market (the flavoured carbonate section). Quatro was launched to the trade in April 1984 and is now selling at an average 1½ million cans per week. The sales target which was to capture approximately 5% of the market share within two years looks like being realised within six months of product launch.

Right Angle Design
One example of Right Angles's approach for effective and simple communication is the design of a product brochure to feature an innovative range of tablets utilising the "The Continus System". The brief was to produce a prestigious brochure, for use by Board Directors, to promote the system and to generate interest from doctors and from other pharmaceutical product manufacturers.

The Hawkeye Studios Limited
Hawkeye is an artwork, production and model-making studio which provides services, mainly to Group companies but also to third parties. Its principal activities are the translation of creative designs into artwork ready for the printer and the production of models for client presentations and/or subsequent manufacture.

The Idea Works Limited
The Idea Works developed a coordinated promotional approach for Alveston Kitchens based on "Alveston Kitchens adds weight to your kitchen".

SLICED BEANS

225

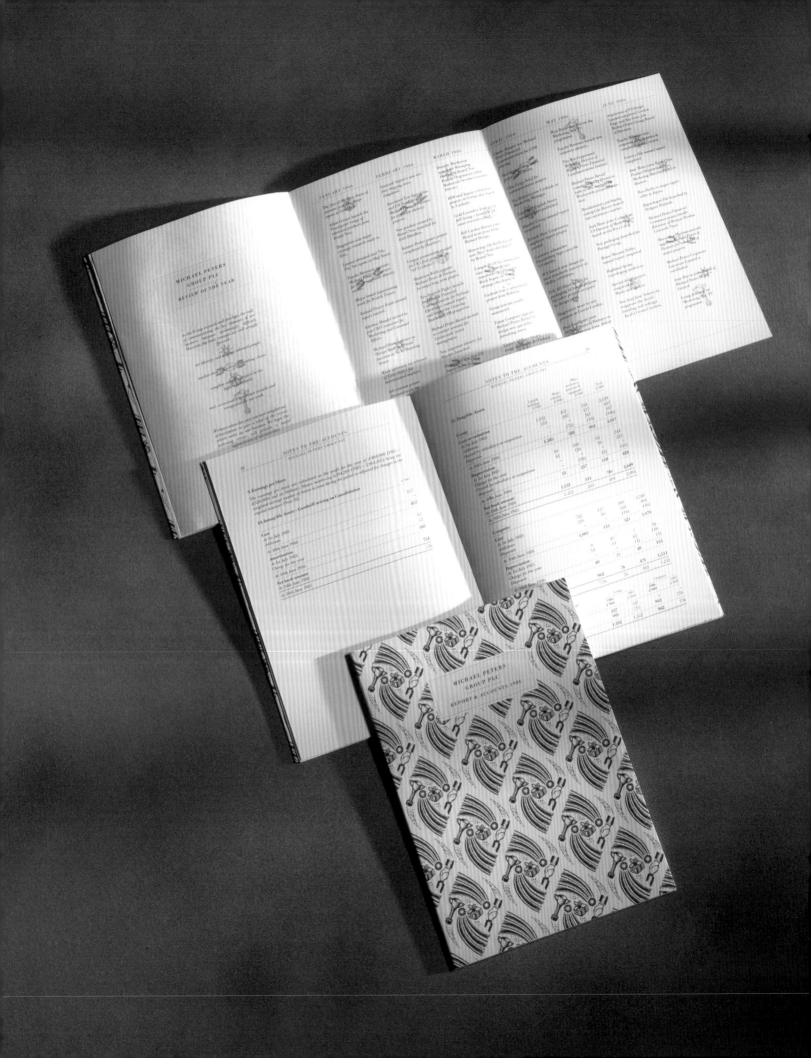

It was a real tribute that in the 'Thank You' Annual Report, produced in 1989, client's endorsed the company's work—e.g. Edgar Bronfman Jr of Seagram, Alistair Grant of Safeway, Ralph Halpern of The Burton Group and numerous others. Other Michael Peters Group Annual Reports are shown opposite and right.

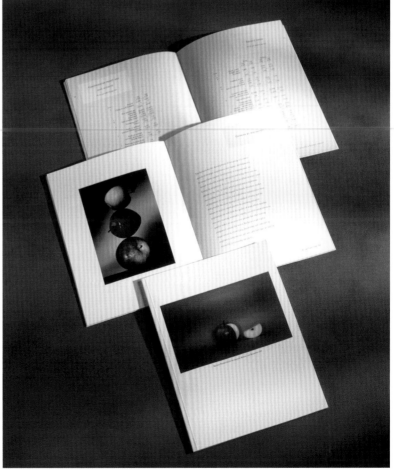

Michael Peters' literature was arguably the best designers of print in the UK. Shown here is a publication for The Science Museum, London (opposite), the annual report for Prestwich Holdings plc (top) and the 'Rorschach ink blot' brochure for recruitment consultants, Saxton Bamfylde (bottom).

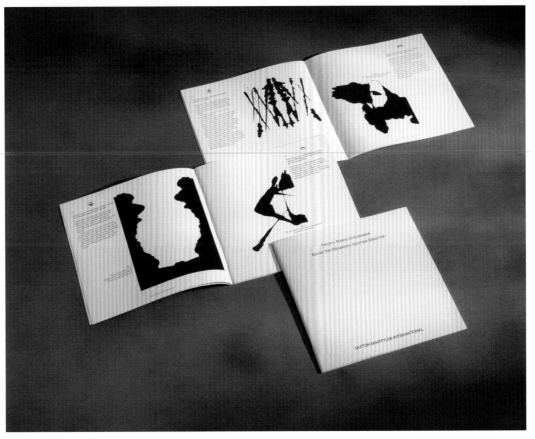

The Seagram Annual Report was a masterpiece of communication. Each corporate message was embodied into the label of each one of its brands—e.g. Mumm Champagne, Chivas Regal, and other products. This Annual Report has won many awards for its creative simplicity in both the US and UK.

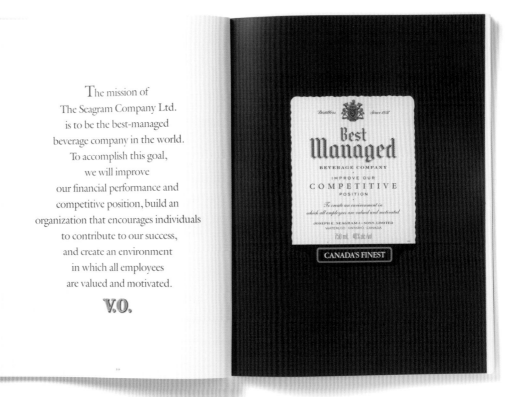

The mission of The Seagram Company Ltd. is to be the best-managed beverage company in the world. To accomplish this goal, we will improve our financial performance and competitive position, build an organization that encourages individuals to contribute to our success, and create an environment in which all employees are valued and motivated.

V.O.

We will strengthen our portfolio of premium brands and focus on improving their profitability and competitive position.

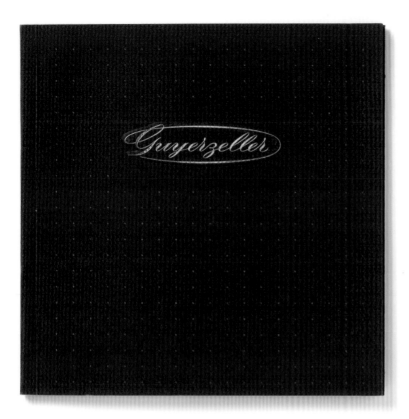

A brochure for a Swiss
Asset Management
Group. The Big Idea
was to depict growth
through nature (and
included actual
wild flowers in the
publication), with
specially produced
papers with petals of
flowers pressed into the
'pulping' of the paper
when manufactured.

RESEARCH AND COUNSEL

The Bank's legal and investment research experts gather and interpret information and opinion from all over the world, enabling them to help the account officers navigate the most appropriate course whatever the client's circumstances.

Guyerzeller advises on all aspects of banking and investment but gives particular emphasis to discretionary portfolios which are managed in accordance with the client's individually defined objectives. The Bank's investment policy is the considered view of a team which studies economic data, market reports and forecasts from institutions in every important financial centre. Asset allocation, carefully translated into timely securities selections, is regarded as the root of portfolio and money management. The speed and precision of Guyerzeller's trading operation is another source of quiet pride.

The Bank's legal department is often called upon to work with a client's other professional advisers. This has resulted in familiarity with legal and fiscal practices in many countries and an invaluable network of contacts. The intricate legal entities sometimes necessary to protect client assets and to ensure that wishes expressed in respect of inheritance or transfers of capital are fulfilled are an area of special expertise.

As the flower is anchored and nourished through its root system, so the Bank's advice and performance are based on a wealth of resources. The legal and investment research departments are central to its services and its success.

6

Consolidations
1991–2008

Carole Laugier, Jimmy Yang, Dana Robertson

I joined Michael in 1992 when he started Identica. We worked together through a decade which saw enormous change, with the international backdrop of the Iron Curtain falling and the rise of global business. Michael's vision was to turn clients' focus onto building their brand. We believed there was an opening for a consultancy that clearly showed how designers could create commercial gold for their clients. It was the beginning of the digital age too, the computer had arrived and many UK design companies, still running on outdated art school philosophies went to the wall. A few agencies like Wolff Olins made it through to this decade unscathed, and new companies like Williams Murray Hamm were appearing but it was a while before the industry rediscovered its confidence. I remember the transition to a hi-tech 'design consultancy' as being pivotal, innovative business solutions were our start point and Michael made buying creativity with technology both fun and profitable for our clients.
Carole Laugier

Michael understood the power of creativity to engage consumers and transform businesses, and he harnessed some of the best talent in the business to apply their skill and craftsmanship to branding. He sold brand strategy combined with creative skills and design application as a single minded offer stealing the ground from the ad agencies and management consultancies. What I remember most is the absolute diversity of it all… the wonderful breadth of clients, the age range and experience of all the designers, all with wildly different skills that we put to work on everything from frozen food packs to airline identities. By taking design into the very heart of businesses we inspired them to be better businesses as well as creating memorable design work for them.
Jimmy Yang

When I joined Michael at Identica, branding as an industry had come of age, and the business had stretched into new and fascinating markets, introducing brands to the emerging Russian and Eastern bloc markets. Creativity and ideas, brilliant thinking and quality of delivery were all important as Identica continued to build an enviable client base. The challenges were enormous but I remember Michael's mantra of re-interpreting the clients' desire for "return on investment" into "return on innovation" being a rallying call that clients and designers both identified with. It was always manic, simultaneously working on such a variety of projects, from banks and law firms to sportswear and vodka. Michael's decision to sell Identica to the Cossette Communication Group was part of his plan for the business, and they continue to run the agency today. Renaming their international design businesses as Identica Branding and Design is testament to the reputation Identica UK had built.
Dana Robertson

	1991	1992	1993	1994	1995	1996
Politics	• The Gulf War begins with Operation Desert Storm and lasts for over a month • Coup plot against Mikhail Gorbachev • Boris Yeltsin elected president of Russia	• Charles and Diana separation announced • South Africa vote for change in apartheid laws	• Bill Clinton elected president • Yitzhak Rabin and Yasser Arafat shake hands agreeing to peace deal • UK recession over	• Nelson Mandela made president of South Africa • Rwandan Genocide begins	• Schengen agreement • Earthquake in Kobe, Japan • Princess Diana gives BBC interview	• Charles and Diana divorce • The Dunblane massacre • Bill Clinton re-elected
Music	• Serge Gainsbourg dies • Miles Davis dies • Freddie Mercury dies	• Nirvana's *Nevermind* released • Grunge • Jungle music in the UK becomes popular	• Michael Jackson accused of child abuse • Prince becomes artist formerly know as Prince after changing his name to an unpronounceable symbol	• Nirvana plays its final show at Munich • Kurt Cobain commits suicide • Britpop/Trip hop	• Oasis vs Blur • Bjork's critically acclaimed *Post* album is released	• Tupac Shakur shot • The Ramones play last ever show at Lollapalooza • Spice Girls/Britpop
Art	• Young British Artists exhibition at the Saatchi Gallery • Damien Hirst has a solo exhibition at the ICA • Arno Breker dies	• Francis Bacon dies • Emma Thompson wins Best Actress at the Oscars • Marlene Dietrich dies	• Audrey Hepburn dies • Steven Spielberg *Schindler's List* • White Cube opens • Rachel Whiteread wins Turner Prize for *House*	• Edvard Munch's painting *The Scream* stolen in Oslo • Gilbert & George's *Cosmological Pictures*	• *Forrest Gump* wins best film at the Oscars • Sol LeWitt exhibition • The Beatles anthology series shown on ITV	• Dan Flavin dies • Douglas Gordon wins Turner prize
Design / Architecture	• Canary Wharf is the tallest building complex in England	• Central Plaza in Hong Kong is built • Collserola Tower is completed in Barcelona • Giancarlo De Carlo wins Royal Gold Medal	• Property developer Urban Splash founded	• Channel Tunnel opens	• San Francisco Museum of Modern Art, designed by Mario Botta opens to the public • Pritzker Prize— Tadao Ando	• Fire destroys La Fenice, Venice's opera house • Stirling Prize established
Innovation	• Stark's Louis 20 Chair	• IPalmtop computers	• Stephen Hawking *A Brief History of Time* • Canon PC-3 portable carrier/pocket memos • Olympus Zoom camera	• Valeriy Polyakov spends 14 months in space, a new world record	• Sony Playstation • Laptops • Trevor Baylis Wind-up radio introduced	• Steve Jobs company 'NeXt' bought by Apple • Dolly the Sheep is cloned • Mobile phones are more readily available • Genetically modified food goes on sale
Fashion	• Vivienne Westwood voted Designer of the Year • Oasis founded	• Calvin Klein creates trend of low jeans and underpants exposed, modelled by Mark Wahlberg • Grunge fashion • Birkenstock sandals	• Body piercing • Extreme sports gear • All-stars logo's shaved on back of head	• Wonderbra, the "heroin-chic" look dominates the catwalks and is the basis of a 1993 advertising campaign of Calvin Klein featuring Kate Moss	• Slogan T-shirts • Combats and camouflage	• Buffalo shoes • John Galliano becomes chief designer for Dior • Hairstylist Max Factor dies aged 91
Sport	• Portugal wins the FIFA World Cup defeating Brazil by 4–2, • Steffi Graf wins Wimbledon	• Michael Schumacher wins his first Grand Prix in Belgium • Denmark wins the FIFA European Cup beating Germany 2–0 • Agassi and Steffi Graf win Wimbledon	• Monica Seles stabbed in back by obsessed Steffi Graf fan • The Zambian national football team dies in an air crash	• Brazil wins FIFA World Cup, defeating Italy 3–2 • Ayrton Senna dies	• Eric Cantona of Man U kicks a Crystal Palace fan in the head • Pete Sampras wins his third Wimbledon title	• Chess computer 'Deep Blue' defeats Kasparov • Glen Hoddle becomes new England coach • Muhammed Ali opens Olympics
Projects						

	1997	1998	1999	2000	2001	2002
Politics	• Princess Diana dies • New Labour win, Tony Blair is prime minister • Mother Theresa dies	• Monica Lewinsky scandal • Iraq refuses to comply with United Nations weapons inspectors	• Columbine High School massacre • The beginning of a newly elected Scottish Parliament	• New millennium is celebrated all over the world amongst Y2K fears • Slobodan Milosevic resigns • George W Bush is elected president	• George W Bush is sworn in as the 43rd president of the USA • Almost 3,000 people are killed in the 9/11, attacks at the World Trade Center in NYC, The Pentagon, and in rural Pennsylvania	• US invasion of Afghanistan: in eastern Afghanistan, Operation Anaconda begins • Euro launched as physical coins and banknotes • Queen Mother dies
Music	• The Spice Girls perform at the Brits • UK win Eurovision song contest • Notorious B.I.G is murdered	• George Michael arrested in public restroom in Beverly Hills • Frank Sinatra dies • Elton John knighted	• Return of Rap—Eminem/Britney • Dusty Springfield dies • Marilyn Manson demonised for apparent influence on the Columbine High School gunmen	• At the Roskilde Festival near Copenhagen, Denmark, 9 spectators die and 26 are injured while the rock group Pearl Jam performs • The Spice Girls break up	• George Harrison dies • Aerosmith, Solomon Burke, The Flamingos, Michael Jackson, Paul Simon, Steely Dan and Ritchie Valens inducted into Rock and Roll Hall of Fame	• Joe Strummer dies • The Streets release *Original Pirate Material* • Reality TV pop groups
Art	• Sensation exhibition opens at the Royal Academy of Art • Roy Lichtenstein dies • Dora Maar dies	• *La vita è bella* • *Saving Private Ryan* • Antony Gormley's *Angel of the North* is completed • *Titanic* wins 11 Oscars	• After 22 years of restoration work, Leonardo da Vinci's *The Last Supper* is placed back on display in Milan, Italy • *The Matrix*	• Tate Modern Gallery opens in London • Peanuts creator Charles M Schulz dies	• Martin Creed wins Turner Prize for *The Lights Going On and Off*	• Kim Howell the culture minister declares Turner nominations are "conceptual bullshit"
Design/ Architecture	• British Library opens	• Hong Kong Chep Lap Kok International Airport opens	• Norman Foster wins the Pritzker prize	• The Millennium Dome closes its doors one year to the day of its opening • Singapore Airlines Flight 006 collides with construction equipment in the Chiang Kai Shek International Airport—83 die	• Daniel Libeskind's Jewish Museum in Berlin opens	• Norman Foster's City Hall opens in London
Innovation	• Digital audio players • Viagra	• Google launches • Sky Digital launches	• Apple computer releases the first iBook • SMS-messaging	• The last Mini is produced	• Apple computer releases the iPod • Wikipedia goes online • Self-contained artificial heart	• Development of Maya, 3-D animation tool
Fashion	• Murder of Gianni Versace • 'Cool Britannia' • John Galliano designs first collection for Dior • Alexander McQueen designs first collection for Givenchy	• David Beckham wears sarong • Alexander McQueen uses disabled model in his show for London Fashion Week	• Levi's announces the closure of 11 of 22 plants and lay off 5,900 factory workers • Gucci purchases Yves St Laurent for $1 billion	• Tom Ford becomes creative director for Yves St Laurent	• Bjork wears swan dress to Oscars • John Galliano awarded a CBE	• Hipster jeans/vests/the parka
Sport	• Tiger Woods wins the Masters	• France defeats Brazil 3–0 in FIFA World Cup	• Michael Jordan announces retirement • In Rome, Hicham El Guerrouj runs the fastest mile ever recorded—at 3:43.13 • Lance Armstrong wins his first Tour de France	• Olympics held in Sydney • France win FIFA European Cup beating Italy	• Beijing wins the bid to host the 2008 Summer Olympics • New York Yankees merge with Manchester United	• The Winter Olympics are held in Salt Lake City, Utah • Serena Williams defeats her sister Venus Williams at the French Open • Brazil win the World Cup
Projects						

2003

- Shoe bomber Richard Reid is jailed for life
- Iraq War begins, Saddam Hussein is brought down and eventually captured
- The Hutton Inquiry

- The White Stripes
- Nina Simone dies
- Johnny Cash dies

- Gustav Klimt's *Landhaus am Attersee* sells for $29,128,000
- Central Saint Martins College of Art and Design takes over the Byam Shaw School of Art

- Emporis Skyscraper Award goes to 30 St Mary Axe
- The last old-style Volkswagen Beetle rolls off its production line in Puebla, Mexico

- Skype launched

- Sarah Jessica Parker in *Sex and The City*
- Miniskirts and celebrities

- Chelsea FC is bought by Roman Abramovich for £140 million
- England win Rugby World Cup

2004

- The largest expansion to date of the European Union takes place, extending the Union by ten member-states
- Terrorist attacks in Madrid
- Tsunami hits South East Asia

- Pete Doherty leaves The Libertines, they split
- Franz Ferdinand

- *Lord of the Rings* wins 11 Oscars
- Filmmaker Theo van Gogh is assassinated
- Momart warehouse burns down in East London

- Taipei 101 opens making it the tallest building in the world
- Foster's Gherkin is completed

- NASA's Spirit, lands successfully on Mars—NASA report that the area where their Mars probe Opportunity touched down shows unmistakable signs of contact with water

- Ugg boots/Ponchos
- Richard Avedon, fashion photographer, dies
- Helmut Newton, fashion photographer, dies

- Lance Armstrong wins 6th Tour de France
- Arsenal finish English Premiership season unbeaten
- Kelly Holmes wins second Gold medal in Olympics

2005

- Prince Charles and Camilla Parker Bowles marry
- 7 July London bombings

- Michael Jackson on trial
- Live 8
- The Arctic Monkeys

- *Dr Who* returns to the BBC
- Patrick Caulfield dies
- Arthur Miller dies
- Caravaggio at the National Gallery

- Rem Koolhaas' concert hall in Porto and Herzog and De Meuron's museums in Minneapolis and San Francisco

- iPod Nano
- Nike Considered boot
- Self-service check-in kiosks

- The term 'bling', hip hop slang that refers to jewellery and other accoutrements, comes into popular usage

- Liverpool wins UEFA championship
- London wins Olympic bid for 2012
- Lance Armstrong wins his 7th Tour de France
- Chelsea wins The Premiership

2006

- Slobodan Milosevic found dead
- Google buys YouTube
- Alexander Litvinenko, is poisoned in London restaurant
- Saddam Hussein executed

- *Top of the Pops* ends
- James Brown dies

- Daniel Craig is James Bond
- Carsten Holler's slides at Tate Modern
- David Hockney's portraits

- Work begins on the Freedom Tower

- The Nintendo Wii comes out in the UK
- Commercialisation of wind technology

- WAGS
- Stylist Rachael Zoe
- Celia Birtwell designs for Topshop

- Michael Schumacher retires/Shane Warne retires
- Chelsea wins The Premiership

2007

- Tony Blair resigns and Gordon Brown takes over as prime minister
- Smoking Ban is implemented in England

- Concert for Diana at Wembley Stadium
- Live Earth
- Led Zeppelin, Spice Girls and Take That reunite

- Final Harry Potter goes on sale
- Terracotta Army at the British Museum

- Renovated St Pancras re-opens/Eurostar moves from Waterloo to St Pancras

- Apple releases the iPhone
- BlackBerry mobile email device

- Kate Moss designs range for Topshop
- Madonna designs for H&M
- Penelope Cruz for Mango

- Lewis Hamilton
- Venus Williams wins Wimbledon

2008

- Fidel Castro resigns
- World Banking Crisis

- Britney Spears and Amy Winehouse dominate gossip columns
- Vampire Weekend
- MIA, Black Kids, Leona Lewis

- Tate Modern's exterior is covered in graffiti
- Man Ray, Picabia, Duchamp retrospective at Tate

- Heathrow's Terminal 5 is officially opened
- Frank Gehry designs Serpentine's Pavilion
- China Design Now exhibition held at the V&A

- £50 hand-powered laptop wins Brit Insurance Design Award

- American Apparel
- Agnes Deyn
- Yves St Laurent dies

- Beijing Olympics, Record British Gold, Silver and Bronze Medals
- Man U win European Championship

AEROFLOT

WHEN THEY ZIG
WE ZAG

IDENTICA

Phoenix from the Ashes

In a peculiar twist, while the Michael Peters Group was experiencing problems, Peters was awarded an OBE (Order of the British Empire) by her Majesty the Queen for his services to design and marketing. He received the award in June 1990, a public recognition for his role as an innovator in establishing design as a business tool, and also for his tireless campaigns to bring socio-economic issues to the attention of the design world.

Peters had played a significant role in advising the Conservative government and the Department of Trade and Industry on design-related issues, and had worked with the Royal Family on initiatives including the Prince of Wales Award for Innovation, Princess Anne's Enterprise Britain, and the Duke of Edinburgh Award. "It was remarkable, especially because I had come from a position of being a young upstart who never got invited into the design echelon", he says. David Hillman further points out that Peters was one of the first designers to receive this kind of acknowledgement. "Some people probably found it negative, because the more successful you are, the more that breeds jealousy. I think it was actually very nice, the fact that someone thought about it is already something to be proud of." And whereas others might have rested on these laurels, Peters went on to set up a new company.

At the time, he was still fulfilling his role of chairman and creative director at Michael Peters Ltd, at the time a subsidiary of Craton Lodge and Knight (renamed The Princedale Group in 1992). After the collapse of the Michael Peters Group, Peters stayed with Michael Peters Ltd for two,

rather unhappy, years. "The company was run by an accountant whom I absolutely despised", he states, "it was clear that we wouldn't get along. He even questioned the £30 I wanted to spend on birthday cards for the staff, asking me to pay for them out of my own pocket. I phoned my friend and lawyer Brook Land nearly every day, moaning about the bastards at the Princedale Group. And he told me that if I had any real balls, I would go out and do it again. That prod was just what I needed. So I simply walked out, much to the upset of people at Michael Peters Ltd, and started Identica."

Peters unveiled his new consultancy in 1992, envisioning it as a small, niche company that operated worldwide, and which would keep a lower profile by being less publicly monitored than the Michael Peters Group, but being driven by the same creative belief. Despite the demise of the group, Peters knew he could rely on his vast experience, his high standing amongst the design community and large network of contacts to attract new business. David Hillman recalls Peters stating that he would never again attempt to build a large company. "We knew full well that within a few months, he'd be back up again. That's what drives him. As a designer, you're either in or out. It's not one of those part-time jobs you can just dip into. Starting a new business after losing your name, bouncing back into the same field with the same people like Michael did, takes a lot of courage."

Identica Ltd (renamed The Identica Partnership in 1995), started off as a small office in Barlby Road in West London. Peters was joined by a handful of employees recruited by Jo Peters, who had started working full-time in design recruitment in 1987. "It was a bit scary for him", she recalls, "having run a large company like the Michael Peters Group and then having to do ordinary things like going to a shop or going to the post office to buy stamps. Michael was used to having people do things for him. But he was also back to doing what he was good at, looking after creative work and dealing with clients—things he had been drifting away from at the Michael Peters Group. And he was very lucky to get large projects right from the start." Within a week of setting up, Peters had secured two major commissions with the drinks company Seagram, and Sage, a computer specialist.

Carole Laugier, who joined as a freelance designer and together with Julie Morris (another designer) and account handler Felicity Hunt helped set up Identica, recalls that her first encounter with Peters via telephone had "a real sense of urgency. He spoke about the future of branding and design and his vision for his new venture with such passion that I knew this was a path I had to take. It was a decision I've never regretted. Almost from the day we started, we were thrown into projects of the highest calibre and greatest variation—from developing software and literature to designing crisp packets."

Jimmy Yang, who came from packaging design experts Lewis Moberly, was the first full-time employee. "For somebody like me, who is used to being quite organised, it was at the same time worrying and exciting, simply because it was the start of something new and very different", he recalls. "The atmosphere was cosy, because there were very few of us, in a relatively new and bare open-plan office. We shared a meeting room with the job club in the building, so every now and then when we booked the room, we would have to change the meeting room door sign to say 'Identica'. The kitchen was basically a little fridge with a kettle on top. Everything was very fluid and allowed to change. And obviously, when Michael later started contacting more and more clients, the business developed from that."

Initially however, Peters wanted to keep his company small, as he told the *Sunday Telegraph* in 1992: "The age of the big design group is over. In the 1980s we lost contact with clients by trying to be all things to all men. This time I am going to stay close to clients." The structure of design

not be zone

Another stretch of Wall crumbles

command. This surrender of its command by the ministry shows that the Government is becoming acutely aware of the importance of ensuring that reunification is carried out in a way which does not — in Mrs Thatcher's words — "make any of us in Eastern or Western Europe feel less secure".

Herr Genscher, who met Mrs Thatcher last week, had understood this point fully. Aides say that he had hardly been able to get a word in after his arrival in Downing Street as the Prime Minister explained her concern at the present pace of reunification. He left the meeting with Mrs Thatcher's support for unity, but with a clear idea that she would try to rally support against any move that appeared to endanger existing security arrangements.

The Foreign Minister therefore reacted angrily to Herr Stoltenberg's statement and eventually enlisted Herr Kohl's support to bring his Cabinet colleague into line.

Herr Kohl managed to win the backing of Signor Giulio Andreotti, the Italian Prime Minister, during a weekend meeting in Pisa, but he remains aware of widespread worries, particularly in France, about the consequences of reunification.

Bystanders watching the dismantling of a watchtower close to the Reichstag in East Berlin yesterday when East German border guards supervised the demolition of part of the Berlin Wall leading up to the Brandenburg Gate.

Modrow vows not to grovel to Bonn

From Anne McElvoy
East Berlin

Herr Hans Modrow, the East German

said the visit had had its successes and spoke of the way being open for speedy reunification.

ment of many East German citizens who now ask themselves whether they are any longer considered brothers

union, Herr Kohl, meanwhile, arrives in Erfurt today to inaugurate the electoral campaign of the right-wing

---

companies and the design industry itself had undergone a significant change with the onset of the 90s. "The 80s were a boom time, and the industry became a bit saturated", Jimmy Yang explains. "There are still large design companies out there, but the difference is that they don't try to run every single office. They give each office autonomy to run their own business in the most effective way."

While Peters made a new start with Identica, Michael Peters Ltd, the company he previously chaired and which still carried his name, ran alongside under the creative direction of Glenn Tutssel. Tutssel then went on to found the design consultancy Tutssels St John Lambie-Nairn with television graphics specialist Martin Lambie-Nairn.

Peters' setting up of Identica concurred with politically turbulent times. After the fall of the Berlin Wall, Germany had been reunited in October 1990, and a few months later, US-led allied forces set out to liberate Kuwait in the so-called "Operation Desert Storm". 1991 also saw the collapse of Soviet Communism as the USSR splintered into ten independent states, a watershed which above all marked a triumph of political and economic liberalism. Economically,

Britain dove headlong into another recession with the devaluation of the British pound following Black Wednesday in September 1992.

This meant that the design industry, which had only just recovered from the strain of preceding years, and despite benefiting from the acknowledgement granted by other industries, had to cope with drastically reduced budgets. Many clients had become more price-conscious when commissioning creative services—no longer were they willing to pay the over-inflated fees demanded in the 80s.

And there was always another design company that did the same work for less. "We've devalued the business ourselves", Peters contends, "and we still flake out when asking for money. I've always insisted on top fees for my work. Because the cheaper you are, the less the client will listen." The 90s were, however, also a decade that saw more and more design companies shift the focus of their expertise and transmute into branding consultancies, or at least engage in certain aspects of the flourishing discipline.

Richard Williams writes a profile on Peters in DesignWeek, in May 1996.

Richard Williams talks to Michael Peters about design, business and the rocky road to success

The outsider

BUDDY HOLLY once said of Elvis that "none of us would have made it if it wasn't for him". I feel that way about Michael Peters. He burst the doors open for brand identity groups like Design Bridge to flourish and allowed people like me to have a decent career. Fortunately, unlike The King, Peters is still well and truly with us and has his mind set firmly on the future.

Four years ago he founded Identica, a business which he describes as "an identity and innovation consultancy, not a design company. I love talking about design and I still lecture on

In the process of making Identica a success, he has cast himself adrift from the traditional design industry. He explains: "Designers are falling so far behind in business because they don't appreciate and admire themselves as people. They feel guilty about what they do. The reason I wanted to start the Design Business Association was to say to people 'If we get everyone swimming, rowing and running together we are going to be a very strong force. The moment that clients can trade us off one against another, it falls down flat'. That's why

Re-fighting the Fight

At the outset, Peters very purposely conceived Identica as a branding consultancy, well aware that he neither could nor should replicate the Michael Peters Group. "I wanted to take the skills and areas I enjoyed most during my work, which were identity, packaging and strategy. I no longer wanted to get involved in the other creative skills of the Michael Peters Group, because at the end of the day, I needed a focus." Creating, developing and managing a brand involved all of these skills and thus, ever since its inception, Identica has been offering brand-related services such as corporate and brand identity, brand strategy, name generation, brand expression, but also new product development, packaging, literature, environmental design and digital media.

By making branding his prime focus, Peters moved on to a territory formerly dominated by advertising, just as he had previously done by encouraging the Michael Peters Group to introduce strategic planning into the design process. He was positive that design provided a more cost-effective and efficient solution to brand-related problems. While Identica employed design as a tool, Peters never considered it a design company. In a 1996 portrait for *DesignWeek*, he described it as "an identity and innovation consultancy. I love talking about design and I still lecture on it, but I don't consider myself a designer anymore. Clients view us as a creative resource to help them develop their business."

The term "branding" stems from the practice of stamping cattle with a hot iron. In a figurative sense, it later came to signify the act of emblazoning a name and character onto a company's products in order to differentiate them from those of other manufacturers. Ever since the mid-nineteenth century, the process of branding sought to establish a close emotional bind between the company and the customer, and to create a sense of loyalty and trust by endowing corporate products and services with strong symbolism and mythology.

Throughout the late twentieth century, branding had grown increasingly important, as more and more multi-national companies were keen to establish their brands on a global scale. Brands and their attributed characteristics became an essential part of modern life, so that one's identity and sense of self was no longer expressed through one's social background or religion, but through a lifestyle supported by the right brands. Addressing both the spiritual and practical needs of their consumers, brands came to symbolise hopes and dreams. In the 90s, the aspirational hedonism of the 80s was then substituted by a mass individualism, which, again through brands, emphasised creativity, non-conformity, and authenticity. No longer did one want to keep up with the Joneses, but to differ from them as much as possible.

In Peters' view, the rise of the brand had strengthened the relationship between design

246

and industry. Design could help manufacturers to develop engaging and compelling brands that expressed their value to the consumer in a variety of ways. "The brand is the interface between consumer and corporation, in essence it is an experience—the way you smell, the way you touch, the way you feel and see what the corporation does." Although other leading brand consultancies shared this perception of branding, Peters' approach was markedly different.

"I have immense admiration for many consultancies including Pentagram, Landor, Enterprise, Interbrand and above all, Wolff Olins, who have been around for a number of years. They have amazing and sometimes very controversial ideas, and I do too, but I like to see it as solving a major business problem, and I like to be measured on the fact that I can actually turn the pencil into a pound sign. I can out-talk all of them in terms of commercial possibilities."

And, as Peters recognised, there was still mileage left in convincing business leaders that a coherent brand package could yield a high commercial benefit. When, in 2000, Identica commissioned a MORI poll to interview roughly 200 leaders of British companies to establish their attitude towards branding, it found that even by the turn of the millennium, only 26 per cent of the interviewed directors linked an investment in brands with higher profits (although a whopping 80 per cent saw a strong brand as essential for business success). Peters therefore found himself re-fighting the fight, when insisting that design and creativity should also possess commercial value in the world of brands.

"It takes a decent piece of bravery to say that", states Dana Robertson, formerly a senior creative director at Identica. "Michael is of that generation that helped define our industry and gave it worth and importance. He has always

unashamedly admitted that we're in this industry to make money. The important thing is that we help make money for other people, and that we offer a service which is of a high value. And especially now, with the rise of the marketing manager who applies the same brush to everything, and the proliferation of the two-man band, it's important for people like Michael to reiterate that our industry offers other companies significant value in lovely, witty, crisp and engaging communication."

Reasserting the commercial worth of design for Peters was always inextricably linked to an exceptionally high quality of work, Jimmy Yang points out. "I think part of the strategy is to be both commercial and creative at the same time. You can have the most beautiful design, but if it's not commercially viable or successful, you will fail your job as a business. And commercial design can also require a lot of crafting, a lot of fine details. For a piece of typography, you can spend a long time on just a few words, for an identity, you can spend months just drawing those letters until you get them absolutely perfect."

A case in point is Identica's rebranding of the Hollywood-based Universal Studios, which at the time had been taken over by Seagram. "The old logo was very old-fashioned and static", Yang states. "It didn't reflect that Universal wasn't just a film business, but also a modern, international theme park and entertainment business." Well aware that they were dealing with a company with a rich history, Identica initially conducted interviews with key people, discovering that the company required the development of a powerful, worldwide brand and new identity without losing the recognition of the old one.

The brief thus called for a delicate balancing of the familiar and the radically new. To update

the identity, designer Geoff Halpin added depth to its pictorial and typographical elements, and a softly glowing halo around the Universal globe to signal "pride and ownership". The tailor-made, three-dimensional lettering was crafted with particular detail, layering a sans-serif typeface, which stood for the modern face of Universal, over a serif typeface, which represented the company's history and tradition. "It symbolised something new emerging out of something old", Peters illustrates.

Peters would also constantly encourage and give fresh impetus to his designers to allow them to produce outstanding design work while, as it had always been his policy, granting them the space and time to test out new solutions. "Michael let designers experiment as much as they wanted to, up to a point where he signalled a direction in which the work should go", Jimmy Yang explains. "A lot of it was pushing designers to come up with the best, most creative solution. He let the leash out a bit, but brought it in when the time was right."

Permitting creative freedom was crucial for the creative overhaul and repositioning of Johnnie Walker, the world-famous Scotch whisky brand owned by United Distillers. The client had initially requested Identica to develop packaging for "Johnnie and Cola", a new product that was to be sold in Australia. "Michael immediately spotted the mistake they were about to make, since Johnnie means different things in different countries", Yang says. "Also, the new product took the brand name in vain, almost devaluing it." These considerations revealed a more fundamental problem: that of having to unite under the Johnnie Walker brand a wide range of products known simply by their blends.

Furthermore, research conducted by the company had shown that the original Johnnie Walker logo, which had been created in 1909 and pictured a striding man with monocles and a top hat, was perceived as rather old-fashioned, snobbish, and therefore unattractive to younger whisky drinkers. Similar to the rebranding of Universal Studios, Identica thus faced the task of having to strike a balance between a modern, expressive style to attract a younger generation, and a style which employed the key elements of a fine whisky brand to appeal to existing customers.

The process of developing the new identity took two years. Jimmy Yang recalls that the design teams literally did thousands of drawings. "They ranged from something more traditional and closer to

the old identity to something so avant-garde that it was beyond recognition." Experimenting allowed the designers to find an appropriate style and manner of execution, which ultimately resulted in a simplified, squiggly mark that expressed a free spirit and successfully accompanied the brand into the twenty-first century.

Driven by Creativity

From the outset, Identica was founded on the notion of an active partnership, both by ensuring that its staff operated as an integrated and mutually supportive team, and by encouraging clients to blend their skills and experiences with those of the consultancy. In addition, Peters would not only take a consulting role, but also one that actively challenged businesses to invest in creativity and blue sky thinking.

"Michael didn't just sit back and think about the most obvious thing", Jimmy Yang states. "He would challenge the clients by telling them, 'you've asked us to do this, but I think you haven't thought it through. You need to look at the bigger picture.' He would consider the whole business, acting almost like a management consultant. It helped that Michael is very astute in terms of seeing straight through problems, cutting through the crap, while many people spend hours explaining something that is quite simple. That's down to his education and experience as a designer."

Avi Eisenstein, an associate professor of visual communications at the Bezalel School of Art in Jerusalem and one of Peters' closest friends, confirms that "Michael has the rare ability to sit

249

Gin Zing and Red Devil were just two of numerous new product development projects that were the brainchild of Blue Science Ltd, the joint venture New Product Development business owned by the Generics Group, in Cambridge, and Identica.

and listen for hours to the most complex issues and deliver an extraordinary and simple solution to the problem. He is one of the most intuitive people I have ever known."

For The Sellotape Company, now under the direction of Neil Ashley (Peters' old client from Birds Eye), which faced the problem of having developed a generic reputation, Identica decided to take a holistic approach, aiming to separate the company from the brand. The idea was to aid Sellotape in utilising its name to become a brand in its own right by launching a new corporate identity, repositioning all of its brands, repackaging every product and developing products for new markets. After the repositioning, the company received overwhelmingly positive feedback from customers and shareholders alike, allowing it to emerge as an innovative market leader and resulting in the sale of the business to a German competitor.

"Michael challenged the clients to think about their ambition, and going about the project properly, not just tickling it around the edges", Dana Robertson points out. "Big companies are risk-averse, especially when they possess large amounts of market share, so transmitting the value of doing something different is a very hard pitch. But Michael could help them realise the value of being brave. In our industry, you can rationalise everything, but there's always that ten to 15 per cent of the design process that is a creative leap. If you don't take the leap, you end up with a mediocre product."

A notable example of Peters convincing his client to go a step further was Identica's work for the law firm Nabarro. The firm had advised Identica in legal matters for several years, enabling Peters to strike up a good relationship to its senior partners. When external research revealed that the firm had become too complacent and understated

to compete in the market, Peters suggested a repositioning to resuscitate the firm's ambitions. He stressed that the project was part of a larger imperative with a significant commercial benefit, and that developing a new corporate identity involved not merely creating a new logo or changing a name (in this case, from Nabarro Nathanson to Nabarro). It instead further involved acting upon the notion of it being an effective tool to communicate a change in corporate personality and strategy, both within the company itself and to the public.

For Nabarro, this meant finding a point of difference in comparison with its competitors and exclusively claiming this territory. "Nabarro were especially good at translating legal issues into plain English", Dana Robertson recalls, "so the signal change was a notion of clarity and 'clarity matters'. It struck a real note with people outside the industry because everyone knows that lawyers will just talk you to death and are happy to bamboozle you when you are actually paying them for clear advice." The new identity, which combined clear, lucid imagery with serene typography, was supplemented by the rather unusual idea of placing highly creative advertisements in the *Financial Times*. "At first they weren't too sure about the commercial benefit", Robertson says, "but it did give them exposure and made their clients feel they are employing the best lawyers around."

Chris Riley, who had started out at Lewis Moberly on a placement and joined Identica as a designer in 1994, points out that Peters was the crucial linkage between both the client and the consultancy side of the partnership. "Market research, for example, can do a lot of things", he explains, "and it can give you pointers as to what is currently out there, but it cannot predict the future.

Olympia Mews in Bayswater, West London, the second of Identica's offices.

That is something for people like Michael to get out of the designers, and then to present it in a format that is acceptable to the client. It provides a lateral point of view for those businesses who don't have someone in charge of the creative aspect, but only brand managers, and for these companies Michael is the external version of a creative director."

For the repositioning of the Irish food company Erin, which sourced a majority of its ingredients in Ireland, such linkage proved vital. "It was a very commercial job. When it came in, it had 'nightmare' written all over it", Chris Riley laughs. Working closely with Erin's marketing director Rob Rees, Identica refreshed the visual identity of the company and repackaged nearly 200 products, highlighting their origin by depicting an Irish landscape on the packs. The project proved a huge success. "A business consultant can tell you a lot about the way market trends are moving", Riley continues, "but in the end, shopping is an emotional thing, and people tend to react on impulse. So the packaging that tends to win out is packaging with a soul. Michael is good at seeing when something is alive, when something has a bit of character to it. He can harvest that and convince someone to put it on the shelf. And invariably, it does well."

As executive creative director of Identica, Peters again permitted himself a high level of involvement with the creative work produced at the company, emphasising and putting into practice his mantra of imbuing each visual identity, each piece of packaging or retail design, with an ingenious idea supported by high quality execution. In effect, he gave it the Peters' touch. "Michael is not exactly a shrinking violet, and that reflects itself in the work",

Chris Riley states. "To each project he brings an open mind and a huge amount of enthusiasm. He likes ideas, and expressive, colourful stuff, and I think that is why he's been so successful with a slightly more commercial type of work that is nevertheless put together beautifully. He's very good at driving that through and does not accept anything mediocre—it can be outrageous, but middle-of-the-road is not where it's at. He's not a compromise person."

"Generally, he is a very good boss", Jimmy Yang adds. "Sometimes he would have an idea at a meeting which was just not right, and we would cringe, thinking, 'No, he has not just said that...!' And at other times he would just come up with the most ingenious things." Remarkably, and in contrast to many other key players in the design industry, Peters always let his personal traits, his charisma and sense of humour, pervade his business personality. "Michael is very self-deprecating, although he is very much the boss. That allowed him a little bit of light-heartedness", Dana Robertson points out. "Michael is like Marmite, you have a real opinion about him. You either love him or hate him. At Identica, he spent his working life getting me into trouble. But even then, it was constructive, because he would push you to solve it, come up with an idea and facilitate the vision."

"Michael inspired me to want to be as good as him in presenting", Carole Laugier adds. "He was and still is the best salesperson I have ever encountered. One time, Michael, Karen O'Neill and I were due to fly up to Scotland to present to Clydesdale Bank. It was a presentation that hinged on various designs which had to be shown on the computer. We did have a laptop, but our projector had broken so we decided to take our computer screen (all 20 pounds of it) up to Scotland with us. The sight of two women carrying presentation boards, mock-ups, computer and screen, with Michael leading the way on the tarmac surely must have caused a few giggles. We couldn't take the computer screen on board, so it went into the hold of the airplane and, of course, broke. But Michael still pulled off the presentation with panache while Karen and I salvaged what we could from our computer to win the account."

Links and Mergers

Cautioned by the fatal overstretching of large design consultancies in the 80s, their 90s counterparts opted for strategic alliances, joint ventures and overseas offices when aiming to expand. For Identica Peters had, with its launch in 1992, already established a link to another discipline by teaming up with The Generics Group. The Cambridge-based science and technology specialists had previously worked closely together with Brand New (Product Origination) Ltd, one of the subsidiaries of the Michael Peters Group; through the alliance, both

Roustam Tariko is the chairman and founder of Roust Inc. Peters and his team worked closely with the owner to create a new premium vodka. This identity (top and bottom) is used across a number of businesses within the group, including Russian Standard Vodka and Russian Standard Bank.

sides aimed to establish a multi-competent, integrated resource for innovation.

Part of the reason why he wanted to work with Peters, Jimmy Yang says, "was the idea of using the knowledge of scientists to formulate new products and to create genuine innovations. Scientists often talk about things in ways that basically nobody understands, and they are not very good marketers, so our job was to help them develop a proposition, a brand name, and maybe a piece of packaging and communication."

In 1999, the association between Identica and Generics was consolidated with the forming of Blue Science Ltd, a joint venture aiming to provide

clients with a full innovation package from a single source. Its initiators Professor Gordon Edge and Peter Hyde of Generics, the former Minister of Design and Technology John Butcher, and Peters, set much hope in the proposed concurrent development of both product and brand—through packaging and branding, consumers could familiarise themselves with technological innovations, while new ideas could more rapidly be brought to fruition.

The collaboration generated various products for United Distillers, for instance the alcoholic "smart drink" Gin Zing, which combined a mixture of Gordons Gin and Korean Ginseng to attract a younger market to the Gordons Gin brand. Another brand extension, Red Devil, was a whisky-based product laced with red chilli peppers. Both were developed "from scratch", involving the creation of the drink formula, the brand names, and product positioning. Red Devil also introduced a packaging innovation by substituting the bottle label with deeply embossed and simultaneously frosted lettering.

This approach reflected Peters' belief that product innovation had to be accompanied by packaging innovation, especially when considering

252

environmental issues. "In Britain we only recycle six per cent of our household waste, whereas in some parts of the US and Canada, 70 to 80 per cent of household waste is recycled", he noted in a 1999 issue of *Graphics International*. Blue Science, therefore, also set upon designing ways to encourage consumers to recycle, to transform waste into new packaging material, or to improve packaging to aid the consumer, for instance by signalling that the product had passed its sell-by-date.

In 1998, Identica merged with TANGO+, a youth marketing and design company set up by well-known advertising agency Bartle Bogle Hegarty in 1987. "My long-time friend and fellow creative John Hegarty, who owned Tango, and I shared the idea of building a bridge between advertising and design", Peters says. "So one day he asked me whether I was interested in buying Tango, and in return, they would receive a stake in Identica. So it was just a swap." TANGO+ specialised in creating design at the point of sale, with a client list including Levi's, Dockers, Gatorade, Ray Ban, Amnesty International, Reebok and Nike. "We thought it would fit nicely with the things we were doing", Peters further explains.

Prior to the merger, Identica had worked closely with Bartle Bogle Hegarty under the watchful eye of its marketing director Paul Donovan, (whom Peters has always considered one of the best in the business), while developing an integrated campaign for the mobile phone company One2One. Initially called Mercury Communication, the company required a repositioning and comprehensive brand language and strategy. Part of this strategy was to address the lack of consumer focus in the mobile phone industry, and to make the brand more accessible. "The emphasis was on human contact", Jimmy Yang states. "That's how the idea of one-to-one was developed, bringing two people together, talking to someone." The result was a bold identity harnessed by a simple visual idea—the connection of two coloured shapes, each containing one word, through a numeral at their point of overlap. Through collaboration with John Hegarty, the One2One brand was then communicated across a variety of media, including packaging, retail and advertising.

One of the accounts acquired through TANGO+ was Nike, the market leader in sportswear ever since the 90s. While also developing own campaigns, packaging and promotional material, Identica worked closely with advertising agency Wieden+Kennedy to convert its campaigns into bespoke retail design. Dana Robertson points out the challenges inherent in this translating process. "You can have a fantastic and unique idea, but I think the challenge also lies in translating this idea into consumer touch points without diluting or compromising it, losing its energy or making it look too corporate. It lies in bringing the brand story to life, and translating it for other media. We were working on a Pan-European basis, and on a lot of different projects, sports performance versus sports culture, Nike Men, Nike Women—so it was never dull and never the same."

On Familiar Terms

Over the years, Identica gradually outgrew its premises, as the increasing volume of commissions required more and more people to be taken on board. After being located in Barlby Road, and renting adjacent offices, the company moved to its own building in Olympia Mews, then to an office in Kensington Church Street, and finally, to Newcombe House at Notting Hill Gate in London. The structure of the company changed simultaneously with its expansion, as Peters worked with different partners at various times. He first led Identica with Alan Bristow, followed by Darryl Phillips, who left after it had become clear that both partners had different visions for the company. "Darryl was very much orientated towards technology and growing the business, and not particularly interested in design or creativity", Jimmy Yang explains.

In 1994, Phillips' position was taken by consultants Tom Austin and Derek Fieldman. Ross Peters and David Robinson joined the board; both had been instrumental in the launch of the Michael Peters Group several years prior, and were important catalysts for the success of both companies. Another key figure for Identica was Karen O'Neill. "Karen without doubt helped to attract the most amazing new business to the company", Peters says, "new business is a very creative job, involving selling to potential clients the wares of our company, quite often when those clients are hostile to being sold to." Yet again, Peters' ability to attract and encourage talented people to work together productively and amicably proved beneficial for the company.

The merger with TANGO+ in 1998 then bestowed Identica with a combined turnover of £10 million and a total of 90 employees. In addition, TANGO+ managing director Sarah Bratt and creative director Peter Rae joined the management team at Identica. The supplementary work then allowed Identica to add to its design, planning and production staff; major recruits of this period were: Geoff Halpin, designer; Richard 'Ginger' Tilley, designer; Gareth Andrews-Jones, planner; and Trevor Willis, production.

Despite Identica's gradual expansion, it was important for Peters to retain the 'Kibbutz' mentality he had encouraged at his previous companies. This meant that all decisions were made by a communal vote through both a business and a creative committee. It also meant that although Peters was nominally the chairman of Identica, he was approachable to his co-workers. "My experience in other design companies was that the people at the top were quite aloof", Chris Riley says, "but Michael would always make sure to say hello to everyone—

New livery as part of the brand identity for Aeroflot—the Russian State Airline.

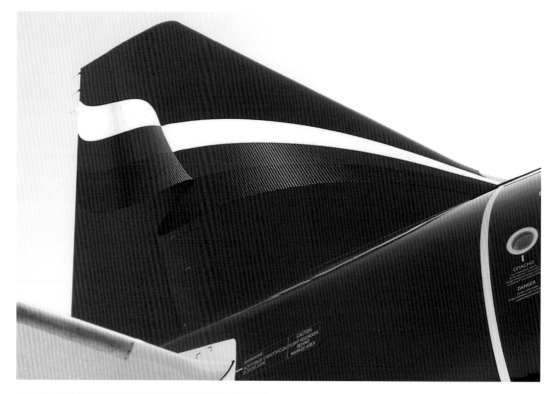

The Identica team, led by Identica Vice-Chairman Tom Austin, took three years to complete this project for Aeroflot. The assignment was a complete repositioning of the Russian State Airline, including the total brand identity, employee communications and brand implementation. The project was extremely complex involving dozens of the airlines staff, from senior management (across every function of the company), and from pilots and crew to ground staff and administration. The airlines management wanted every aspect of the brand to be considered, from the training of staff, to the design of the interiors of the aircraft, complete livery, uniforms, ticketing, and food presentation.

whether they want to talk to him or not—and he also expected a response to that. In terms of office hierarchy, there wasn't any when I came in the mid-90s. No one had a title. Even Jimmy Yang, who to all intents and purposes was a creative director, wasn't called a creative director."

Shamoon, who joined as Peters' personal assistant in 1997, first mistaking him for the office boy, "because it was a hot day, and he was only wearing informal shorts", and whose job it was to keep the office running smoothly while taking care of Peters' official and personal appointments, confirms that he permanently cultivated a family atmosphere. "Michael was very accessible, and it was never difficult for anybody to come into his office. He would also always show his appreciation with flowers or notes. People at the office were quite close to each other, they bonded, went out for drinks together."

Identica also saw its fair share of Magical Mystery Tours, leading its staff to visit the English countryside in Kent, Northampton and Leicestershire, and eventually (when the company began to prosper) the European cities of Dublin, Bilbao and Berlin. "These outings used to take place after a particularly heavy period of work—Michael was very good at working out when people needed a lift, and delivering on that in some way, whether it was drinks out, a good Christmas party, the D&AD awards, or the Magical Mystery Tours", Chris Riley says. "The tours were usually centred around something cultural, so in Bilbao, we visited the Guggenheim Museum. Or there would be some sort of fact-finding, team-building exercise where you had to go around and search for something or produce something, and afterwards, there was always one victim who had to do an after-dinner speech."

Riley himself once had to deliver one of the infamous speeches. "It was less complimentary to Michael, since we had found a picture of him as a young boy, dressed as a cowboy, with socks and sandals on. We projected it onto the wall and made a lot of jokes about cowboys in the design industry, and him coming from Luton. He got his revenge by making me down a half-pint of Guinness and three oysters the next morning."

Jimmy Yang adds that having fun and playing practical jokes was very much part of the company ethos at the time. "A great story was when Michael was about to go to a meeting to present a mock-up for a new ceramic bottle we designed for Seagram's Royal Salute. So he stopped the car outside the office to meet Kevin Johnson, who was a designer at Identica. Kevin walked up to the car, and just at the moment when Michael had got out, dropped the box, and watched the blood drain out of Michael's face. Of course, we had prepared the box by putting broken glass inside."

Foreign Relations

Aeroflot hires Briton to give its image a lift

Mark Franchetti
Moscow

RENOWNED for surly staff, inedible food and ageing planes, Aeroflot has a reputation as one of the world's worst airlines. More than 10 years after the collapse of the Soviet Union, its logo is still a winged hammer and sickle. Not, perhaps, for much on autopilot and going for a stroll. They had to force their way back in with an axe.

On another occasion an American couple crossing Siberia found one of the passengers cooking his own meal on a portable stove at the back of the plane. Aeroflot stewards have been known to serve vodka during take-off.

After the fall of commu-

On another occasion, the company conspired to make one of its designers falsely believe he was about to leave the country for a longer period of time. "We told him he had to help one of his clients develop a brand in Poland", Yang continues. "We got him to wake up at three in the morning, took him to Stansted airport—we had a fake ticket made up waiting for him at the information desk—and when he opened up the ticket envelope, he only found a Polaroid with the entire staff holding up a placard saying, 'You sucker!' That was actually Michael's idea."

And sometimes, the fun resulted simply out of unforeseen circumstances: "When I turned 30", Chris Riley recounts, "Michael brought a birthday cake into the building, which has a no-smoking policy, with 30 candles on it. All the candles were alight and of course, by the time Michael had got it out of his office and into the studio, it was a towering inferno. The smoke alarms went off, and the whole building had to turn out into the car park to wait for the fire brigade. And the fire brigade charge you if there is a false alarm. That's why I like to call it the £7,000 birthday cake."

Identica continued the tradition of being a "university of design" headed by Peters; its alumni who set up their own companies after developing their expertise at Identica include both Jimmy Yang and Dana Robertson, who head the design and branding consultancies Yang Rutherford and Neon, respectively, Karen O'Neill, who launched the fruit juice and smoothie company RDA Organic, as well as Kevin Johnson (Innovus), Glen Harrison (Next Big Thing), Deborah Beradi (Inaria), Stuart McKay (Ergo), Kevin McGuirk (Indigo), Sophie Fenton (Sophie Fenton Design), Tim Barson (Pack My Bag), Simon Manchipp (NoOne, SomeOne) and Peter Rae (Curious).

The end of the 90s in Britain was marked by two spectacular events: the tragic death of the Princess of Wales and "Queen of Hearts", Lady Diana Spencer, and the election of Labour Party leader Tony Blair as Prime Minister in 1997, concluding nearly 20 years of Conservative administration. As part of the Labour Party's political agenda, Blair hailed Britain as "Cool Britannia", emphasising his links to the Britpop establishment (which had created 90s' anthems such as "Parklife" and "Wonderwall"). The British fashion magazines *i-D* and *The Face* now guided the fashion-conscious worldwide, *Wallpaper** covered the domestic front by introducing the concept of loft living to non-artists. The art world found its new icons in the protagonists of the Young British Art movement, which culminated in Saatchi's landmark Sensation exhibition at the Royal Academy in London, attracting hundreds of thousands of visitors.

Britain also became one of the principal exporters of design, leading Blair to dub the United Kingdom the "design workshop of the world". Exemplary of this development and highly regarded internationally due to its branding and design expertise, Identica received a significant amount of its overall income, approximately 60 per cent, through overseas commissions. Peters had also added to the company's management board senior managers with relevant market experience, including deputy chairman Tom Austin, senior creative director Carole Laugier and finance director Ruth Goddard.

Laugier recalls having a share of interesting projects and clients all over Europe. "I remember one time flying to Amsterdam to work with a client on a gaming website called Whizzworld. This was right before the 'dot com crash' when clients were confident of their ideas and happy to employ us to help realise them. It was meant to be a meeting to present our creative ideas to date. Imagine my surprise when, after seeing the work, the client was so delighted that he handed me the payment for half of the project in cash! I was a bit unclear as to what I would do coming back from Amsterdam with so much cash and no suitcases, but luckily I had a big handbag and made it back 'home' with payment in hand."

Also in the late 90s, a visible sign of the concurrent creation of the European Union, the Euro currency, had entered the financial market and in 2002, the lives of many Europeans. Although Identica worked for a large number of European clients, mainly in Italy, Switzerland and Scandinavia, Peters could not call himself a Europhile. "I enjoy being part of Europe, and trading with European companies", he states, "but being part of the common market is the fastest way for us to reach annihilation. I don't think we should be governed by anonymous people in Brussels who make our law." In an issue of *Marketing* in 1994, he voiced

After the successful launch of One2One, the marketing director, Paul Donovan, moved to Vodafone, taking Identica with him to work on all promotional activities, including retail communications and packaging.

Vodafone image shift by Identica

By Alexandra Jardine

Vodafone, the UK's largest mobile telecoms company, has hired Identica – the consultancy that originally created the One 2 One brand – to revamp its brand communications and ad strategy in an effort to make Vodafone more appealing to consumers.

his opinion about the design of the proposed European currency notes by wryly suggesting that they should incorporate educational content: "On one side of the tender, let's learn to count from one to ten in the languages of Europe, say please and thank you and ask for a beer. On the reverse, national maps will be printed which fit together across denominations to produce a geographical jigsaw of Europe...."

Apart from Europe, Identica worked predominantly in Israel and Russia, two countries which presented Identica with the additional challenge of necessitating a design approach tailored to the respective cultures. Peters had found that whereas most brand strategies for the Russian market entailed focusing on notions of tradition and heritage, most Israeli clients requested an orientation towards the future.

Bank Leumi, one of Israel's leading financial institutions and one of the first independent Zionist banks, for instance had commissioned Identica, through its marketing director Yona Fogel, to re-design its corporate identity to symbolise the bank's ethos of progression and aspiration—"the dawn of a new era". This positive image was visualised by a sunrise, incorporated in blocks of turquoise and dark blue. As the bank had faced strong international competition moving into the Israeli banking market, it was, after the new identity had been launched and implemented in branches and corporate literature, more than pleased to discover that 80 per cent of all Israeli banking customers expressed themselves positively about the change.

Identica's work in Russia was spearheaded by Tom Austin, who as vice chairman ran the company on a day-to-day basis and was

responsible for ensuring that it remained profitable during growth. "Tom was the person who both in good and bad times was able to wear his very creative business hat and sort out some thorny problems", Peters states. "He was often, in football parlance, referred to as my defender, as he would collect the ball from the opposition and allow me to score goals." Austin would commute almost weekly to Russia to develop new business and open the market for branding and design projects.

The benchmark within the Russian market was then formed by Identica's work for the Russian Standard vodka brand, which it developed together with the management consultancy company McKinsey. Noticing the lack of premium quality vodkas produced in its home country, Roust Inc, a leading Russian distributor of spirits, had approached Identica to aid the company in establishing a super-premium vodka of its own. Identica extensively analysed both the country's history and the Russian vodka market, learning that the proposed brand would have to compete with 200 others, albeit of a lower quality.

This analysis ensured that the project could be supported by a clear and meticulously planned strategy, which was to reflect the premium, aspirational quality of the product and to combine it with a modern interpretation of its Russian heritage. The Kremlin-inspired and embossed bottle, together with its extraordinary wrap-around label, designed by Chris Barber, successfully distinguished the product to the extent that it was soon able to position itself as the leading premium vodka in Russia.

The fundamental difference in working for Russian clients as compared to British clients, Dana Robertson states, lies in the fact that "in the UK, we have a very media-savvy audience, whereas Russia is still a kind of virgin territory.

256

There are a lot of former state companies that have to reinvent themselves to avoid disappearing, and a lot of entrepreneurs that want to build a brand but have no idea how to go about it." The advantage of working with such companies, Chris Riley points out, "is that you can make quite radical changes because people there want new, exciting things. After years of not being able to buy certain products, they actually want change, whereas people in the UK are probably more suspicious.

Of course, this depends also on the clients and on how open-minded they are."

Russia was very keen to shed its staid, Soviet-era image and also to rid itself of the less complimentary stereotypes that surrounded its culture. "One of the funnier stories is that when Michael first went to Russia, he insisted on having two bodyguards", Jimmy Yang recalls. Realising that he wasn't going to be kidnapped by the Russian mafia, Peters after subsequent travels sorely regretted his *faux pas*. Fortunately, it did not derogate his Russian business relations. Identica soon won the project of rebranding Russia's national airline, Aeroflot, on the back of its work for Russian Standard.

The airline presented Identica with a major strategic task, since, as Peters states, "it had the reputation for crashing every five minutes, although it in fact possessed one of the best safety records in the airline industry as defined by IATA". Led by Tom Austin and Gareth Andrews-Jones, the project involved making the airline look more contemporary, professional and friendly by means of a newly designed, comprehensive identity programme. "We re-designed everything—the badges and livery for the crew, the ticketing, the interiors and exteriors of the planes, and so forth." Peters says. A key element of the new identity was a stylised national flag, signifying the airline's traditional roots, on the tailfins of its planes. Various tailfin designs like those sported by British Airways (a design put forward by Interbrand Newell and Sorrell with the input of Michael Wolff) would have not benefited Aeroflot, Peters says. "The work for British Airways was a brilliant idea, but Aeroflot was a different proposition altogether. British Airways, as the world's favourite airline, wanted to have its tailfins decorated with all its various destinations. Aeroflot, however, needed to get back to the basics, it was dusty and grey, and first and foremost required style and a monolithic brand identity."

A project for which a Russian client deliberately sought a "Western look and feel" was emax/cafemax, a business enterprise that combined an online portal with a network of internet cafes—the first of their kind in Russia. In collaboration with Alex Reznokovitch and Lev Nikolau—the founders, Identica was asked to develop a branding strategy that supported and linked both sides of the business, while reflecting the youthful and optimistic attitude of the New Russia. "They provided the brand name and we thought it would be good to create a fun, dynamic and flexible figure, a mix between a cartoon character and MTV", Jimmy Yang states. Central to the new identity created for emax/cafemax was an "egg-head" icon which, depending on the portal content and subject, changed its facial expression, and was executed in a bold and colourful style to effectively set the brand apart from its competitors.

A New Millennium

In 2002, Peters, in addition to his OBE, received recognition for his lifetime achievements by being nominated for the Prince Philip Designer's Prize, along with furniture designer Michael Marriot, architect Edward Cullinan and Geoff Kirk, the former chief design engineer at Rolls Royce (who ultimately won the award). The prize had been initiated by the Duke of Edinburgh to publicly acknowledge designers who through their work had advanced the public perception of design and raised the profile of design practitioners within society.

A year later, Peters with the help of Tom Austin sold The Identica Partnership and its sister consultancy TANGO+ to Canada's largest marketing communications network, the Cossette Communications Group. The takeover allowed the Cossette Group to take up a European presence in light of a development that saw more and more clients aiming to establish their brands globally. The BBH share was taken out of Identica, ending a partnership that Peters describes was "less than a holy alliance. John Hegarty went to America, and with him, we lost the ethos and contact which this partnership represented. But BBH learnt a lot from us and we learnt from them."

By acquiring Identica, the Cossette Group added Identica's expertise in successfully developing and managing international brands to its portfolio of communication services, which included advertising, sales promotion, interactive solutions, strategic planning, ethnic and urban marketing. In turn, the takeover enabled Identica to create an extensive, worldwide network of affiliated offices in New York, Toronto, Vancouver, Montreal, Moscow and Shanghai. Peters retained his role of chairman and chief creative director, and led the London office.

When Dana Robertson joined the company just after it had been bought by the Cossette Group, he found it extremely heterogenous, made up of seemingly irreconcilable elements. This fragmentation of the company structure owed much to the fact that Identica had grown to a significant size in the late 90s, employing nearly 100 people. However, the political and economic climate changed dramatically after the 11 September terrorist atrocities in New York and the declaration of the "War on Terror" by the US government. The commercial pressures grew even stronger after the terror attacks reached London with the suicide bombings of July 2005, putting many UK businesses under intense strain.

It was inevitable, therefore, that Identica during these years rapidly cut back on staff. "Some of my sadder memories comes from our 'lean years' during the times of recession", Carole Laugier recalls. "Over the years, I had progressed from designer to creative director and partner and not only designed, but had a hand in day-to-day and future decisions made for the good of the company. When it was announced that we had to cut back to ensure that Identica would continue to be a profitable company, I had to see many good friends leave. It was an incredibly sobering time, but one which made me reflect on the nature of our business and our roles within it."

Peters had been planning to sell Identica for several years prior; the planned sale was in fact one of the reasons that had led him to consider expanding the company in the late 90s. "I was very ambitious. I wanted to grow it to such a size and profitability that I could sell it. Why have a business? So that you can, one day, either hand it to your children or sell it to somebody else. I wanted Identica to have premium value, to be seen as a symbol of excellence, just as Michael Peters and Partners and the Michael Peters Group had been."

For Identica, this meant that Peters ensured that it stayed at the forefront of its discipline, capable of managing imminent changes within the creative industries. He was certain that advertising would diminish, while design and communication would increase in importance. He also envisioned companies with "designers on their boards, so that clients will finally recognise the importance of creativity and design, and of taking risks with their products."

He furthermore anticipated that brands would move significantly further into the field of interaction, thus replacing many of the services traditionally offered by advertising. Keenly aware of the fact that technology increasingly played a key role in design practice, he insisted that digital design could help raise the standing of the design industry, as it possessed skills that allowed companies to create whole—albeit virtual—worlds around their brands and products. Although the burst of the "dotcom bubble" around the turn of the millennium had somewhat dampened the proliferation of companies seeking an internet presence, the importance of the World Wide Web as an alternate platform to express brand values remained uncontested.

One of Identica's relatively recent projects involved the creation of a new identity and way-finding system for the national sports and entertainment venue Wembley Stadium. The project accompanied the opening of a new building designed by architects Foster + Partners and HOK Lobb in 2004, and involved the rebranding of the stadium as a destination, the creation of signage, and the design of its merchandising and marketing elements. Jimmy Yang recalls that it was very important for Identica to win the project, "because the stadium is a national symbol for football, and Michael is a great fan". Sure enough, the company secured the job, pitching against 11 other design groups. The new visual identity created by Identica then utilised the stadium arch creatively and very effectively, rendering it a symbol and ultimately, a London icon.

The Shape of Things to Come

In October 2007, Peters resigned as chairman and executive creative director of The Identica Partnership, thus carrying out the plans he had made while closing the deal with the Cossette Communications Group four years prior. Upon leaving Identica, Peters is able to look back on having successfully established four design companies (including one design empire),

spawning scores of start-ups and playing a key part in the professionalisation of British graphic design by furthering the merge of design and commerce. Remarkably, Peters' principles of excellence, ingenuity, and giving clients a return on their investment in design have throughout their various corporate manifestations remained constant. And crucially, these principles were supported by Peters' unique ability to act as a catalyst, to discover and bring together some of the brightest talents of the design industry.

Even after 40 years, his dedication to the design business has not ceased. "I'll never leave the business; I'll go on with it until the day that I drop. Because for me, it is not a job, it is a vocation, it's part of my DNA", Peters says. A passionate advocate of innovative and highly creative design at all times, he also, in 2007, started sponsoring an award for multi-disciplinary collaboration, as part of the Design for Our Future Selves awards scheme for students of the Royal College of Art in London. "I was blown away by what the students at the Royal College of Art were doing in terms of innovation. It gives me great hope for the future of our industry."

As for his own future, Peters has definite plans. "I've always wanted to re-write the rules and right now, I'm at the beginning of a new chapter, brimming with new ideas. I love with a passion what I have done to date, but I'm not complacent. So I'm going to take all of this experience into my new venture. Most of all I want to take the concept of collaboration, blending the finest talents in the business, wherever they are in the world, to produce even greater work, both creatively and commercially. I know I can convince people of the importance and value of design."

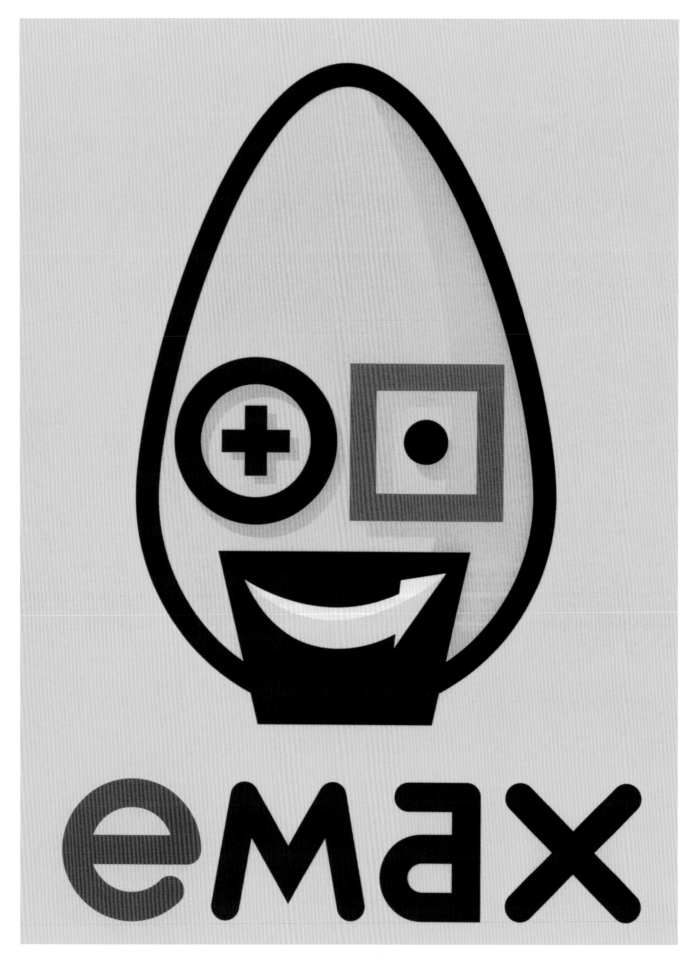

Cafemax was the brainchild of Alex Reznokovitch and Lev Nikolau, two ex-McKinsey consultants who had worked with Identica on the creation and launch of the Russian Standard Vodka brand. Part of the project idea was to create the look and feel for the emax brand both on- and off-line, including the creation of category icons to speed up downloading of information. The whole identity was then developed through the cafe chain in partnership with a Russian interior design team.

Russian Standard Vodka is now one of Russia's most famous premium brands. Together with the client, and McKinsey, Identica created this 'Kremlin Bell'-shaped bottle. This has become an icon in the Russian Vodka sector. The logo—the bear and eagle—was a key part of the promotion of the brand and is today used across all products within the Russian Standard portfolio.

Smirnov Vodka was originally launched in Russia in 1860. After a painful family split, the brand fell behind its competitors. With the support of new investors (and led by Alex Reznokovitch, ex-McKinsey) a new and evolved brand look was launched in 2004 to wide acclaim. The Smirnov brand is now part of the Diageo portfolio.

The dream for many years whilst working with Seagram was to re-design the 'star' of its business—The Chivas Regal brand. In 2000, Identica was briefed to look at the entire Chivas portfolio, in order to give all products within the range a distinct and cohesive family feel. These projects are challenging and extremely complicated, especially in terms of packaging production. The Chivas Regal re-design took nearly four years to complete, with every detail examined and re-designed in order to preserve the integrity and pedigree of one of the most famous whisky brands in the world. Although the brand has a loyal customer base, it was vital to attract new consumers by creating a more 'contemporary' look and feel within a very traditional sector.

266

Where the law is complicated...

Where the mind is boggled
by gobbledegook...

Clarity

Nabarro launch material for all employees.

Nabarro—the new name for the prestigious law firm previously known as Nabarro Nathanson—recognised that the changes in the way law firms promote themselves coincided with the many changes in the sector.

The firm had grown over 50 years and developed a strong practice in all fields of commercial law. However, it had been held back by a dislike of trumpeting its abilities and the fact that the premier reputation it had developed in certain fields, especially real estate, tended to overshadow its accomplishments in other fields. There was

a growing recognition that the firm should take more control of its reputation to redress these factors, and promote itself in a way that reflected its practice as a whole, and by reference to the qualities the partners and established clients saw in it.

With this in mind, Identica was selected to help position the firm to reflect the particular qualities of business-like and user-friendly service delivery.

Along with this, a total revamp of the identity, both internally and externally, was developed with a consistent and coherent approach to everything the firm does, especially

in the recruitment of new graduates and newly qualified lawyers.

As part of the positioning of Nabarro, Identica created promotional advertising campaigns to coincide with seasonal activities.

Clarity is egg-shaped.

Geometrically speaking, the chocolate confection traditionally given at Easter is a three-dimensional ovoid whose shape is that of half each of a prolate and oblate ellipsoid joined at the equator and sharing a principal axis of symmetry. Enjoy.

Looking for a law firm that calls an egg an egg?
www.nabarro.com

NABARRO
CLARITY MATTERS

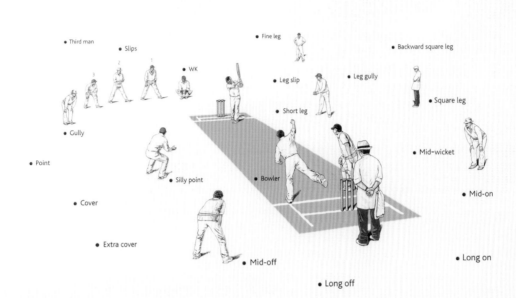

The cricket season?
Or the silly season?

Cricket is a game of two sides. The off side and the on side. The on side is also called the leg side.
The on (or leg) side is the side to the batsman's left. Or right, if he is left-handed. The fielding side
is made up of eleven players, two of whom are the bowler and the wicket-keeper. The other nine
can be either short, long, fine, wide, deep, square, backward, forward or silly.
And now, the lbw rule...

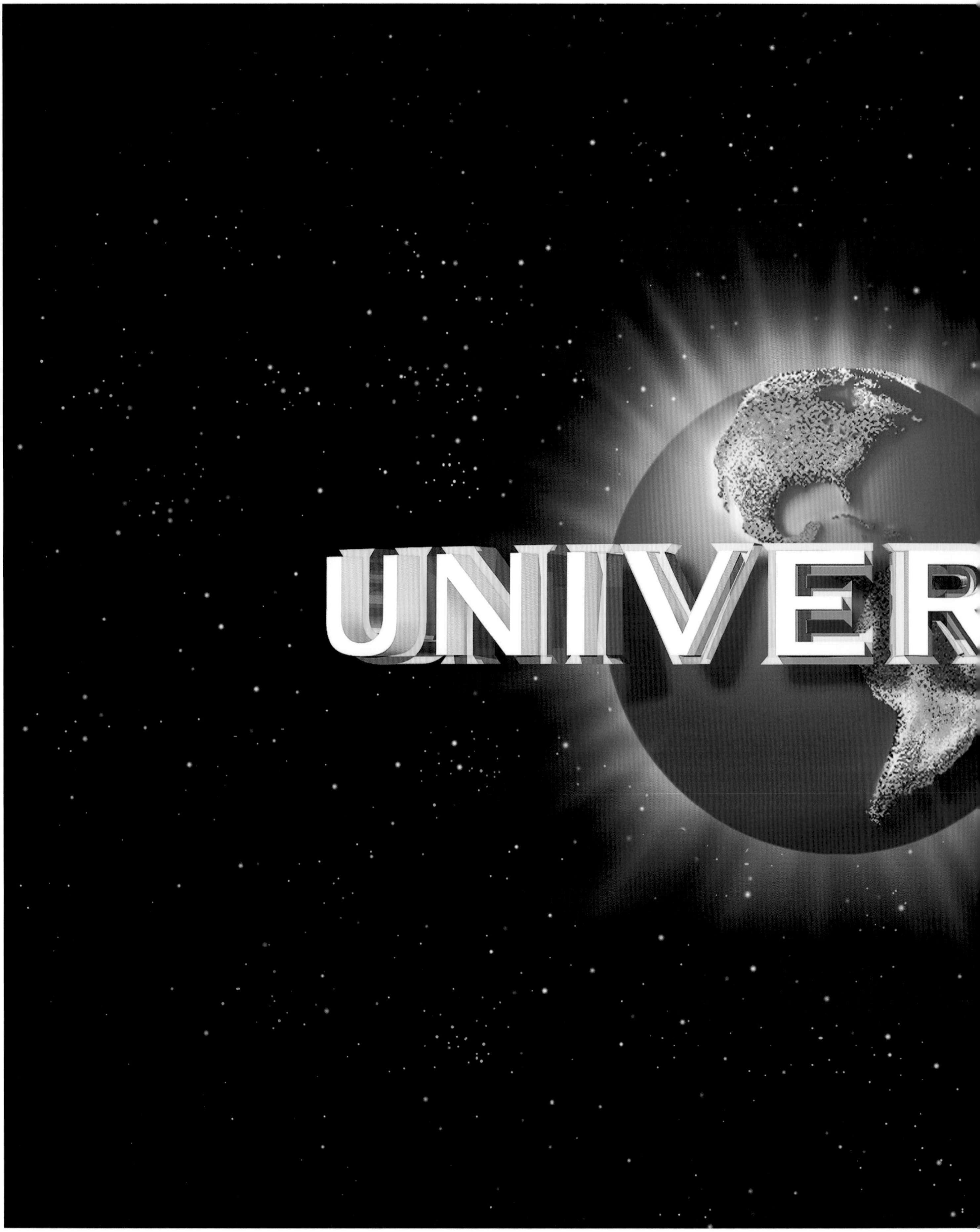
UNIVER

Undoubtedly, this was one of the most exciting and prestigious projects that the Identica team worked on. The 12-way pitch was won in 2002; with Identica being the only non-American branding and design business to compete for this contract.

With such an incredible reputation in so many areas of entertainment, the Universal management team planned to reorganise the business, in parallel with a revitalised brand initiative. While Identica was given a 'clean sheet of paper' to 're-launch' this famous brand, it was felt that the history and pedigree of the organisation was key to the development of the Brand idea. It was decided not only to evolve the existing identity, but to also create a new visual language that would encompass all theme parks, merchandise, retail, publishing, music and the film studios.

The creative talent at Universal was a huge influence on the success of the re-branding, including the famed architect Rem Koolhaas (who endorsed Identica's ideas), while he himself was working on the masterplan for the development of the Hollywood studio theme park complex. Peters said, "that to sit in a cinema or to watch a film on TV from Universal Studios and see the 21-second Universal animation and the sonic brand working in sync made him feel very proud of all the work that was done over a two year period." "That project" he says, "was one of the most explosive (politically) and exciting (creatively) assignments I have worked on in many years."

The Johnnie Walker brand is one of the most famous whisky brands in the world, with the striding man, one of the most well-known icons in that sector. The original symbol of the striding man was created around 1908. But it was felt that in the quest to grow the brand worldwide a more contemporary look was required. The move from the original to the new was a brave move by the brand's team. The new 'icon', along with new signature and evolved packaging was part of a three year branding and packaging design programme.

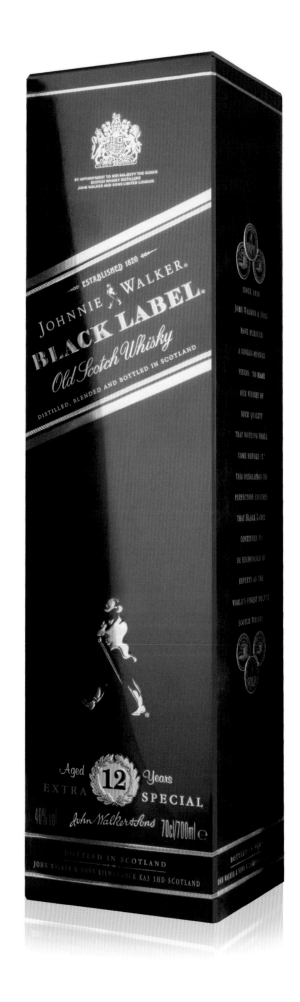

274

Captain Morgan is one of the largest Rum brands in the world. Over a three year period, Identica worked on the Captain Morgan brand, including new products—e.g. Tattoo and the recently launched Morgan Spice. This was an extremely complex job, since the intention was to retain all the attributes of the "beloved Captain character", adapting it to a more contemporary look and feel—from the old (bottom left) to the new (bottom right).

277

Conad is one of the largest supermarket chains in Italy. Identica worked for over seven years, to re-design every part of its private label. This was an extremely demanding project with some of the work being designed and produced within 14 days. Yet the Conad clients embraced great work, and this made the project one of the most stimulating in the complex world of private label packaging.

278

*DanceEast is a small
dance company based
in East Anglia, UK.
This new identity is
part of the rebranding
exercise to support
a major promotional
effort to attract finance
in support of all
DanceEast's activities,
including its own theatre
and dance studios.*

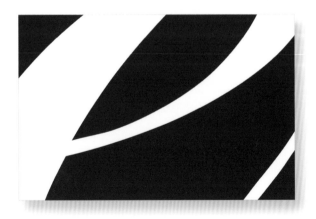

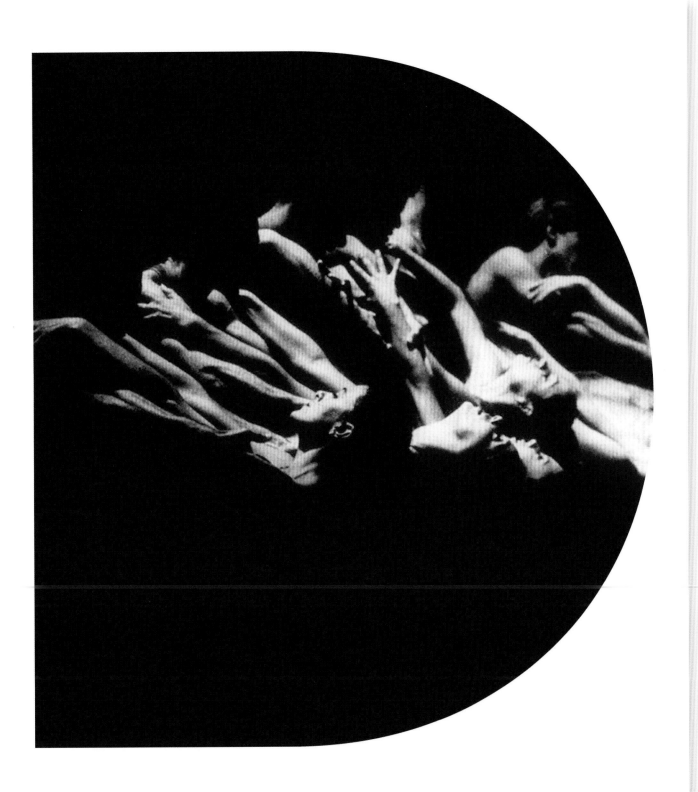

 DanceEast

Contemporary Dance 10.06.07
BRINGING THE HIGHEST QUALITY DANCE
OPPORTUNITIES TO THE EAST OF ENGLAND

Presant luptatum zzril delenit augue duis dolore te feugait nulla facilisi,
consectetuer adipiscing elit, sed diam nonummy nibh euismod tincidun.

Flagman is one of Russia's largest selling mid-price vodka brands. The brand has traditionally had a naval heritage, both in terms of colour and iconography. Like most brands in the sector, new entrants have adopted a more aggressive look and feel. This prompted Flagman, to completely review its position within its 2007 relaunch, 'remixing' many of the elements of the original design, with the introduction of a new glass bottle. The range has now regained its recognition and position in this very competitive sector.

Simon Seaton, a property lawyer, together with his partner, decided to launch a new business specialising in high-speed conveyancing. They recognised that the importance of building a brand, even at the beginning of a new business was key to realising their objectives, especially in a sector that has not traditionally felt the need to communicate. They required a name and brand identity that was different to set them apart from their 'competition'.

Fridays

284

Fridays

PROPERTY LAWYERS

David Sampson
Marketing Manager

8-16 Cromer Street
London
WC1H 8LH

dl +44 (0) 20 7239 1368
m +44 (0) 78 9409 6324
f   +44 (0) 87 0487 2859
e   davidsa@fridaysmove.com
w   fridaysmove.com

Cromer Street London WC1H 8LH   (Registered Office same)
(0)845 644 0337   F +44 (0)207 278 5486   DX 37900 Kings Cross
& Licensed Conveyancer: Simon Seaton   Dir: Natasha Bhatia
ys Property Lawyers Limited trading as 'Fridays'   Company No. 5403952
s is regulated by the 'Council for Licensed Conveyancers' to Provide Conveyancing Services

We use 100% recycled paper – do you?

Ocean Spray is a
world famous brand.
Craisins (opposite
below right) was
originally launched in
the UK with a US pack
design appropriate
to the baking sector
(bottom right), where
it enjoyed great
success. However,
the marketing team at
Ocean Spray decided
that the real opportunity
for this product was
to reposition it and
enhance its position
as a natural snack in
a different category.
The brief for the
Identica team was
that the 'new snack'
was to be part of
children's lunch boxes
and for after-school
healthy snacking, with
a look and feel that
enhanced its position
in this 'new' category.

The company now
known as Passaggio
began its life as SSG
(Schweizerische
Speisewagen-
Gesellschaft) a supplier
of food for the Swiss
travel industry. Working
directly with Peter
Herzog, their CEO—the
idea was to create a
totally new brand, as
the SSG banner was
no longer able to carry
the weight of their
expanding business
and was seen as being
rather negative in a very
competitive market.
The new name, the
new icon and a totally
new brand identity was
enthusiastically received
by all its customers
and stakeholders and
has now been sold to
a competitor which still
retains the Passaggio
name, look and feel.

288

PharmaMed is one of Russia's largest manufacturers of vitamin supplements for men, women and children. Over the years the company had grown dramatically, but now felt that they were in need of a totally new, consistent look and feel for all their packaging. The key was to create a range of simple and bold packaging designs that in the crowded supermarkets formed a 'banner' of PharmaMed products that could be instantly recognised.

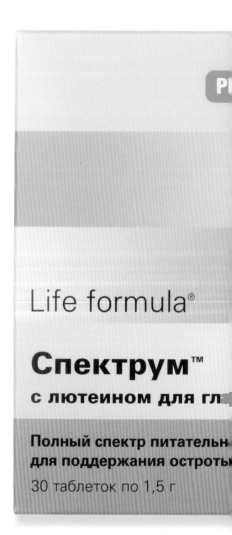

PharmaMed®

Lady's formula®

Антистресс™

Натуральное успокаивающее
средство для женщин

30 таблеток по 0,85 г

PharmaMed®

Kid's formula®

Ацидофилис-
Бифидум™
плюс витамин C

Для нормализации
микрофлоры кишечника
у детей и подростков
30 жевательных таблеток по 1,3 г

ADD WATER KEEP COOL DRY NATURALLY

LEVI'S 501 THE ORIGINAL SHRINK-TO-FIT JEANS

When Identica acquired Tango, Levi's was an important part of the Tango client list, and the combined Tango/Identica teams worked on all in-store promotions over a number of years. With so many different configurations of point of sale, the key issue was in-store flexibility for Levi's and its retail customers.

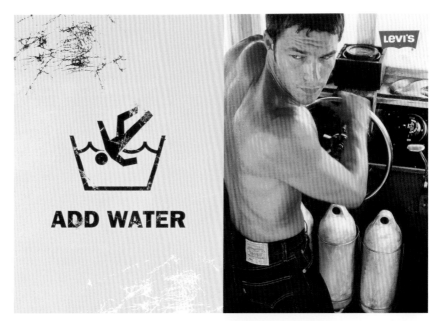

Over a number of years the Identica team worked with Planters on the development of a variety of its products. This particular project was one of the favourites of the design team at Identica, given the challenge of it being designed and artworked within five days.

Emphasising the word nuts (in peanuts), the design and production team sourced stock photography to create an eccentric packaging presentation.

295

Xtreme Information
is led by chairman
John Gordon. Xtreme
Information captures
and archives over
25,000 TV and press
advertisements every
month from over 60
countries, as well as
cinema, radio, outdoor
and internet banner
ads. The identity
has helped to create
immense interest with
a new network of
potential customers.
The client wanted the
new look and feel to
be creatively edgy and
different from that of
its competitors.

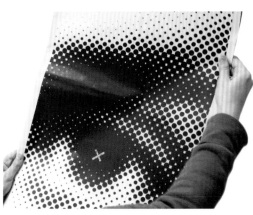

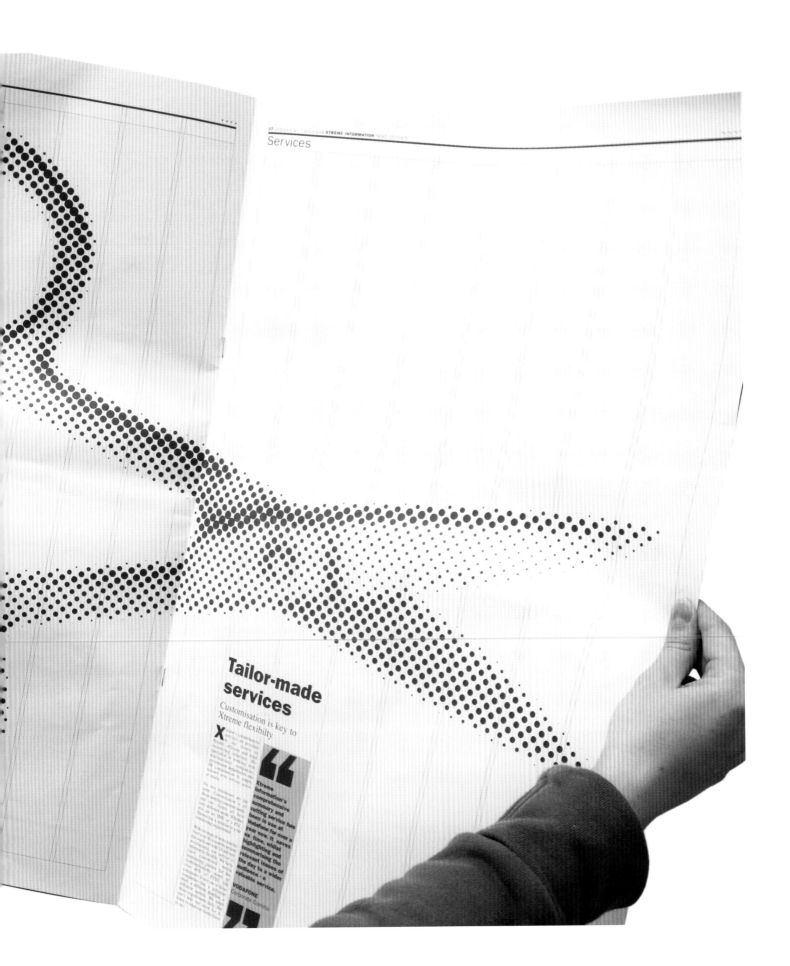

Tailor-made services

Customisation is key to Xtreme flexibilty

X treme customises services to provide clients the greatest choice and flexibility in selecting, viewing and tailoring content. As customised workflow, with content alignment and integration with your workflow, drive benefits at many levels.

At the forefront of any Customisation is the time. Customisation can help drive efficiencies and save considerable effort. Whether you are an SME or a FTSE monitoring a diverse range of industries, Customisation is key.

With a range of services available, including a news viewing tool that allows you to select, view and tailor content, customisable workflow, and to ensure clients can easily access the content they need, Xtreme provide the greatest flexibility and efficiencies possible.

FTSE 100 to FTSE 40 firms have the same...

> **Xtreme Information's comprehensive summary and cutting service has been in use at Vodafone for over a year now. It saves us time, whilst highlighting and summarising the relevant issues of the day to a wider audience - a valuable service.**
>
> **VODAFONE**
> Corporate Comms

New identities, branding and names for a variety of Identica clients.

First row, left to right:
• Leumi—new brand identity for Israel's leading bank.
• Mediarena—identity and name for a Swiss portal.
• Astra—new identity for a Diamond company.
• At Bristol—naming and logo for a millennium project in Bristol.
• Kitchen & Pantry—new identity for a coffee shop in Notting Hill Gate.

Second row, left to right:
• Life—new identity for a Russian bank.
• One 2 One—new identity and naming for a mobile telephone business.
• Discover—identity for a children's centre in East London.
• ICO—new identity for a worldwide satellite.
• The Marketing Society—new logo.

KITCHEN & PANTRY

scover
the children's discovery centre

ICO

THE MARKETING SOCIETY

Campbell's Soup is one of the largest companies in its sector in the UK. It decided to appraise its look and feel in the increasingly competitive retail market by repositioning the brand from its old packaging to this new presentation (right).

Working with architects
Foster + Partners
and HOK LOBB, the
Identica team won
the pitch for the new
brand identity for this
iconic stadium. The
three shapes making
up the logo formed
a visual language for
all promotion, while
the logo exquisitely
symbolised the design
of the stadium itself. A
key part of the project
was the signage system
that now forms an
important part for all
directions to the seating
and restaurant areas in
the stadium.

WEMBLEY

STADIUM

icesave

PART OF LANDSBANKI, REYKJAVIK, ICE

This Icesave project is deliberately the last case history in the Yes Logo book. It encapsulates and points the way, according to Peters, to the future in the world of brand and brand communication. Landsbanki, one of Iceland's largest banks, decided to launch an online savings product initially in the UK, but with an eye to a bigger international market. Identica was commissioned to create and develop a new brand and total brand communication to support this. Research indicated that although similar competitive products were relatively successful there was a degree of scepticism and nervousness for a new product (albeit with a generous interest rate) especially from a bank based in another country. The key strategic issue was to develop a brand that was easy to understand (by way of a big communication idea) and that would be consistent across all media. It became clear through the research that the naturalness, purity and perceived simplicity of Iceland was a key factor in the development of the name Icesave. This was led by the client team (CEO Mark Sismey-Durrant and his marketing director Alan Gilmour) to be the most exciting approach. This concept, with the colourful overlapping lettering for the logo and its distinct personality, has been applied to all communication including online, print advertising, posters, promotions—such as London Taxis. The initiative has been an enormous success, both in terms of new customers and financial return. All targets have been exceeded and, as of 2008, Icesave, in just under two years, has achieved huge recognition with this bold and innovative approach.

e.co.uk

ND

...ching!

...ccess Savings Account. We guarantee
...2011 and at least match it until May 2013.

icesave.co.uk
PART OF LANDSBANKI, REYKJAVIK, ICELAND

Darling.

The Chancellor may want lower interest rates, but our savers don't.
Open an Icesave Fixed Rate Savings Account today.

icesave.co.uk
PART OF LANDSBANKI, REYKJAVIK, ICELAND

...ainer.

...save Fixed Rate Savings Account today.

icesave.co.uk
PART OF LANDSBANKI, REYKJAVIK, ICELAND

Gobsmacked.

The only surprises you get with an Icesave Easy Access Savings Account are nice ones. Like our guarantee
to beat the Bank of England Base Rate by at least 0.35% until May 2011 and at least match it until May 2013.

icesave.co.uk
PART OF LANDSBANKI, REYKJAVIK, ICELAND

305

Designer Index

Page 25
Jefferson's
—Michael Peters

Page 26
Festival of Britain logo
—Abram Games

Page 27
RoSPA
—Arnold Rothholz

Page 28
Gillette
—Tom Eckersley

Page 29
GPO
—Hans Schleger

Page 30
London Transport
—Harry Beck

Page 31
Arnold Cook
—Michael Peters

Page 33
*Man with the
Golden Arm*
—Saul Bass;
Harper's Bazaar
—Henry Wolf;
McCalls
—Otto Storch

Page 34 IBM
—Paul Rand

Page 38
Change of Address
—Michael Peters;
Yale project
—Michael Peters

Page 39
B'nai B'rith
—Michael Peters;
Yale Law Report
—Michael Peters

Page 40
Weniger Lärm
—Joseph Müller-
Brockmann;
Portfolio
—Alexei Brodovitch;
Schweiz
—Herbert Matter

Page 42
Alphabetica™
—Michael Peters

Page 44
Yale Project
—Michael Peters

Page 46
Harvey Probber
Advertisement
—George Lois

Page 47
Greetings Cards
—Michael Peters;
Time Magazine
—Michael Peters

Page 48
Harris and Sloan
—Michael Peters

Page 49
CBS Mural
—Lou Dorfsman

Page 50
The Last Angry Man
—Michael Peters

Page 51
George Rose Entertains
—Michael Peters

Page 52
"RX for the Losers"
—Michael Peters

Page 53
"On a note
of understanding"
—Michael Peters

Page 54
KickOff 65
—Michael Peters

Page 56
*What happened to
Goldwater?*
—Michael Peters

Page 68
Birds Eye Foods
—Keith Bowen
and photographer
James Agar

Page 69
Birds Eye Hidden Centres
—Michael Peters

Page 69
Birds Eye Cheesecakes
—Jane Seager
and photographer
Tony Copeland

Page 70
Winsor & Newton
—Geoff Hockey/
John Gorham

Page 71
White Elephant
Sandwich
—Michael Peters

Page 71
Cotman
—Jan Stringer/
Michael Peters

Page 72
Abbey Life
—Michael Peters/
Peter Brookes;
Bull Hatcher
—Howard Milton

Page 74
Spong
—Howard Milton

Page 75
Ormo
—Michael Peters/
Tony Meuwissen

Page 77
Virgin
—Howard Milton

Page 78
J Cloth
—Jane Seager

Page 79
Gauloises
—Fred Fehlau

Page 80
Penhaligon's
—Madeleine Bennett

Page 80
Yellow Can Company
—Bev Whitehead

Page 81
Lacroix
—Klaus Schultheiss

Page 82
Artus
—Klaus Schultheiss

Page 83
Batchelors Soups
—Bev Whitehead

Page 84
Packaged for Success
—Michael Peters;
Logoptics
—Michael Peters

Page 85
Thresher Exhibition
—Michael Peters

Page 87
International Coffee
Organization
—Madeleine Bennett

Pages 88, 89
Adams
—Bev Whitehead/
Howard Milton/
Claire Tuthill

Page 90
Post International
Productions
—Glenn Tutssel/
Bush Hollyhead

Page 91
Hayter
—Mark Wickens;
Creative Excellence in
Newspaper Advertising
—Madeleine Bennett;
CC Soft Drinks
—Madeleine Bennett

Pages 92, 93
Snopake
—Mark Wickens

Page 94
Chesterfield Socks
—Michael Peters

Page 95
Louis Féraud
—Michael Peters

Pages 96, 97
Elsenham
—Madeleine Bennett

Page 98
Piper's Whisky
—Madeleine Bennett

Page 99
Fine Fare Dark Rum
—Glenn Tutssel

Page 100
Yorkshire Tea
—Fred Fehlau/
Pat Perchal

Page 101
Taylors of Harrogate
—Pat Perchal

Pages 101–105
Winsor & Newton Inks
—Geoff Hockey/
Michael Peters

Pages 106, 107
Winsor & Newton
Alkyd Colours
—Bev Whitehead

Pages 108, 109
Winsor & Newton
Calendar
—Michael Peters/
Jan Stringer

Pages 110, 111
Winsor & Newton
Poster Colours
—Howard Milton

Pages 112, 113
Winsor & Newton
Advertising
—Michael Peters

Pages 114–117
Brocks Fireworks
—Claire Tuthill/
Geoff Halpin

Pages 118–123
Penhaligon's
—Madeleine Bennett

Pages 124, 125
Michael Barrie
—Madeleine Bennett/
Gerry O'Dwyer

Pages 126, 127
Yellow Can Company
—Bev Whitehead

Pages 128, 129
AF Cricketer's
—Howard Milton/
Michael Peters/
Jooce Garrett

Pages 130, 131
Seagram/Crocodillo
—Jim Groark

Pages 132, 133
International
Coffee Organization
—Madeleine Bennett

Pages 134, 135
Thresher
—Bev Whitehead/
Howard Milton

Pages 136, 137
Lyons the bakers
—Mark Wickens

Pages 138, 139
Fürstenberg
—Madeleine Bennett

Pages 140, 141
Hamleys
—Michael Peters

Pages 150, 151
Michael Peters Group
—Jackie Vicary/
Michael Peters

Page 152
Sculpture
—Takenobu Igarashi

Page 153
Olaf Street Interiors
—John McAslan/
Troughton McAslan

Pages 154–159
Signs and Doors
—listed on Page 153

Page 160
Arthur Scargill/Maggie
Thatcher Cartoon
—Peter Brookes

Pages 162, 163
Michael Peters Group
Annual Report
—David Stocks

Page 164
Hawkeye Studios
—Klaus Schultheiss

Page 165
Isabel Bird
—Paul Browton

Page 166
BP Oil can
—Glenn Tutssel/
Garrick Hamm

Page 167
Shell Oil can
—Glenn Tutssel/
Graham Thompson

Page 168
Burton Annual Report
—David Stocks

Page 169
Sandeman Port
—Pat Perchal;
Royal Mail Stamps
—Mark Pearce

Page 171
K-Cider
—Glenn Tutssel/
Jonathan Ford

Page 173
Alliance and Leicester
—Paul Browton

Page 175
Conservative Party Logo
—Jonathon Ford/
Michael Peters

Page 176
Illustration of
Michael Peters
—Ralph Steadman

Page 178
Design Business Group
—Glenn Tutssel

Pages 180–185
Peters/Duffy Book
—Glenn Tutssel/
Joe Duffy/Garrick
Hamm/Sharon Werner/
Haley Johnson/
Chuck Carlson

Page 186
Michael Peters Group/
Duffy Design Groups
—Fallon McElligot

Page 189
Sculpture of
Michael Peters
—Jake McCall

Pages 190–191
Cordon Bleu
—Glenn Tutssel

Page 192
Joseph Perfume
—Madeleine Bennett

Page 193
Törq
—Paul Mullins/Rob Davie;
Wardrobe Perfume
—Madeleine Bennett

Page 194
Ross Radio
—Graham Thompson

Page 195
Ross Electronics
—Karen Welman/
Graham Thompson

Pages 196–199
Sweet Factory
—Paul Mullins/
Rob Davie/Bill
Carden-Horton

Page 200, 201
Leopardi Ice Cream
—Mark Wickens

Page 202
Royal Mail Stamps
—Mark Pearce

Pages 204, 205
Georgio Armani
—Madeleine Bennett

Page 206
Tsaritska Vodka
—Glenn Tutssel

Page 207
Carling
—Garrick Hamm

Pages 208–211
Arthur Bell & Sons
—Glenn Tutssel

Pages 212, 213
Martell Packaging
—Mark Pearce/
Glenn Tutssel

Pages 214, 215
Clarke's Icecream
—Glenn Tutssel

Pages 216, 217
Lyons Maid Icecream
—Garrick Hamm

Pages 218, 219
Consilia
—Pat Perchall/
Barry Gilliebrand

Pages 220–223
Bremworth Carpets
—Paul Browton;
British Museum
—Madeleine Bennett;
ESRB
—Glenn Tutssel;
Powergen
—Michael Peters Group;
National Children's
Bureau
—Madeleine Bennett;
Danisco
—Michael Peters Group;

Fort William Fish Co
—Michael Peters;
TEN
—Madeleine Bennett;
DH Evans
—Madeleine Bennett;
Eurohub
—Bill Carden-Horton;
Safeguard
—Glenn Tutssel;
MD Foods
—Tony Blurton;
Leonard
—Madeleine Bennett;
Four Corners
—Glenn Tutssel;
V&A
—Glenn Tutssel;
Ideas
—Madeleine Bennett;
Touche Remnant
—Paul Browton;
Body
—Madeleine Bennett;
BBC
—Glenn Tutssel/
Mark Pearce;
ATS
—Glenn Tutssel

Pages 224, 225
Michael Peters' Pop Up
Annual Report
—Peter Chodel

Pages 226, 227
Michael Peters
Annual Reports
—Jackie Vicary/
Peter Chodell/
Jonathan Davies/
Kate Hutchison

Page 228
The Science Museum
Annual Report
—Jonathan Davies

Page 229
Prestwick Annual Report
—Peter Chodel;
Saxton Bamfylde
Brochure
—Paul Bagshawe

Pages 230, 231
Seagram Annual Report
—Jackie Vicary

Pages 232, 233
Guyerzeller Brochure
—David Stocks

Page 248
Lounge Lizard
—Michael Peters/
Julie Morris

Page 249
Nabarro
—Dan Calderwood;
Erin
—Chris Riley

Page 250
Ginzing and Red Devil
—Jimmy Yang

Page 252
Russian Standard
—Chris Barber

Page 254
Aeroflot
—Carole Laugier

Page 257
Nike
—Dana Robertson/
John Geery/Hamish
Campbell

Pages 260, 261
E-max
—Jimmy Yang/TNC

Pages 262, 263
Russian Standard
—Chris Barber

Pages 264, 265
Smirnov
—Nina Fortune/
Geoff Halpin

Pages 266, 267
Chivas Regal
—Geoff Halpin/
Ginger Tilley

Pages 268, 269
Nabarro
—Dan Calderwood

Pages 270, 271
Nabarro
—Dan Calderwood/
Richard Foster/
Michael Peters

Pages 272, 273
Universal
—Jimmy Yang/
Geoff Halpin

Pages 274, 275
Johnnie Walker
—Jimmy Yang

Pages 276, 277
Captain Morgan Rum
—Chris Barber/
Geoff Halpin

Page 277
Morgan's Spiced
—Ian Firth

Page 278, 279
Conad
—Jimmy Yang/Chris
Barber/Melissa Smith

Pages 280, 281
DanceEast
—Dana Robertson/
Ian Firth

Pages 282, 283
Flagman
—Chris Riley/John
Hughes

Pages 284, 285
Fridays
—Dana Robertson

Pages 286, 287
Ocean Spray
—Dana Robertson/
John Hughes

Pages 288, 289
Passaggio
—Nina Fortune/
Geoff Halpin

Page 290, 291
PharmaMed
—Chris Riley/
Roger Ackroyd

Pages 292, 293
Levi's
—Glen Harrison/
Kieran Malloy

Pages 294, 295
Planters
—Chris Riley

Pages 296, 297
Xtreme Information
—David Jones/
Geoff Halpin

Page 298, 299
Leumi
—Ginger Tilley/
Geoff Halpin/
Michael Peters;
Mediarena
—Roger Hardy;
Astra
—Dana Robertson;
At Bristol
—Carole Laugier;
Kitchen & Pantry
—Nina Fortune;
Life
—David Jones;
One2One
—Jimmy Yang;
Discover
—Jimmy Yang;
ICO
—Lisa Feitelson/
Geoff Halpin;
The Marketing Society
—Geoff Halpin

Pages 300, 301
Campbell's Soups
—Chris Riley

Pages 302, 303
Wembley Stadium
—Jimmy Yang/
Roger Hardy/
Geoff Halpin

Pages 304–307
Icesave
—Ian Firth/Dan
Calderwood/
Richard Foster

Index

4AD 76

A
Abbey Life Assurance 72, 151
ABC Television 39
Acanchi 188
Adams Childrenswear 88, 89
George Adams 29
Michael Adams 89
Addison 179, 185, 188
Aeroflot 13, 254, 258
Aerosols International 83
AF Cricketer's Gin 84, 128, 129, 145
Otl Aicher 84
Josef Albers 11, 34, 39, 40, 41
Virginia Alexander 160, 161
Woody Allen 11
Zelig 11, 12, 13
Alliance and Leicester and Alliance and Leicester Building Societies 173
Allied Breweries 86
Allied International Designers 79, 87, 149, 185–187
American Institute of Graphic Arts (AIGA) 181, 185
Amnesty International 253
Amos and Partners 68
Ted Andresakes 47, 49
Gareth Andrews-Jones 253, 258
Annual Reports Ltd 72, 73, 74, 75, 86, 149, 164, 173
Michelangelo Antonioni *La Notte* 32
Sam Antupit 33, 152, 153
Apple Macintosh 152
Arienheller 83
Armani 205

Bernard Armstrong 37
Art Deco 81
Art Directors Club of Germany 83
Art Directors Club of New York 71
Arthur Andersen & Co 187
Arthur Bell & Sons 208, 209
Artus 83
Neil Ashley 69, 250
ATS 222
Nick Austin 188
Tom Austin 253, 254, 256, 258
Austria 163
Autumn/Winter Football Schedule 54, 55

B
B'nai B'rith 38, 39
Babycham 86
David Bailey 9
Ban the Bomb 17
Bank Leumi 256, 298
Barmitzvah 22
Chris Barber 256
Michael Barrie 83, 124, 125
Stuart Barron 73
Tim Barson 255
Bartle Bogle Hegarty (BBH) 58, 253, 258
Harold Bartram 32
Baskerville 152
Saul Bass 17, 33, 71, 152, 153
Batchelors Food 83, 86
Bauhaus 11, 26, 34, 38, 40, 86, 164
Bay of Pigs 41
Herbert Bayer 39
Brian Bayliss 170, 191
BBC 22, 75, 168, 172, 174, 174, 177, 223
BBC National Design Awards 174

Richard Beaumont 70
The Beatles 9, 12, 17, 49, 57, 59
Sgt. Pepper 9
Harry Beck 11, 17, 30, 31
Beethoven 21
Madeleine (Maddy) Bennett 73, 81, 83, 169, 170
Jimmy Benson 179
Benton and Bowles 163
Berlin Wall 185, 245
Bill Bernbach 49
John Bernbach 49
Bezalel School of Art, Jerusalem 249
Biba 81
Isabel Bird 165, 173
Birds Eye Foods 68, 69, 70, 250
Derek Birdsall 17, 32, 79
Black Monday 185
Black Mountain College 40
Black Wednesday 245
Mischa Black 17
John Blackburn 63
Tony Blair 255
Peter Blake 57
Blue Science Ltd 250, 252, 253
Blue Way 81
Blueprint 177
Boase Massimi Pollitt 9, 67
Bodoni 152
James Bond 57
Bonjour Tristesse 33
Bonnie and Clyde 9
Keith Bowen 72
David Bowie 63
Boy George 145, 170
BP 145, 166
Brand House WTS 188
Brand New (Product Origination) Ltd 86, 149, 164, 172, 251
Brand New Product Development Ltd 172, 188
Mike Branson 166, 188
Georges Braque 26
Sarah Bratt 253

John Brimacombe 63
Alan Bristow 253
Britain Can Make It 175
British Airways (BA) 168, 173, 222, 258
British Museum 220
Brixton race riots 87
Brocks Fireworks 114, 117
Alexei Brodovitch 11, 34, 38, 39, 40
Edgar Bronfman Jr 227
Peter Brookes 72, 160
Bob Brooks 34
Robert Brownjohn 34
Paul Browton 73, 173
Duncan Bruce 179
Robin Budish 179
Bull Hatcher/Bull Hatcher Haulage 72
Will Burtin 39
Burton Group Annual Report 168
The Burton Group 168, 173, 227
John Butcher 174, 252

C
Cadbury's Smash 9
Cafemax 260, 261
James Callaghan 87
Margaret Calvert 57
Campaign 59
Campbell's Foods 249, 300, 301
Canterbury 163
Captain Morgan 277, 278
Bill Carden-Horton 172
Carling 206, 207
Chuck Carlson 179
Debbie Carter (née Catford) 73, 76, 188
Giovanni Caselli 72
Philip Castle 71, 104, 105
Fidel Castro 29
Cato Peters O'Brien 57
Ken Cato 153
Mac Cato 57

CC Soft Drinks Ltd 91
Central Electricity Generating Board 220
Change of Address Card 38
Arthur (AL) Chattell 34, 35, 37, 41, 153
Ivan Chermayeff 152
Chernobyl 178
Chesterfield Socks 94, 95
Chicago 34, 40, 185
Chivas Regal 231, 266, 267
Peter Chodel 151, 161, 163, 188
Sir Winston Churchill 57
Seymour Chwast 70, 152, 153
Cincinnati 56, 57
Civilian Clothing 1941 21
Henry Clarke 214–217
The Clash 87
Stafford Cliff 153
Clio Award 170
Clydesdale Bank 251
Cockade Ltd 165, 179, 187
Arthur Cohen 49, 56
College of Further Education, Dunstable 37
Collett, Dickenson, Pearce (CDP) 57, 58, 67, 69, 75
Ron Collins 59
Columbia Broadcasting Systems (CBS) 12, 46, 47, 49, 51, 53, 54, 55. 56, 57, 68, 77
"commercial Bauhaus" 11, 40, 86, 164
Communication Arts 26
Communication Arts Award of Excellence 170
Communiqué 26
Communism, fall of 145, 170
Conad 278, 279
Concorde 13, 173, 188
Terence Conran 57, 79, 87, 175, 185
Conservative Party 13, 73, 174, 175, 243, 255
Conservative Party identity, new 175
Conservative Party logo, old 174, 175
Consilia 218, 219
Container Corporation of America 33
Pamela Conway 86, 168
Arnold Cook 31, 32
Cool Britannia 255
Cooper-Hewitt Museum 83

Gary Cooper 26
Cordon Bleu 170, 190, 191
Cossette Communication Group 237, 258, 259
Council of Industrial Design (CoID) 175
The Country Diary of an Edwardian Lady 12, 81
County Education Authority 34
Crabtree & Evelyn 81
Alan Cracknell 57
Crafts Council 179
Craisins 286, 287
Cramer Saatchi 9, 67
Ross Cramer 58, 59
Craton Lodge & Knight 183, 243
Creative Excellence in Newspaper Advertising, The Annual Award 91
Creative Review 25, 77
Crocodillo 86, 130, 131
Crosby/Fletcher/Forbes 25, 58, 63, 81
Jim Cross 153
Cuba 29, 41
Cuban Missile Crisis 41
Edward Cullinan 258
Keith Cunningham 32, 34
Curious 255

D
Daily Mirror 11, 34, 149
Terence Daly 72
DanceEast 280, 281
Danisco 220
The Danish Dairy Cooperative 222
Rob Davie 165, 172, 187
David Davies 152, 153
George Davies 175
Alain Delon 32
Mike Dempsey 153
Catherine Deneuve 11
Department of Trade and Industry (DTI) 174, 177, 243
Design 13, 175
Design Business Association (DBA) 13, 178
Design Business Group 178
Design Council 177
Design Effectiveness Awards 178

Design for Our Future Selves 259
Design for Recovery 13, 177
Design Matters 177
Design Museum, London 177
Designer 75, 79, 151
Design and Art Directors Association (D&AD) 57, 58, 59, 70, 71, 76, 81, 145, 161, 169, 170, 174, 178, 254
DesignWeek 13, 177, 179, 246
Diagnostics Market Research 165, 187
Dick Barton; Special Agent 22
Franklin W Dixon 22
Dockers 253
Ivan Dodd 32
Dome of Discovery 28
Paul Donovan 253, 256
Terence Donovan 9, 59
Lou Dorfsman 12, 46, 47, 49, 77
Dromoland Castle, Ireland 163
Duffy Design Group 174, 179, 181, 185, 187
Joe Duffy 179, 187, 188
Duke of Edinburgh 258
Duke of Edinburgh Award 243
Duke of Edinburgh's crest 81
Bob Dylan, "Blowin' in the Wind" 41

E
Charles Eames 12, 46
Charles and Ray Eames, Mathematica exhibition 46
Tom Eckersley 28, 30, 34, 152, 153
The Ed Sullivan Show 57
Dr/Prof Gordon Edge 164, 252
EH Gomme and Sons 26
Alvin Eisenman 34, 41
Avi Eisenstein 152, 153, 249
El Greco 22
Ella Fitzgerald 32
Duke Ellington 32
Tony Elliot 59
Elsenham Jams and Preserves Limited 96, 97

Emax 258, 260, 261
Enterprise 247
The Entertainment Network 220
Ergo 255
Erin 249, 251
Esquire 33
ESRB 220
European Economic Community 73
Eurythmics 170

F
Fallon McElligot 179, 181, 187
Pat Fallon 179, 181
Ian Farnfield 188
Susie Faux 193
Fred Fehlau 81
Lord Basil Feldman 174
Federico Fellini, La Dolce Vita 32
Sophie Fenton 255
The Face 255
Festival of Britain 11, 25, 26, 28
Derek Fieldman 253
Fine Fare's Dark Rum 99, 169
Fine Fare 99, 168, 169
First Things First manifesto 58
Fitch 79
Fitch-RS 179, 185
Rodney Fitch 79, 175
Jim Fitzpatrick 72
Flagman 283
Mike Flanagan 169
Alan Fletcher 11, 34, 38, 71, 79, 80, 152, 153, 165
Fletcher/Forbes/Gill 12, 34, 58, 81
Yona Fogel 256
Colin Forbes 34, 152
Jonathan Ford 160, 161, 163, 164, 170, 179
Fortune 34
Foster + Partners 259, 302
Foster's Menswear 163
David Freedland 29, 34
Jonathan Freedland 319
Michael Freedland 34
Freedom Marches 41
French, Cruttenden, Osborne (FCO) 135
Richard French 79
Fridays Solicitors 284, 285
Betty Friedan 41
The Feminine Mystique 41

Adrian Frutiger 39
Fürstenberg 138, 139
Futura 152

G
G-Plan 26, 29
Abram Games 26, 29
Ken Garland 30, 58
Jooce Garrett 84
Gatorade 253
Gauloises 79, 81
Generics Group 164,
166, 178, 250–252
*George Rose
Entertains* 51
Gesell Institute of Child
Development, Yale
University 41–43
Julian Gibbs Ltd 74
Gill Bold 152
Gill Light 152
Bob Gill 33, 63
John Gillard 9, 32,
172, 178
Gillette 28
Fiona Gilmore 145,163,
166, 173, 174, 178, 188
Alan Gilmour 304, 305
Gin Zing 250, 252
Milton Glaser 58, 70,
79, 181
Jeff Glazer 161
Ruth Goddard 255
The Golden Egg 58
Barry Goldwater 56
John Gordon 296. 297
John Gorham 63, 71,
104–107
Fritz Gottschalk 153
Graphics International 253
Lynette Grass 86
Alistair Grant 169, 226,
227
Milner Gray 17
Great Exhibition 25
April Greiman 152,
153, 161
Jim Groark 86
George Grosz 29
Guinness 138, 139, 254
Guyerzeller 232, 233

H
Bill Haley 33
Sir Ralph Halpern 13,
173, 226, 227
Geoff Halpin 248, 253

Hambrecht Terrell
International 174, 179,
185, 187
Garrick Hamm 179
Lucy Hammer 38
Lionel Hampton 32
Harper's Bazaar 33,
39, 40
Harris and Sloan 49
Glen Harrison 255
Harvard University 40
Harvey Probber 46, 47
Aubrey Hastings-Smith
86, 160
Hawkeye Studios Ltd
86, 149, 164
Haymarket Publishing
172, 178
Sir John Hegarty 9, 58,
172, 178, 253, 258
Heldenbräu 83
Helvetica 17, 39
FHK Henrion 29, 152
Tony Hertz 149, 151
Peter Herzog 288, 289
David Hillman 11, 17,
30, 32, 37, 39, 56, 71,
152, 153, 168, 169,
187, 243, 244
Eileen Hillman 30
Hillsdown Holdings 187
George Him 29
Charles Hobson 34
Jeff Hockey 71
David Hockney 57, 63
Edouard Hoffman 39
HOK Lobb 259, 302, 303
Billie Holiday 32
Holt, Rinehart &
Winston 49, 56
Lena Horne 32
"House of Monsanto" 57
Barbara Hulanicki 57
Hundred Pipers Whisky
169
Felicity Hunt 244
Peter Hyde 252
Hyman Peters
Foundation 178, 179
Hayter 90, 91

I
i-D 255
IATA 258
IBM 34, 39
Icesave 304–307
Identica 13, 226, 227,
237, 243, 256, 257, 259,
261, 262, 266, 270–273,
276–279, 286, 287, 292,
293, 298, 299, 302–305

Identica Branding and
Design 237
Identica Partnership
244, 258, 259
Identica UK 237
IDEO 58
Idlewild Airport 38
Takenobu Igarashi 152
Inaria 255
The Independent 187
Indigo 255
Industrial Relations Act 74
Innovus 255
'Institute of Higher
Learning' 37
Interbrand 247, 258
International Coffee
Organisation 86, 87,
132, 133
IRA 63, 76
Isotype System 84
Norman Ives 34

J
Robin Jacques 72
Jaeger 75
Jefferson's Menswear
25
Jersey 163
Jewish Board of
Guardians 11, 26
John Nicholson
Associates 179
Johnnie Walker 248,
249, 274, 275
"Johnnie and Cola" 248
Johnson & Johnson 77
Haley Johnson 179
Kevin Johnson 254,
255
Lyndon B Johnson 56
Gray Jolliffe 243
Grace Jones 170
Joseph 170
Joseph Ettedgui 192,
193
Joseph Perfumes 192,
193
Journey into Space 22

K
K-Cider 171, 173
Tibor Kalman 181, 185
Wassily Kandinsky 26
Rory Kee 169
John F Kennedy 41
Stuart Kershaw 169

Kiev 21
Martin Luther King 17, 41
"I Have a Dream" 41
King's Cross tube
station fire 185
Kingsley Manton and
Palmer 58, 174
David Kingsley 58, 174
Jock Kinneir 57
Geoff Kirk 258
Paul Klee 26
Klein Peters 9, 58, 59, 67
Lou Klein 12, 34, 58,
59, 67, 71
Kraft Cheese Slices 78
Stanley Kubrick
A Clockwork Orange 74
Mervyn Kurlansky 153

L
L'Or 212, 213
Labour Party Red Rose
logo 174
Lacroix Soups 83
Fred Lambert 32
Martin Lambie-Nairn
161, 245
Brook Land 187, 243
Landor 247
Landsbank 304, 305
Paul Langsford 161,
165, 187, 188
Barry Lategan 74
Carole Laugier 237,
244, 251, 255, 258
Laura Ashley 81
Stan Laurel 174
Lee Cooper Jeans 29
Lee Jeans 179
Peggy Lee 32
Leopardi 200, 201
Annie Lennox 170
Levi's 253, 292, 293
Herb Levitt 49
Lewis Moberly 187,
188, 244, 250
Barbara Lewis 178
Mary Lewis 187
Lippincott and
Margulies 73
Liverpool 21
Loftleidir 37, 38
Logoptics Ltd 30, 84, 86
George Lois 46
Joan Lombardi 49
London Blitz 21
London Business
School 75
London College of
Printing (LCP) 77

London Fund Management Company 222, 223
London School of Printing and Graphic Arts (LSP) 9, 11, 17, 29, 30, 32, 34, 37, 39, 41, 70, 172
London Underground map 11, 30
Louis Féraud 94, 95
"Love, Money and Power" 185
Herb Lubalin 17, 49, 58
Elaine Lustig-Cohen 49, 56
Alvin Lustig 56
Luton News 25
Luton Pictorial 34, 36
Liz Lydiate 179, 187, 188
Lyons Corner House 28
Lyons Maid 214–217

M

Harold Macmillan 25, 57
Mademoiselle 39
Madonna 145
Magical Mystery Tour(s) 76, 161, 163, 254
Simon Majaro 75
John Major 187
Simon Manchipp 255
Alan Manham 72, 100, 105
Jane Mann 188
Romek Marber 57
Marcello Mastroianni 32
Marcello Minale 58, 71, 152, 153
Marketing 255
Ross Marks 194, 195
Brian Marshall 30
Thurgood Marshall 38
Martell 212, 213
John Massey 32
Lindsay Masters 172, 178
Herbert Matter 11, 34, 38–40
Andrew McCall 75, 80
Jake McCall 188
McCall's 33
John McConnell 63, 71, 152
Sherman McCoy 164
Kevin McGurk 255
Stuart McKay 255
Dorothy McKenzie 164, 178, 188
McKinsey 256, 260–265

McKnight Kauffer 124, 125
Fernando Medina 153
Tony Meeuwissen 70, 71
Mercury Communication 253
Metropolitan Police 161
Michael Manwaring 153
Michael Marriot 258
Michael Peters and Partners 12, 59, 63, 67–69, 70–72, 74, 75, 76–79, 80, 81, 83, 84, 86, 99–103, 118, 119, 130–133, 145, 149, 151, 152, 160, 163, 164, 165, 168–170, 172, 174, 178, 190, 191, 218, 219, 259
Michael Peters Corporate Literature 164
Michael Peters Financial Communications 165
Michael Peters Group 13, 128, 129, 149, 151–153, 160, 162, 164–166, 172, 175, 177–179, 181, 185, 187, 188, 194–197, 212, 213, 243, 244, 246, 251–253, 259
Michael Peters Group—Annual Senior Management Conference 173
Michael Peters Group Annual Report 224, 225
Michael Peters Group Pop-up Annual Report 224, 225
Michael Peters Group Thank You Annual Report 227
Michael Peters Ltd 187, 243, 245
Michael Peters Retail Ltd 165, 172, 187, 196, 197
Max Miedinger 39
Ian Miller 72
Millets 29
Howard Milton 76–78, 81, 84, 153, 163
Colin Millward 57
Minale Tattersfield & Partners 12, 58, 63, 160
Ministry of Food 22
Minneapolis Star Tribune 181
Bill Moggridge 58
László Moholy-Nagy 40
Monsanto-Chemstrand 57

Jean Moreau 32
MORI (Market & Opinion Research International) 151, 247
Julie Morris 244
Mozart 21
MTV 258
Müller-Brockmann 39, 40
Paul Mullins 165, 172
Mumm Champagne 230, 231
Quentin Murley 73
Jeremy Myerson 11

N

Nabarro 250, 268–271
Nabarro Nathanson 250, 268, 269
National Children's Bureau 220, 221
National Socialist regime 40
NBC 181
Neon 255
Otto Neurath 84
"New Advertising" 47
New Bauhaus 34, 40
New York 11, 12, 34, 40, 46, 47, 49, 56, 57, 68, 71, 77, 80, 83, 152, 174, 179, 188, 258
Newell and Sorrell 258
New Haven, Connecticut 34, 37, 38, 47
Next Big Thing 255
Nicholas Thirkell Associates 63
Nike 13, 253, 257
Lev Nikolau 258, 260, 261
NoOne, SomeOne 255
Bob Noorda 31
Northern Ireland 75, 76, 173
Jim Northover 58
Notting Hill race riots 87
Nova 17, 79

O

Dick O'Brien 57
Gerry O'Dwyer 73, 78, 83, 84
Karen O'Neill 251, 253, 255
Occhiali 204, 205

Ocean Spray 286, 287
Ogilvy Group 179
Bruno Oldani 153
Wally Olins 58, 175, 187
Vaughan Oliver 73, 76
"On a note of understanding" 53
"Operation Desert Storm" 245
Lee Harvey Oswald 41
Sarah Owens 13
Oxo 29

P

"Packaged for Success" 84, 86
Pack My Bag 255
PA Design Corporate Identity 165
Fred Palmer 38
Papert, Koenig, Lois (PKL) 46
Parfum de Jour 170
Paris 21, 74, 76, 163
Alan Parker 9, 12, 57
"Parklife" 255
Passaggio 288, 289
Passover 22
Pat Perchal 73, 169, 188
Adele and Gabriel Patashnik 21, 25
Art Paul 152, 153
John Pearce 57
Mark Pearce 160, 172, 174, 188
Pearlfisher 188
Alan Peckolick 80, 153
Penguin Books 57
William Henry Penhaligon 80
Penhaligon's 80, 81, 118–121, 145, 170
David Penny 81
Pentagram 11, 58, 79, 81, 87, 152, 165, 247
Perrier 178
Jo Peters 47, 76, 187, 244
Claire Peters 21
Elaine Peters 21, 25
Gary Peters 49, 243
Hyman Peters 21
Rosalind Peters 21, 25
Ross Peters 253
Sarah Peters 243
Lock Pettersen 160
PharmaMed 290, 291
Darryl Phillips 253
Di Picard 162
Pablo Picasso 22

Sheila Pickles 81
Abe Pievsky 21
Pievsky, Mr and Mrs Herschel 21
Piper's Scotch Whisky 98, 99
PJ Amos & Partners 63
Plakat Paints 28, 29
David Pocknell 152, 153
Porsche North America 179
Colin Porter 153
Post International Productions 90, 91
Post Office (Royal Mail) 169, 174, 202, 203
Powergen 220, 221
Elvis Presley 17, 34
Prince Charles and Lady Diana Spencer, wedding of 87
Prince Charles, Prince of Wales 170, 195
Prince of Wales Award for Innovation 243
Prince Philip Designer's Prize 258
The Princedale Group 187, 243
Princess Anne's Enterprise Britain 243
Lady Diana Spencer, Princess of Wales 87, 255
Profumo scandal 57
Push Pin Studio 70
David Puttnam 9, 12, 57, 59, 67
Chariots of Fire 57
The Killing Fields 57
Rita Pyzdrowski 84

Q
Mary Quant 57
Queen Victoria 80
Queen's Silver Jubilee 81

R
Peter Rae 253, 255
Ralph Lauren 179
Ralph Selby 152
Ayn Rand, *The Fountainhead* 26
Paul Rand 11, 17, 33, 34, 38–40, 44–47, 78, 165,
Raphael Rations Books 22

Peter Rauch 49, 153
Ravensbourne College of Art and Design 81
Ray Ban 253
Man Ray 11
RDA Organic 255
Reaganomics 164
Red Devil 250, 252
Reebok 253
Carolyn Reed 170
Rob Rees 249, 251
Research International 151
"return on innovation" (ROI) 168, 237
Reykjavik 38
Reynold Ruffins 70
Alex Reznokovitch 258, 260, 261, 264, 265
Rheims 163
Simon Rhind-Tutt 188
Stella Richmond 171
Chris Riley 250, 251, 253, 254, 255, 257
Arthur Robbins 104, 105
Dana Robertson 237, 247, 250, 251, 253, 255, 256, 258
David Robinson 253
Anita Roddick 161
Rolls Royce 258
'Rorschach Ink blot' 229
Jerry Rosentsweig 153
Ross Electronics 172, 177, 194, 195
Ross Radio 145, 172
Rotary Club 34
Hans Arnold Rothholtz 11, 26
Roust Inc 252, 256
Royal Academy 255
Royal College of Art 59, 259
The Royal Family 87, 243
Royal Philharmonic Orchestra 21
Royal Society for the Prevention of Accidents (RoSPA) 27–29
Rubik's-Cube 12, 63, 164, 165
Jack Ruby 41
Rudi Ruegg 153
Paul M Rudolph 39
John Rushton 153
John Rushworth 169
Russian Standard Bank 252
Russian Standard Vodka 252, 256, 260–263
"Rx for the Losers" 52, 53

S
Saatchi & Saatchi 9, 179
Charles Saatchi 12, 57, 58, 255
Safeway 169, 227
Sage 244
John Salmon 57, 59
Peter Sampson 165
Sandeman Port 169
Sandvik 160
Sandwich in the Bag 71
Saxton Bamfylde 229
Hans Schleger (Zéro) 29
John Schlesinger *Sunday Bloody Sunday* 74
School of Communication Arts 32, 178
Franz Schubert 21
Klaus Schultheis 83
Arnold Schwartzman 71, 152, 153
The Science Museum 229
Scope 39
Scotland 163, 173, 220, 221, 251
Jane Seager 80
Seagram 128–131, 168, 169, 212, 213, 226, 230, 231, 244, 248, 254, 266, 267
Seagram's Royal Salute 254
Second World War 21, 22, 27, 28, 30, 68
The Sellotape Company 250
Sensation 255
Sexton Shoe Company 58, 59
Rodney Shackell 72
William Shakespeare *Romeo and Juliet* 81
Shamoon 254
Shell Helix pack 172
Shell International 172
Shostakovich 21
Showerings 170, 171
Jeremy Sice 188
Robert Silver 75, 86, 87, 149, 174
Tony Simmons-Gooding 69
Simon and Garfunkel, "Bridge Over Troubled Water" 73
Simon Seaton 284, 285
Mark Sismey-Durrant 304, 305
Smith & Milton 78, 188
Charlie Smith 75

Jay Smith 78, 163
Paul Smith 161
Snopake 92–93
Lord Snowdon 9
Sophie Fenton 255
Edward Sorel 70
Paul Southgate 178, 188
Soviet Communism 245
David Sowden 75, 80
Spectrum Communications 179, 187
Herbert Spencer 152, 153
Erik Spiekermann 31
Spong 74
Springett Wuttke 63
Rod Springett 58
Springpoint 188
Sputnik 26
SSG (Schweizeriche Speisewagen-Gesellschaft) 288, 289
St George and the Dragon 22
Starpack Award 81, 170
Ralph Steadman 153, 176, 177
Henry Steiner 153
Sterling Design 188
Stevenage 163
Martin Stevens 73, 74
David Stuart 153
Stocks Austin Sice 188
David Stocks 173, 188
Otto Storch 33
Studio Art Associates 57
Sunday Telegraph 58, 244
The Sunday Times 11, 17, 79, 83
The Sunday Times Magazine 11, 37, 57, 79
"Support for Design/ Design for Profit" 177
Deborah Sussman 153
Sweet Factory 145, 172, 196–199
John Swannell 173
Swiss design 17, 39
Swiss typography 39, 79

T
Talmadge Drummond 68
Talmud 22
Tandy Halford Mills 68
TANGO+ 253, 258
Roustam Tariko 252

Brian Tattersfield 58, 152, 153
Taylors of Harrogate 100, 101
TBWA 58
Margaret Thatcher 12, 87, 145, 164, 174, 175, 187
Thatcherism 164
The Idea Works Ltd 165, 149
The Last Angry Man 50, 51
The Man with the Golden Arm 33
Nick Thirkell 63, 71, 104, 105
Bradbury Thompson 39
Graham Thompson 172
Thresher 78, 86, 134, 135
Richard 'Ginger' Tilley 253
Time 47
The Times 71, 160
Tit-Bits 22
Torah 22
Mel Tormé 32, 71
Toronto 179, 258
Townsend Thorenson ferry disaster 185
Trade Description Act 70
Lynn Trickett 152, 153
Troughton McAslan 153
Tsaritska Vodka 206, 207
Barry Tucker 153
Glenn Tutssel 145, 160, 161, 169, 170, 172, 174, 179, 187, 245
Tutssels St John Lambie-Nairn 245
Claire Tuthill 73, 88, 89, 163
Twiggy 17

U
Unilever Group 168
United Distillers 242, 248
United States Information Service 38
Universal Entertainment Network 220, 221, 248
Universal Studios 13, 233, 249, 272
Univers 39
"University of Design" 145, 160, 255
Unlisted Securities Market (USM) 149, 164
USSR 245

V
Van Den Bergh 59
Michael Vanderbyl 153
Yarom Vardimon 153
Sarah Vaughan 32
Jackie Vicary 151, 165
Victoria & Albert Museum 222, 223
Vietcong 57
Vietnam War 41, 57
Massimo Vignelli 17, 31, 152, 153
Virgin Records 76–78
Luchino Visconti, *Rocco e I suoi Fratelli* 32
Vogue 173
Volkswagen 70, 77

W
Wall Street Journal 181, 187
Wallpaper* 255
Wardrobe 193
"War on Terror" 258
Watergate 63
Michael Waters 58
Brian Webb 153
John Webster 9
HG Wells 25
Karen Welman 160, 162, 163, 179, 188
Wembley Stadium 259, 302, 303
Sharon Werner 79
Rod Weston 71
What Happened to Goldwater? 56
White Elephant Club 71, 72
Whitbread 134, 135
Bev Whitehead 60, 63, 71, 73, 77, 78–80, 83, 84, 86, 152, 163
Whizzworld 255
Wickens Tutt Southgate 188
Mark Wickens 188
Wieden + Kennedy 253
Williams Murray Hamm 237
Trevor Willis 253
Harry Willock 81
Harold Wilson 57, 58, 73
Winchester 75
Peter Windett 81, 153
Winsor & Newton 12, 70, 71, 76, 81, 102, 103, 108, 109–113, 145, 174

Brian Winterflood 149
Henry Wolf 33, 152, 153
Tom Wolfe 58, 59, 174, 178, 258
Michael Wolff 58, 175
Wolff Olins 12, 58, 63, 79, 165, 187, 237, 247
Women's Liberation 17
"Wonderwall" 255
WPP Group 179, 185
Frank Lloyd Wright 29
Klaus Wuttke 58

X
XMPR 187
Xtreme Information 296, 297

Y
Yale Law Report 38, 39
Yale School of Art and Architecture 34, 37
Yale University 11, 12, 39–43, 57, 80
Yale University Press 38
Yang Rutherford 255
Jimmy Yang 237, 244, 245, 248, 249, 251–255, 257, 259
Yellow Can Company 80, 83, 126, 127
Yeshiva 22
Young British Art movement 255
Lord David Young 153

Z
Donald Zec 149
Franco Zeffirelli 81, 118, 119

Credits

**Michael Peters
and Partners**

Richard Beaumont
Barbara Lewis
Jeff Hockey
Bev Whitehead
Rod Westin
Vaughan Oliver
Howard Milton
Jay Smith
Jane Seager
Madeleine Bennett
Fred Fehlau
Klaus Schultheis
Gerry O'Dwyer
Rita Pyzdrowski
Jim Groark
Andrew McCall
David Sowden

**Illustrators at
Michael Peters
and Partners**

Tony Meeuwissen
Philip Castle
Nick Thirkell
John Gorham
Arthur Robins
Harry Willock
Jooce Garrett
David Penny

**Illustrators
for Abbey Life**

Keith Bowen
Alan Manham
Robin Jacques
Peter Brookes
Jim Fitzpatrick
Giovanni Caselli
Ian Miller
Terence Daly
Rodney Shackell
David Rowe

Annual Reports Ltd

Martin Stevens
Robert Silver
Benjamin Rowntree

Hawkeye Studios

Aubrey Hastings-Smith
Lynette Grass

Brand New

Debbie Carter
Pamela Conway
Dorothy McKenzie
Jane Mann

**The Michael
Peters Group**

Karen Welman
Jonathan Ford
Glenn Tutssel
Mark Pearce
Peter Chodel
Paul Langsford
Virginia Alexander
Di Picard
Claire Tuthill
Jackie Vicary
Rob Davie
Paul Mullins
Mike Branson
Pat Perchal
John Rushworth
Carolyn Reed
Graham Thompson
Bill Carden-Horton
Paul Browton
David Stocks
Paul Southgate
Jo Duffy
Garrick Hamm
Sharon Werner

Haley Johnson
Mark Wickens
Simon Rhind-Tutt
Nick Austin
Jeremy Sice
Ian Farnfield

**Hyman Peters
Foundation**

Liz Lydiate

Identica

Jimmy Yang
Dana Robertson
Geoff Halpin
Chris Riley
Alan Bristow
Darryl Phillips
Tom Austin
Derek Fieldman
Karen O'Neill
Sarah Bratt
Peter Rae
Richard 'Ginger' Tilley
Gareth Andrews-Jones
Trevor Willis
Shamoon
Shoena Mlchie
Kevin Johnson
Max Dubois
Glen Harrison
Deborah Beradi
Stuart McKay
Kevin McGurk
Sophie Fenton
Tim Barson
Simon Manchipp
Carole Laugier
Ruth Goddard
Chris Barber
Julie Morris
Felicity Hunt

Thanks

Acknowledgements

Colophon

Roger Ackroyd
Gareth Andrews-Jones
Madeleine Bennett
Paul Browton
Debbie Carter
Peter Chodel
Paula Cresswell
Rob Davie
Jonathan Ford
Nina Fortune
Jonathan Freedland
Barry Gilliebrand
Fiona Gilmore
Glen Harrison
Sir John Hegarty
Polly Iannaccone.
David Jones
Paul Langsford
Carole Laugier
George Lois
Luke Lois
Brendan Martin
Chris Barber
Carly Michael
Shoena Michie
Howard Milton
Paul Mullins
Robin Munden
Jeremy Myerson
Karen O'Neill
Sarah Owens
Pat Perchal
Chris Riley
Dana Robertson
Stephen Rothholz
Paula Scher
Mrs Pat Schleger
John Scorey
Shamoon
Ginger Tilley
Nick Turner
Glenn Tutssel
Jackie Vicary
Trevor Willis
Karen Wellman
Bev Whitehead
Jimmy Yang
Ivri Verbin

I would like to thank my oldest friend (from our Art School days), **David Hillman**. Throughout this project he has been a tower of strength from the very inception of the idea until the delivery of the book. As the designer of *Yes Logo*, he has pushed me very hard especially with work that I was unsure about and it is to him that I send my heartfelt gratitude and thanks.

Also to **Jeremy Myerson**. Jeremy has for years tried to persuade me to produce a book of my experiences, but until now I never felt ready. His persistence has now paid off and I would like to thank him for his continuing support, especially as the 'architect' of *Yes Logo*.

Sarah Owens, who wrote this book, was a marvellous and patient partner and to her I owe a great deal of thanks, especially as she, through her research, uncovered so many things that I had forgotten.

To my publisher **Duncan McCorquodale** a huge thank you for guiding me through the labyrinth of fear and frustration, with his experience and charm and this has resulted in a beautiful book; also to his designer **Emily Chicken** who has the patience of Job. Between my endless calls and meetings she fielded, with elegance and calm, the tension that occurs when someone like me is so pedantic. And to **Sophie Hallam**, Duncan McCorquodale's PA—a thank you for taking every call and soothing my brow when I needed her advice and help.

And finally to two of my old colleagues **Maddy Bennett** and **Bev Whitehead**—a thank you for sharing with me and obtaining work that I had completely forgotten about, they were, and are, a tower of strength.

And finally, finally, to my PA of over ten years—**Shamoon**. She was the ringmaster of some of the most exciting times in Identica. She was, in football parlance, my defender who tackled problems when they occurred and help me to score goals. She was unbelievably helpful in the early stages of this book and to her a huge thank you.
Michael Peters, London 2008

© 2008 Black Dog Publishing Limited, London, UK, Michael Peters and the authors.
All rights reserved.

Black Dog Publishing Limited
10A Acton Street
London WC1X 9NG
info@blackdogonline.com

Designed by David Hillman
Main text written by Sarah Owens

All opinions expressed within this publication are those of the authors and not necessarily of the publisher.

British Library Cataloguing-in-Publication Data. A CIP record for this book is available from the British Library
ISBN 978 1 906155 377

Black Dog Publishing Limited, London, UK, is an environmentally responsible company. *Yes Logo* is printed on Sappi Magno Satin, an FSC certified paper.

michael@michaelpetersandpartners.com

architecture art design
fashion history photography
theory and things

black dog
publishing

www.blackdogonline.com   london uk

Joseph Mitchell Sophie Rae Kieron Sarah Louise Ford Julie
Morris Ruth Sykes Simon Morton Hannah Kerton David Rowe
Rob Munden Lucy Drew Jeremy Holden Oliver Murphy Robin
Jacques Jackie Vicary Simon Porteus Chris Murray Neil Wood
Anatt Narkiss Jennifer Newell Alan Bristow Adam Levene John
Nicholson Allen Luther Sarah Turner Natalie Norris Ian Oliver
Lisa Feitelson–Gifford Vaughan Oliver Sarah Waybright Deborah
O'Neill Roi Brooks Maria Nicholson Karen O'Neill Fiona Warr
David Sowden Georgie Papadopoulos Dominic Sullivan Stefan
Pateman Toby Norris Peter Horridge Catherine Hogg Jim
Paterson Bev Whitehead Alex Paver Howard Milton Silvia
Avanzi Alisdair King Deborah Dare Sally Munro Steven Peng
David Beare Marc Ten Burggen Pat Perchal Nina Fortune Kathy
Miller Michael Waters Susan Israel Abby Reed Michael Prestor
Andrew Davies Mike Bainbridge Rod Westin Marcia Grunberg
Debbie Roberts Rita Pyzdrowski Peter Rae Dornie Watts David
Pearman Andrew Westgate Jon Neal David Revell Brenda
Lardner Tim Worsley Tamsin Rickeard Chris Riley Carolyn
Lindsey Ian Rippington Clare Bainbridge Emily Heath Allison
Scott Martin Roberts Clare Dawson Caroline Hamlyn Paul
Mullins Gail Romanes Peter Knapp Janina Rudin Chris Wakeling
John Rushworth Peter Sampson David Melton Emma Saunders
Jonathon Ryder Janet Fransen Gerry O'Dwyer Johannes
Schulzhenko Val McCrum John Scorey Duncan Bruce Olga
Sedova Alice Moore Kevin Allan Claire Turner Harry Sangster
Leo Slocombe Jo Montgomery David Pike Matt Smith Kathryn
Chamberlain Glenn Tutssel Marren Steffans Stephen Thomas

Jessica Woodburn Martin Stevens Lisa McWilliam Dana Ro

Jules Convery Robbie Stringer Nicole Worth Sherrine Raouf Jo

Paterson Kate Irving Nick Thirkell Tim Pearce Graham Thoms

Lisa Dennis Trevor Willis Claire Tuthill Jonathan Vanderberg Ho

Caroline Bish David Tyrell Tim Ward Ian Stokes Karen Welma

Rhind-Tutt George Peters Ed Hebblethwaite Mia Whitmore

Laurence Gunzi Sophie Winch Paul Sillers Jennie Withers A

Michael Wright Mia Svensson Joanne Veronneau Becky Taylo

McVee Camilla Tengvall Chantel Purdon Rob Turner Adrian Sle

Dawn Ferrier Steven Hutson Dennis Bryan Zachary Hogg Patt

Aileen Robertson Kate Newby Eric Balledux Gayle Thompson

Bishop Jane Stevenson Gerard Murtagh Brian Bailey Gillian

Langman Alan Briefel Helen Lindsay Jo Buckley Hilary Spence

McGee Caroline Smyth Jeff Gomez Suzanne Carradice Jere

Boukje Bannenberg John Lewis Hayley Worrall John Shephe

Vizard Martin Swaine Julie Simpole Alysen Harvey Julie Smith

Robina Lillecrapp Jo Rowbotham Karin Ambrose Paul Good

Amanda Bligh Wall Kin-Ip-Yu Sandra Wight Krystina Hunter-C

Abery Loris Neophytides Steve Jude Jane Winckley Amanda

Marina Elena Cusick Julie Cox Mary Caulfield Yvonne Gary M

Hollingsworth Amanda Ross Keery Melonie O'Hara Tracey

Zebedee Pamela Sampson Paul Foley Sarah Stanford Marjori

Jonathan Taylor Paul Willis Jonathan Davis Chris Norman A

Mortensen Ros Payne Sarah Heaslip Helen Sanders Sarah Ha

Deborah Harris Sian Ricketts Nicki Cleaver Simon Freer Chris

Sue Price David Goodman Sue Wedderburn Tim Shorten Reb

Metson Sharon De Lucca Wendy Moys Antonella Moroni